Advances in Computation: Theory and Practice
Volume 16

APPLIED PARALLEL AND DISTRIBUTED COMPUTING

ADVANCES IN COMPUTATION: THEORY AND PRACTICE

Volume 16 – Applied Parallel and Distributed Computing
Yi Pan and Laurence Tianruo Yang
ISBN 1-59454-174-4

Volume 15 – Parallel and Distributed Scientific and Engineering Computing: Practice and Experience
Yi Pan and Laurence Tianruo Yang
ISBN 1-59033-956-8

Volume 14 – Technology Supporting Business Solutions
Rafael Corchuelo, Antonio Ruiz-Cortés and Robert Wrembel
ISBN 1-59033-802-2

Volume 13 – Implementation of Term Rewriting-Based Programming Languages
Nadia Nedjah and Luiza de Macedo Mourelle
ISBN 1-59033-645-3

Volume 12 – Practical Application of Parallel Computing
Laurence Tianruo Yang and Marcin Paprzycki
ISBN 1-59033-532-5

Volume 11 – Numerical Solution of Nonlinear Elliptic Problems via Preconditioning Operators: Theory and Applications
I. Faragó and J. Karátson
ISBN 1-59033-376-4

Volume 10 - Constructive Methods for Parallel Programming
Sergei Gorlatch and Christian Lengauer
ISBN 1-59033-364-0

Volume 9 - Imaging and Vision Systems: Theory, Assessment and Applications
Jacques Blanc-Talon and Dan CPopescu
ISBN 1-59033-033-1

Volume 8 - Machines that Learn to Play Games
Johannes Furnkranz and Mirsolav Kubat
ISBN 1-59033-021-8

Volume 7 - Scientific Computing and Applications
Peter Minev and Yanping Lin
ISBN 1-59033-027-7

Volume 6 - Weak Intelligence: Through the Principle and Paradox of Multiple Knowledge
Matjaz Gams
ISBN 1-56072-898-1

Volume 5 - Parallel Program Development for Cluster Computing: Methodology, Tools and Integrated Environments
José C. Cunha, Peter Kacsuk and Stephen C. Winter
ISBN 1-56072-865-5

Volume 4 - Structured Matrices: Recent Advances and Applications
Dario Andrea Bini, Eugene Tyrtyshnikov and Plamen Yalamov
ISBN 1-56072-890-6

Volume 3 - Recent Trends in Numerical Analysis
Donato Trigiante
ISBN 1-56072-885-X

Volume 2 - High Performance Algorithms for Structured Matrix Problems
Peter Arbenz, Marcin Paprzycki, Ahmed Sameh and Vivek Sarin
ISBN 1-56072-594-X

Advances in Computation: Theory and Practice
Volume 16

APPLIED PARALLEL AND DISTRIBUTED COMPUTING

YI PAN AND LAURENCE TIANRUO YANG
EDITORS

Nova Science Publishers, Inc.
New York

For permission to use material from this book please contact us:
Telephone 631-231-7269; Fax 631-231-8175
Web Site: http://www.novapublishers.com

Library of Congress Cataloging-in-Publication Data

ISBN 1-59454-174-4

Published by Nova Science Publishers, Inc. ✢ New York

CONTENTS

PREFACE

In the not too distant future, every researcher and professional in science and engineering fields will have to understand parallel and distributed computing. With hyperthreading in Intel processors, hypertransport links in AMD processors, multi-core silicon in today's high-end microprocessors from IBM and emerging cluster and grid computing, parallel and distributed computers have moved into the mainstream of computing. To fully exploit these advances in computer architectures, researchers and professionals must start to design parallel or distributed software, systems and algorithms for their scientific and engineering applications. Parallel and distributed scientific and engineering computing has become a key technology which will play an important part in determining, or at least shaping, future research and development activities in many academic and industrial branches.

We would like to use this edited book to report the recent important advances in the area of parallel and distributed computing for science and engineering applications. This book contains selected best papers from prestigious workshops such as PACT-SHPSEC, IPDPS-PDSECA and ICPP-HPSECA together with some invited papers from prominent researchers around the world. The book is basically divided into five main sections. We believe all of these chapters not only provide novel ideas, new experimental results and handful experience in this field, but also stimulate the future research activities in the area of parallel and distributed computing for science and engineering applications.

Section 1: Distributed Applications

In chapter 1, *Pan et al.* argue that sequential computations can benefit from distributed computing through the use of self-migrating threads. They demonstrate that using their self-migrating threads to implement distributed sequential programs is almost as efficient as using message passing, because they have made thread migration almost as efficient as message passing. *Tadel* describes an implementation of a hierarchic server--client model written in C++ in chapter 2, and have an outside form of an object-oriented framework. In chapter 3, *Casola et al.* first present the results of their analysis on policies and policy languages used to formally express security statements in distributed systems; then they illustrate their framework and finally a policy-based approach to solve security interoperability problems that arise in un-trusted distributed domains is proposed. *Di Martino et al.* describe a hybrid semantic and statistical technique, and its prototypical implementation, for information retrieval of text documents and web pages and sites in chapter 4. In chapter 5, *Bonifacio et al.* describe architectures and solutions for the accessibility of telecommunications networks from external client applications, and the fast implementation of telecom enabled applications.

Section 2: Numerical Applications

In chapter 6, *Aubanel et al.* propose an asynchronous parallel algorithm for the linear Boltzmann transport equation in three dimensions, for Boron Neutron Capture Therapy (BNCT) radiation therapy planning, which can be implemented efficiently on shared memory parallel computers. The use of object-oriented programming techniques in development of parallel, finite element analysis software enhances software reuse and makes application development more efficient. In chapter 7, *Henz* et al. describe an object-oriented programming framework for developing parallel finite element software. A numerical approach for grounding analysis embedded in stratified soils and its implementation in a high-performance parallel computer are presented by *Colominas et al.* in chapter 8. *Lätt et al.* introduce VLADYMIR, a matrix library in chapter 9 that permits the development of array-based code in C++. It is especially useful for numerical simulation tasks and parallelizes automatically, without any need for parallelization-specific instructions. *Fujio* presents in chapter 10, a finite element method (FEM) software repository tool called feelfem. The work by *Trinitis et al.* described in chapter 11 presents first experiences with electromagnetic field simulations on a cluster with Infiniband interconnect. A real world example from the area of power transformer design, which has served as benchmark problem in previous publications, has been simulated on the Infiniband cluster. In chapter 12, *Yang* proposes the improved parallel version of the Conjugate Gradient Squared method (ICGS) for solving the time-varying sparse linear differential-algebraic equations arising at each linearization step of the waveform Newton method for the transient simulation of semiconductor devices on parallel distributed memory computers. In the final chapter, namely chapter 13, *Chen et al*. develops a distributed parallel solver for multiphase flow in porous media. In the solver they parallelize an iterative flexible GMRES (FGMRES) and use a block ILU as its parallel preconditioner. The corresponding numerical results for realistic simulation models on Linux parallel PC clusters are fully described as well.

Acknowledgments

Of course, the proposed division into sections is one of the possible partitioning strategies. The represented areas, as well, are not an exaustive representation of the world of parallel and distributed scientific and engineering computing. Nonetheless, they represent the rich and useful practice and experience, that we have the pleasure of sharing with the readers. We would like to thank the authors, for their contributions, and patience in assisting us. Finally, the fundamental work of all the reviewers is also very warmly acknowledged.

Yi Pan
Georgia State University, USA
Laurence Tianruo Yang
St. Francis Xavier University, Canada

SECTION 1: DISTRIBUTED APPLICATIONS

In: Applied Parallel and Distributed Computing
Editors: Yi Pan and Laurence T. Yang , pp. 3-19
ISBN 1-59454-174-4

DISTRIBUTED SEQUENTIAL COMPUTING

LEI PAN, LUBOMIR F. BIC, MICHAEL B. DILLENCOURT, AND MING KIN LAI *

Abstract. Sequential computations can benefit from distributed computing through the use of self-migrating threads. On large problems, significant performance improvement is achieved by eliminating disk paging completely, trading off against a modest amount of data communication. The key idea is to have computation and small-sized data move to meet with large-sized data rather than the other way around. Using self-migrating threads with strong mobility provides a flexible way of grouping computations into programs. One of the benefits of this flexibility is ease of application-level programming. Sequential programs are easily augmented into distributed sequential programs for solving large problems, and the distributed sequential programs serve as a good starting point for incremental parallelization. Using our self-migrating threads to implement distributed sequential programs is almost as efficient as using message passing, because we have made thread migration almost as efficient as message passing.

Key words. Distributed sequential computing, Navigational programming, Self-migrating thread, Computation mobility, Principle of pivot-computes, Algorithmic integrity, Incremental parallelization

1. Introduction. One of the major goals of distributed computing is using networks of workstations to solve large problems quickly. The most obvious way of achieving this is through parallel computation, when the problem lends itself to parallelization. This can make the computation faster in several ways. Speedup is achieved by distributing the total computational work over multiple workstations; this is the fundamental advantage of parallelism. But in addition, the computation on each workstation may use a smaller working set, leading to fewer or no page faults. Since dealing with page faults is part of the work that must be performed, distributing a computation over multiple workstations thus decreases the total amount of work required by the computation. In some cases, the efficiency advantages due to the second effect—reducing total work—may dwarf the efficiency advantages due to distributing the workload. This observation suggests that even for algorithms that are not easily parallelizable, distributing the data and the sequential computation over multiple workstations can potentially result in significant increases in efficiency. In this chapter, we consider **distributed sequential computing (DSC)**, defined as computing with distributed data using a single locus of computation, and describe a new approach to DSC based on the use of self-migrating threads.

In order to be practically useful, DSC must be efficient and scalable, and it must also be easy to program. Neither of the two classical approaches to distributed programming—Distributed Shared Memory (DSM) or Message Passing (MP)—satisfies both requirements. DSM is easy to use, but it is inefficient and unscalable [23]: the gain from eliminating disk paging may be overshadowed by the cost of network communication. MP is efficient and scalable, but it is in general hard to use [16]. MP is particularly ill-suited for DSC, for reasons that will be explained later on. Our approach to DSC is based on the use of self-migrating threads. The basic idea is to have the sequential computation, carried by a self-migrating thread, run on a network of workstations. The data is distributed; in essence, we use the network as a data farm. Rather than having the data migrate to the computation, the computation (not code) follows the data. The programming of self-migrating threads is called **Navigational Programming (NavP)**.

DSC when implemented using the NavP approach has two major advantages:

1. Improved and Scalable Performance: The overhead of disk paging is eliminated completely: we can achieve this simply by making sure that each data partition fits in the main memory of a workstation. Communication through the network is handled by the

*School of Information and Computer Science, University of California, Irvine, Irvine, CA 92697-3425, USA ({pan,bic,dillenco,mingl}@ics.uci.edu)

self-migrating threads that carry small-sized data to meet with large-sized data in every sub-computation of the entire execution. Moreover, the thread doing the computation can send out auxiliary threads to other machines to post-write computed data and pre-fetch data for subsequent computation. In this way, the DSC program works even when the amount of data that needs to be processed is much larger than the amount of memory available in the entire network.

2. Good Programmability: An existing sequential algorithm does not have to be substantially rewritten; it merely needs to be augmented with navigational statements (e.g., *hop*()) to migrate the computation from one machine to another at the appropriate points in the algorithm. As described above, pre-fetching and post-writing may be done in parallel with the computation, but this parallelism is very easy to introduce and does not require modifying the sequential algorithm being executed. The thread doing pre-fetching and post-writing typically consist of only a few lines of code, and their synchronization with the main computing thread is straightforward.

We describe DSC, and the reasons why it is not a good fit with DSM or MP, in §2. Our NavP approach to DSC, along with some simple examples, is presented in §3. Section 4 contains three case studies of DSC: matrix multiplication and two algorithms for solving linear system of equations. A comparison of other possible approaches with ours is given in §5. Section 6 provides some additional remarks.

2. Distributed Sequential Computing. We define **distributed sequential computing (DSC)** as computing with distributed data using a single locus of computation. There are several reasons for using sequential computing in a distributed environment. First, only very few algorithms (referred to as "embarrassingly parallel") can be perfectly parallelized. Many parallel algorithms have inherently sequential portions, often over distributed data, that become bottlenecks for speedup (this phenomenon is the basis of Amdahl's law and its variants), so it is important to be able to handle these sequential portions efficiently and easily. Second, when solving problems on distributed-memory systems, programmers may choose to decompose a problem into coarse-grained sequential sub-tasks that run in parallel, even if fine-grained data parallelism is an option [16]. Third, distribution and parallelization are two major components in distributed parallel programming [14]. The job of distribution is to map the task onto different machines so that the overall communication overhead is minimized, while the job of parallelization is to identify sub-tasks that can be performed concurrently. If we can find an easy and efficient approach to handle distribution for distributed sequential computing, we can then build parallelism using concurrent DSC sub-tasks in an incremental fashion. Finally, DSC programs can be used to solve large problems when parallelization is impossible or unaffordable for any reasons [1]. It is important to note that DSC is not being proposed as a competitor to parallel computing; rather, it is a complementary programming method that can be used in conjunction with parallelism.

Both DSM and MP fail to provide good underlying support for efficient, scalable, and easily developed DSC programs. A single process running on DSM is, conceptually at least, a DSC program, but it is not scalable. This is because although disk paging is eliminated, new communication through the network is introduced, and the size of the communicated data is proportional to the network memory farm and can be arbitrarily large compared to the main memory on the workstation on which the process is running. The DSM approach moves more data than needed. Moreover, when the size of the problem working set is larger than that of the main memory, thrashing is going to happen no matter what paging device is being used; paging to remote main memory does not reduce the number of page faults, it only improves the service time for each page fault. In fact, a special case of DSM, "remote main memory paging," works under the assumption that the working set of a problem cannot be larger than the main memory of the workstation [4].

Message passing provides efficient and scalable programs, but distributed programming with MP is hard, and is not amenable to incremental parallelization. The transformation from a sequential program into an MP program is an "abrupt break" since the code must be completely restructured [16]. So in situations where full parallelization is impossible or too expensive, re-implementation of a sequential algorithm in MP is usually inappropriate, as it requires paying the cost of re-implementing the program without gaining the advantage of parallelism.

To be viable, distributed sequential computing must be both scalable and easy to use. The key to scalability in distributed computing is reducing the amount of data being moved. The principle of **pivot-computes**, defined as the principle under which a (sub-)computation takes place on the node that owns the large-sized data, is necessary to achieve the goal of minimizing communication. The node that owns the large-sized data is called the **pivot node**. The scope of the principle of pivot-computes is code building blocks that can have one or more statements. It is obvious that DSM-based DSC violates the principle of pivot-computes because at any point of execution the large-sized data can be anywhere in the workstation farm but the stationary sequential process always pulls in the data, large or small in size, from the farm for computation. This explains why DSM-based DSC is not scalable.

Moving computation locus across machine boundaries is unavoidable if we follow the principle of pivot-computes in distributed memory. This observation is an immediate consequence of the following two basic facts: (1) in order for a computation to be performed on some data pieces, the data pieces and the locus of computation need to be together; and (2) the pivot nodes that host large-sized distributed data pieces change as different sub-computations of a program are carried out. We define **computation mobility** as the ability for the locus of computation to migrate across distributed memories and continue the computation as it meets the required data. This migration is controlled by a programmer either explicitly using navigational statements in the programs or implicitly through data distribution.

Computation mobility can be supported in at least two ways. Message passing can be used to transfer locus of computation from one machine to another. In fact, since the metaphor of message passing suggests pivot-computes strongly, an MP programmer usually does not make the mistake of moving large-sized data. This is why MP is efficient and scalable, and hence popular in the high-performance commercial software market [10]. But, moving locus of computation from one machine to another with MP is cumbersome. In an SPMD (single program multiple data) style, an MP program imposes "artificial constructs" that are usually in the form of **If/Else** blocks that define which line of code runs on which workstation according to how data is distributed in the network. Thus, with MP, distributing data means restructuring code. When transforming a sequential algorithm to an MP implementation, code restructuring can be in the form of reordered and regrouped code lines that are assigned to different artificial constructs, or broken small loops that each runs on a different machine but altogether mimic the original large loop spanning the entire data. This code restructuring usually causes the MP implementation to look dramatically different from the original algorithm, and it is unnecessary because it does not contribute directly to performance improvement. Moreover, explicit synchronization is needed among the processes even if the MP program is a (distributed) sequential application.

Self-migrating threads that provide strong mobility [5] are another means to facilitating computation mobility. A NavP programmer can "drive" the computation to wherever wanted by augmenting the code with navigational statements (e.g., *hop*()). These augments will keep the original code structure of the sequential program unchanged, thus making code development and maintenance easy. Small-sized data can be "carried" to meet with large-sized data in the workstation farm. This makes it possible to follow the principle of pivot-computes and hence achieve scalability.

3. The Navigational Programming Approach. Self-migrating threads are conceptually similar to mobile software agents [15, 17, 13]. Mobile agents are programs that move autonomously among networked machines, carrying their data and execution states. A mobile agent, with strong mobility [5], can halt its execution, encapsulate the values of its variables, move to another machine, restore the state, and continue executing. This sequence of actions is referred to as a *hop*() statement.

Navigational programming using self-migrating threads with strong mobility provides a flexible and powerful way of grouping distributed computations into programs. Computations, represented by code lines in a program, can be "chained" using *hop*() statements. This allows programs to execute a particular computation on one participating node, then a second computation on another node, and so forth. In contrast, the SPMD programming style used by the MP approach has only one way to group computations. That is, computations are grouped by their execution locations, and the different groups are then put together using **If/Else If** constructs. This flexibility of the NavP approach simplifies the programming task considerably. Transforming a sequential algorithm into its NavP-based DSC implementation requires introducing only minor changes, namely the insertion of the appropriate navigational statements. The original code structure is preserved. We say that such a transformation preserves **algorithmic integrity**.

Of course, algorithmic integrity is beneficial only if the original code structure has the right properties (e.g., locality of reference). For this reason, it may be useful to rearrange the sequential code before inserting the navigational commands. The important point is that once a good starting point is chosen, there is no reason why the conversion from sequential code to DSC code requires making unnecessary or undesirable changes in the code structure.

3.1. A brief overview of the MESSENGERS system. All of the examples of DSC presented in this chapter were implemented using the MESSENGERS mobile-agent system [6, 7]. In this system, MESSENGERS code (with strong mobility) is translated by the MESSENGERS compiler into C code communicating using message passing with sockets. As part of this translation, the MESSENGERS program is broken into small C functions, so that each small function represents a unit of computation [25]. In essence, the navigational statements form the boundaries of these small functions. This C code is then further compiled into machine native code for execution. The MESSENGERS system allows code to be either loaded from a shared disk or, in a non-shared file system, sent across the network at most once, irrespective of how many times the locus of computation moves across the network [8].

As a result of this architecture, the additional overhead incurred by thread migration is quite small. When a thread migrates, the state of its computation needs to be sent over the network but the code itself does not. In the MESSENGERS implementation, thread migration is almost as efficient as message passing. The additional overhead of a *hop*() (other than the data, which would also have to be sent in a message-passing computation) is about 200 bytes [25].

3.2. Two simple examples. We use two simple and somewhat artificial examples to illustrate our NavP-based DSC approach. More realistic examples are provided in §4. In our first example, we assume that A and B are two large $N \times N$ matrices and we compute the vector $A\,(B\,diag(A))$, where $diag(A)$ is a vector consisting of the diagonal entries of A and both multiplications represent a matrix multiplied by a vector. We assume there are two nodes, with A located on node0 and B located on node1. The pseudocode is listed in Fig. 3.1(a). The diagonal entries of matrix A are extracted and assigned to a vector $v1$ of size N at line (1). Matrix B is then multiplied by $v1$ to obtain a vector of size N assigned to $v2$ at line (2). Finally, A is multiplied by $v2$ to obtain $v3$ at line (3). In the MP version, listed in Fig. 3.1(b), lines (1) and (3) are executed on node0 because they both require

```
(1)    v1 = diag (A)
(2)    v2 = B v1
(3)    v3 = A v2
```

(a)

```
(1)    v1 = diag (A)
(1.1)  hop (node1)
(2)    v2 = B v1
(2.1)  hop (node0)
(3)    v3 = A v2
```

(c)

```
(0.1)If μ == node0
(1)       v1 = diag (A)
(1.1)   Send (v1, node1)
(1.2)   Recv (v2, node1)
(3)       v3 = A v2
(3.1)ElseIf μ == node1
(3.2)   Recv (v1, node0)
(2)       v2 = B v1
(2.1)   Send (v2, node0)
(2.2)EndIf
```

(b)

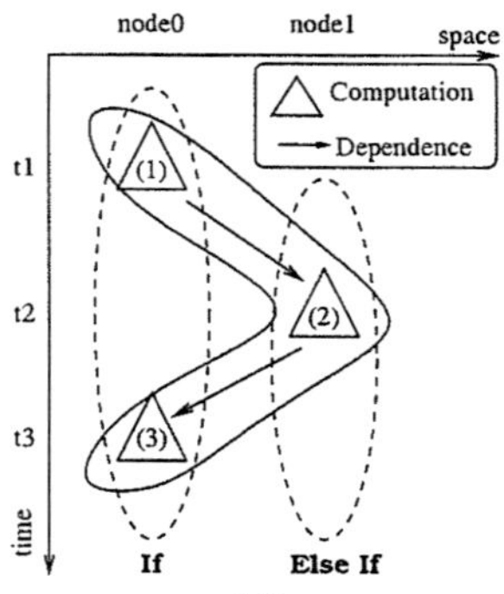

(d)

FIG. 3.1. *Computing on distributed data. (a) Sequential. (b) MP. (c) NavP. (d) Two ways of grouping computations.*

matrix A, while line (2) is on node1 because it computes with B. As a result, the three lines in the original algorithm is now reordered and regrouped - lines (1) and (3) are in one group and line (2) is in another, as depicted by the ovals in dashed lines in Fig. 3.1(d). The groups are then assigned to one of the **If/ElseIf** constructs (μ is the ID of the current node). This demonstrates that with MP distributing the data requires restructuring the code. Communication and synchronization between the two nodes are done through *Send* () and *Recv* () (lines (1.1), (1.2), (3.2), and (2.1)). Explicit synchronization is needed among the computations even if the MP program is (distributed) sequential. This MP implementation follows the principle of pivot-computes. The pivot nodes for lines (1) and (3) are node0, and for line (2) is node1. In the NavP implementation, with code shown in Fig. 3.1(c), $v1$ and $v2$ are **agent variables**, which are "carried" by a mobile agent to whichever node it visits, and A and B are **node variables**, which are stationary to nodes, on node0 and node1 respectively. The NavP code is basically the same as the sequential code except for the insertion of two *hop*() statements, which enable the thread to navigate between the two nodes. The NavP implementation also follows the principle of pivot-computes, and the amount of communication incurred, namely vectors $v1$ and $v2$, is the same as in the MP code. The NavP approach provides a flexible way of grouping computations into threads, as depicted in Fig. 3.1(d) by the angular shape in solid line. As a result, communication and synchronization among the sequential computations are intra-thread, and therefore are subsumed in the execution flow.

```
(1)   For i = 2 .. n
(2)      A[i] = A[i − 1] + 1
(3)   End For
```

(a)

```
(1)    For i = 2 .. n
(1.1)  x = A[i − 1]
(1.2)  If i == n/2 + 1  hop (node1)
(2)       A[i] = x + 1
(3)    End For
```

(c)

```
(0.1)If μ == node0
(1)       For i = 2 .. n/2
(2)          A[i] = A[i − 1] + 1
(3)       End For
(3.1)   x = A[n/2]
(3.2)   Send (x, node1)
(3.3)ElseIf μ == node1
(3.4)   Recv (x, node0)
(3.5)   A[1] = x + 1
(1')      For i = 2 .. n/2
(2')         A[i] = A[i − 1] + 1
(3')      End For
(3.6)EndIf
```

(b)

FIG. 3.2. *Looping over distributed array. (a) Sequential. (b) MP. (c) NavP.*

The second example is a simple sequential loop over a 1-D array $A[1..n]$, shown in Fig. 3.2(a). Because of the dependency between $A[i]$ and $A[i-1]$, this loop is hard to parallelize [18]. For data distribution, we assume the first $n/2$ elements of A are on node0 and the second $n/2$ elements on node1. The sequential MP code is shown in Fig. 3.2(b). The loop is broken into two parts in order to follow the principle of pivot-computes, one in **If** block (lines (1), (2), and (3)), another in **Else If** block (lines (1'), (2'), and (3')). At the array boundary with $A[n/2]$ on node0 and $A[n/2+1]$ on node1, communication of $A[n/2]$ and synchronization are needed (lines (3.2) and (3.4)). The NavP implementation, listed in Fig. 3.2(c), on the other hand, preserves the loop structure. The loop index i and the temporary variable x are agent variables. The arrays $A[.]$ on both nodes are two node variables acting as one distributed shared variable (DSV) [19].

4. Case Studies. In this section, we present case studies with three real-world applications, namely matrix multiplication, Gauss-Seidel iteration, and Crout factorization. Our focus will be on the comparison of performance and programmability between the NavP-based and the other approaches to DSC.

When the total memory use of an application exceeds the size of the main memory on one node, virtual memory is used and hence disk paging occurs. When the working set cannot fit into the main memory, heavy disk paging, or thrashing, happens. Both paging and thrashing can dramatically degrade the performance, although the exact point at which the performance deteriorates may vary depending on the details of the implementation and the data access patterns. One way to reduce paging is to continue to use a sequential program and augment it with *ad hoc* "spill logic" that uses the knowledge of the future data access pattern to reduce disk paging overhead. But this solution is application dependent, cumbersome, and non-scalable.

To eliminate disk paging, we use network-connected machines, and code the applications using the NavP approach. The basic idea is simply to decompose the entire data into smaller pieces each fitting completely into the main memory of a workstation, and therefore all computations on all the machines will be paging free. Self-migrating threads carrying relatively small amounts of data, such as loop indices or intermediate result, hop among the machines to perform computations.

In addition to the performance gained from eliminating paging, the NavP approach is easy. In principle, it is possible to mimic the behavior of the NavP code with message passing, using stationary processes that transfer the locus of computation by sending wake-up messages that contain the state of the computation. In two of our examples (matrix multiplication and Crout factorization), we provide MP-based DSC pseudocode to illustrate the additional burden placed on the programmer when MP is used rather than self-migrating threads.

The NavP implementations used MESSENGERS. All the performance tests were run on SUN Sparc Ultra-1's with 64MB of main memory, 1GB of virtual memory, and 10Mbps of Ethernet connection. These workstations have a shared file system (NFS).

4.1. Matrix multiplication. The first example is matrix multiplication, i.e., $C = AB$, where A, B, and C are assumed to be square dense matrices for simplicity. We use a block-fashion coarse-grained algorithm, and partition the matrices into p horizontal and vertical strips, as depicted in Fig. 4.2 with $p = 3$. Each piece C_{ij} is the product of two slices A_i and B_j. Sequential pseudocode is listed in Fig. 4.1(a).

The DSC implementation of matrix multiplication assumes that a sequence of sub-matrix multiplications are performed, and each multiplication in the sequence requires a pre-fetching (to obtain the two sub-matrices being multiplied) and a post-fetching (to store the resulting sub-matrix). Performing fetching in parallel with computations provides some speedup, even if the computations are strictly sequential. To explore further parallelism in

```
(1)  For i = 0..p-1
(2)      For j = 0..p-1
(3)          Cij = Ai Bj
(4)      End For
(5)  End For
```

(a)

```
(1)    For i = 0..p-1
(2)        For j = 0..p-1
(2.1)          inject (WR (i, j))
(2.2)          waitEvent (IO_b(i,j))
(3)            Cij = Ai Bj
(3.1)          hop (!μ)
(4)        End For
(5)    End For
```

(b)

```
(1) WR (int i, int j)
(2)   hop (!μ)
(3)   write (C_i''j'')
(4)   read (A_i', B_j')
(5)   signalEvent (IO_b(i',j'))
(6) End
```

(c)

FIG. 4.1. *Pseudocode for matrix multiplication. (a) Sequential. (b) NavP. (c) Fetching.*

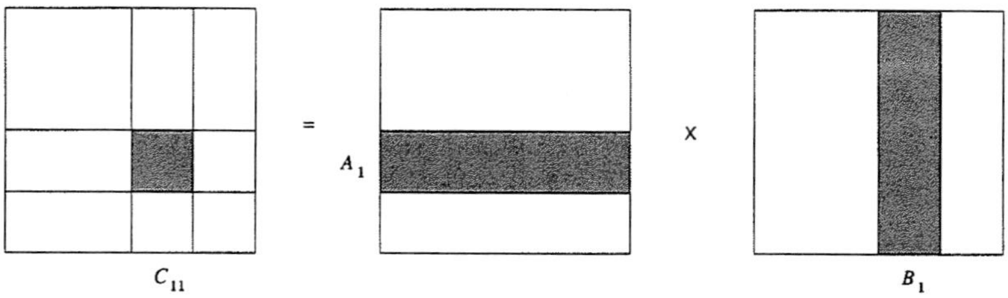

FIG. 4.2. *Matrix decomposition.*

matrix multiplication, one can use, e.g., Gentleman's algorithm. In the interest of clarity and simplicity in presenting the idea of DSC, we focus on the first source of parallelism coming from parallel fetching. We use two networked workstations. There are two threads carrying out the task. One thread called *Multiplier*, with the pseudocode listed in Fig. 4.1(b), calculates C_{ij} on the node where A_i and B_j reside. This thread hops between the two nodes alternately carrying its computation state, the loop indices i and j which indicate which C_{ij} is being calculated. The computation locus is only on a single node, either node0 or node1, at any particular time. A second thread, called *WR* (writer and reader, with code listed in Fig. 4.1(c)), injected (i.e., spawned) by the *Multiplier* at line (2.1) on one node, hops to the other node ($!\mu$), post-writes $C_{i''j''}$ computed from the previous iteration to disk, and pre-reads $A_{i'}$ and $B_{j'}$, the next pair of slices to be computed after the pair A_i and B_j. Obtaining (i'', j'') or (i', j') from (i, j) is trivial, and the details are thus omitted. These two threads synchronize among themselves using local "events." For example, *Multiplier* will need to, on either node, wait for *WR* running on the same node to finish before it can start computing; so at line (2.2) it waits for an event, $IO_{b(i,j)}$, signaled by *WR* (at line (5)) after reading A_i and B_j. In MESSENGERS, *signalEvent*() and *waitEvent*() implement the classical operations of process blocking and wakeup. Only program state (e.g., loop indices i and j) that is tiny compared to the data (i.e., matrix slices), migrates between the two nodes. Provided the total size of A_i, B_j and C_{ij} does not exceed the size of the main memory on either node, the computation will not cause disk paging.

Fig. 4.3 lists the pseudocode for MP implementation. The code is much longer, and more importantly the code lines are regrouped according to where they are executed. For example, line (3) in the original code Fig. 4.1(a) is repeated in the MP implementation (lines (6) and (23) in Fig. 4.3) because this code line is executed on both nodes. The two nested loops are duplicated on both nodes, with the one on node1 being a *While*() loop that is a semantically equal translation of the loop nest. Here node0 has all the loop state information and node1 is acting as a slave by doing what it is told to do. Another way of implementing is to have both nodes compute redundantly the loop state information. In

```
If μ == node0
  For i = 1..p
    For j = 1..p
      If (i*p+j)%2 == 0
        Send("read", (i,j), node1)
        C_ij = A_i B_j
      Else
        Send("comp", (i,j), node1)
        write(C_i''j'')
        read(A_i', B_j')
      End If
      Recv(sync, node1)
    End For
  End For
  Send("stop", (0,0), node1)
ElseIf μ == node1
  While(1)
    Recv(s, (i,j), node0)
    If s == "read"
      write(C_i''j'')
      read(A_i', B_j')
    Else If s == "comp"
      C_ij = A_i B_j
    Else If s == "stop"
      exit
    End If
    Send(sync, node0)
  End While
EndIf
```

FIG. 4.3. *Pseudocode for matrix multiplication in MP.*

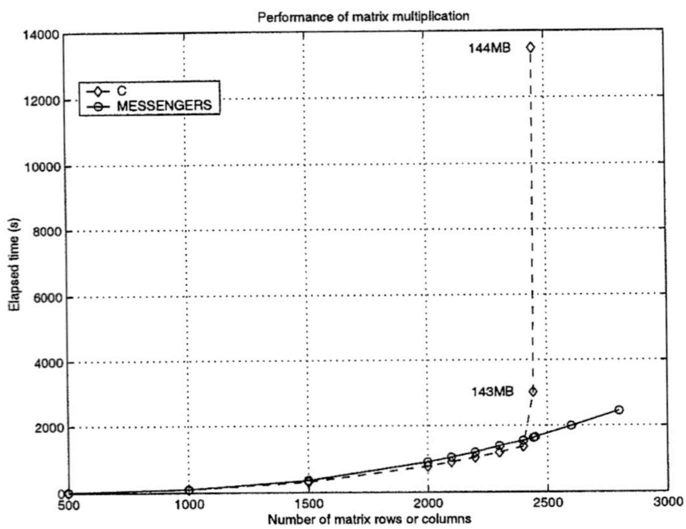

FIG. 4.4. *Performance of matrix multiplication.*

this way, the amount of communication will be slightly smaller, but both nodes will have to maintain two full loops. It is not clear which way is better, but in either case significant code restructuring is unavoidable.

While the MP pseudocode represents a significant departure from the original algorithm, the NavP implementation leaves the code structure essentially unchanged (Fig. 4.1(b)); the algorithm is augmented with three statements: a *hop*() (line (3.1)), a *waitEvent*() (line (2.2)), and an *inject*() (line (2.1)). The code for fetching (Fig. 4.1(c)) is written separately and it is not tangled with the code for computing at all.

Fig. 4.4 shows that the performance of the sequential C code deteriorates dramatically after the total size of the matrices reaches a certain critical value (around 140MB). Our NavP implementation has performance almost identical to that of the C implementation when the total size of the matrices is below this critical value, and it continues the same performance trend after the total size exceeds this critical value.

4.2. Gauss-Seidel iteration. Much of the CPU time spent in executing numerical analysis programs is used in solving linear systems of equations. In this and the next subsections we consider two classical methods for solving linear systems: namely, an iterative method based on Gauss-Seidel iteration and a direct method based on Crout factorization.

Let $Ku = f$ be a system of linear equations, where K is an $N \times N$ matrix, u and f are vectors of size N. Matrix K can be decomposed into $K = D - L - U$, where D is the diagonal of K, and $-L$ and $-U$ are the strictly lower and upper triangular parts of K. Gauss-Seidel iterative method [2] can be expressed as

$$u^{n+1} \leftarrow P_G u^n + (D-L)^{-1} f, \tag{4.1}$$

where $P_G = (D-L)^{-1}U$ is the Gauss-Seidel iterative matrix.

We update the components of the solution vector u in ascending order. Components of the new approximation u^{n+1} are used as soon as they are computed. In other words, we solve the jth equation for u_j using new approximations for components $1, 2, ..., j-1$. The initial value of u can be arbitrary, e.g., $u^0 = [0, 0, ..., 0]^T$. Gauss-Seidel iteration can be done in a block fashion, in which only a portion of the solution vector u^{n+1} is updated given a slice of the matrix K and the entire solution vector from the previous iteration u^n, as illustrated in Fig. 4.5. This is a coarse-grained algorithm. The stopping criteria is $\|e^n\|_2 < TOL$, where $e^n = u^n - u^{n-1}$ is the error at iterative step n, TOL is a user defined tolerance, and $\|\cdot\|_2$ is the L^2 norm defined by $\|e\|_2 = \{\sum_{j=0}^{N-1} e_j^2\}^{\frac{1}{2}}$.

Since matrix K is usually banded, we do not store the leading and trailing zeros of the rows. This is referred to as the "compact row storage scheme," under which the rows are stored in a 1-D array, and an integer array of size N is used to store the positions, in the 1-D array, of the first nonzero terms of all rows.

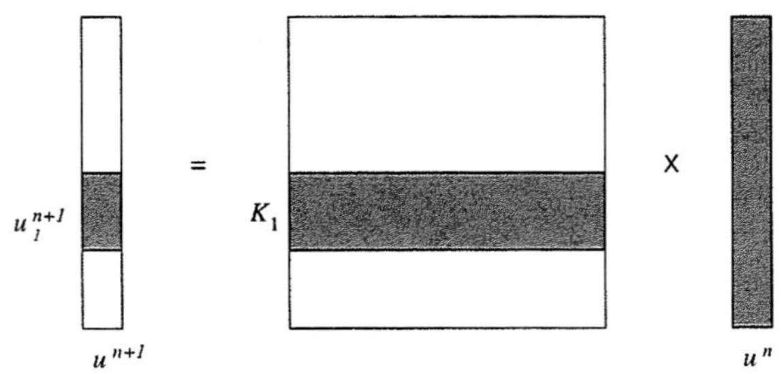

FIG. 4.5. *Matrix decomposition and block fashion of Gauss-Seidel iteration.*

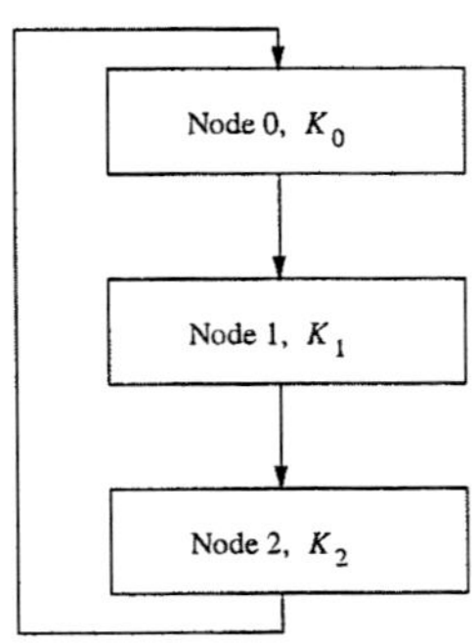

FIG. 4.6. *The network for Gauss-Seidel iteration.*

```
u1 = {0}; err = 1
While err > TOL
   u0 = u1
   For j = 0..p-1
      u1 = block_gs (Kj, u0, f)

   End For

   err = check_error (u0, u1)
End While
```

(a)

```
u1 = {0}; err = 1
While err > TOL
   u0 = u1
   For j = 0..p-1
      u1 = block_gs (Kj, u0, f)
      hop ((j + 1)%p)
   End For

   err = check_error (u0, u1)
End While
```

(b)

FIG. 4.7. *Pseudocode for Gauss-Seidel iteration. (a) Sequential. (b) NavP.*

The matrix K is partitioned into horizontal slices, as illustrated in Fig. 4.5. Each slice of K is used to update the components of u corresponding to row positions of the slice. The network used by the NavP implementation is a ring, where the number of nodes is equal to the number of slices, p, into which K is partitioned; the case of $p = 3$ nodes is shown in Fig. 4.6. A thread carrying the solution vector u can visit a node, use the slice of K on that node to update the corresponding entries of u, and then hop to the next node, repeating this until the error satisfies the stopping criteria.

The pseudocode is shown in Fig. 4.7. The function $block\_gs()$ runs one step of Gauss-Seidel iteration Equ. (4.1) in the block fashion. Notice that the NavP code (Fig. 4.7(b)) is almost identical to the sequential code (Fig. 4.7(a)); the only difference is the $hop()$ statement. In the NavP implementation, j and u_1 are agent variables, and other variables are node variables.

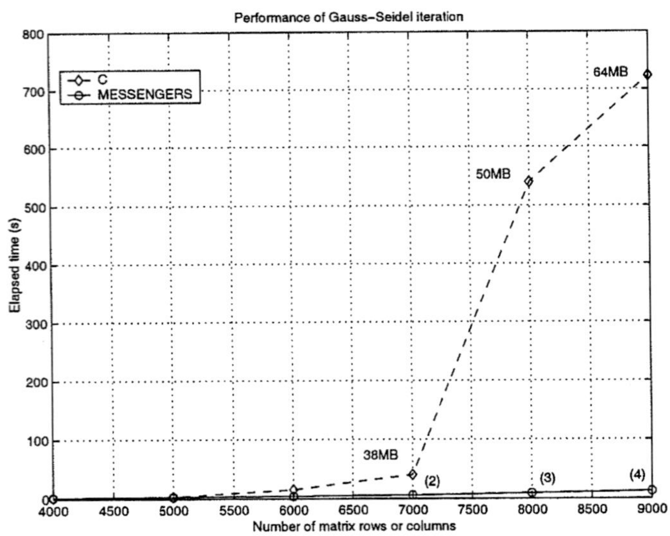

FIG. 4.8. *Performance of Gauss-Seidel iteration.*

Performance data is shown in Fig. 4.8. The K matrices used are banded, and their bandwidth is 10% of their dimensions. The numbers in parentheses by the MESSENGERS curve indicate the number of workstations used, and the amount of total memory required is marked by the C code curve. It would also be possible to implement the NavP version of Gauss-Seidel method using only two workstations, with one pre-fetching the sub-matrix slice

(1) *For* $j = 1..N$
(2) *For* $i = 2..j-1$
(3) $K_{ij} \leftarrow K_{ij} - \sum_{l=1}^{i-1} K_{li}K_{lj}$
(4) *End For*
(5) *For* $i = 1..j-1$
(6) $T \leftarrow K_{ij}$
(7) $K_{ij} \leftarrow \frac{T}{K_{ii}}$
(8) $K_{jj} \leftarrow K_{jj} - TK_{ij}$
(9) *End For*
(10) *End For*

(a)

(1) *For* $j = 1..N$
(1.1) *hop* (*node*[j])
(1.2) *If* (*hopped across node*)
(1.3) *inject* ($WR(j)$)
(1.4) *waitEvent* ($IO_{b(j)}$)
(1.5) *End If*
(1.6) *load* (*column* j)
(2) *For* $i = 2..j-1$
(2.1) *hop* (*node*[i])
(2.2) *load* (K_{ii})
(3) $K_{ij} \leftarrow K_{ij} - \sum_{l=1}^{i-1} K_{li}K_{lj}$
(4) *End For*
(4.1) *hop* (*node*[j])
(4.2) *unload* (*column* j)
(5) *For* $i = 1..j-1$
(6) $T \leftarrow K_{ij}$
(7) $K_{ij} \leftarrow \frac{T}{K_{ii}}$
(8) $K_{jj} \leftarrow K_{jj} - TK_{ij}$
(9) *End For*
(10) *End For*

(b)

FIG. 4.9. *Pseudocode for Crout factorization. (a) Sequential. (b) NavP.*

to be used next while the other performing the computation, similar to the implementation of matrix multiplication described in §4.1.

4.3. Crout factorization. When matrix K is symmetric and positive-definite, there exists a non-singular lower triangular matrix L, with unit diagonal entries, and diagonal matrix D such that $K = LDL^T$. The process of obtaining matrices L and D is called *factorization.* One possible way of conducting factorization is due to Crout [11], and the pseudocode is listed in Fig. 4.9(a).

Only the upper part of the matrix K is stored due to its symmetry. To further save storage for a banded matrix, a "skyline" storage scheme is used, in which we link the first non-zero items in every column together to form a "skyline," and we do not store the zero values above this line. Zero values under the skyline are stored, since they could become non-zero during Crout factorization. No additional storage is necessary in the factorization process since the algorithm works in place and K is overwritten by L and D at the end.

In line (3) of the Crout algorithm listed in Fig. 4.9(a), the summation over l corresponds to a dot product of two sub-vectors of columns i and j. These are the two shaded vectors in Fig. 4.10(a). The computation of the jth column depends on the previously computed columns, which constitute the working set. Fig. 4.10(b) is an example for a banded matrix, with the shaded area being the working set for the jth column.

Crout factorization is an algorithm with good locality of access. There does not need to be sufficient memory to hold the entire half matrix; as long as the working set fits in memory, performance is good. However, when the size of the working set exceeds the size of the main memory on a single workstation, extensive thrashing occurs. In Fig. 4.12 the dashed line shows how bad the performance can be when the size of the working set exceeds the size of main memory.

The basic idea of the NavP implementation is for a self-migrating thread to carry the jth column to the working set, which is distributed among several workstations, and compute the terms of the column on these machines. The amount of communication overhead incurred by this approach is obviously much smaller than if the working set is brought in to meet

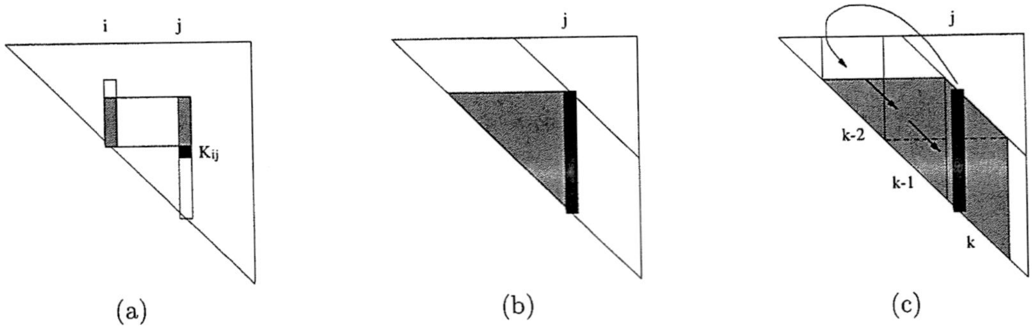

FIG. 4.10. *Crout factorization. (a) Computing of K_{ij} requires the dot product of the two shaded vectors. (b) Working set for column j. (c) Working set decomposition.*

with the jth column. The working set is decomposed into several pieces each consisting of several matrix columns, where the number of pieces is chosen so that each piece can fit into the main memory of one workstation thus avoiding paging overhead. Fig. 4.10(c) shows an example for which the working set is subdivided into three pieces. The arrows indicate how a thread, carrying the jth column which it is computing, moves through the pieces of the working set.

Fig. 4.11(a) shows the network, again assuming that the working set is decomposed into three pieces. The network consists of four nodes. Three of the nodes are used to hold the three working set pieces shown in Fig. 4.10(c), and a fourth node is used to pre-fetch the next piece that will be used later. All four nodes are fully connected, so that a thread can hop to any node from anywhere in one step. As indicated by the arrows, a thread would load from a node variable and carry the jth column in its agent variable, and hop from node 1 to node 3 where piece $k-2$ resides; after it finishes computing using piece $k-2$, it hops forward along the link to node 2 where piece $k-1$ resides (note that $k-2$ and $k-1$ are pieces that have been already computed in the previous loops); finally, it hops back to node 1, computes the rest of column j using piece k, and unloads the jth column from its agent variable to the node variable, and then scales the jth column using the diagonal terms it carries back from the other nodes. These loops go on and on until all columns in piece k are computed, at which time the thread moves on to the next node (4 in the example) to compute piece $k+1$. Again, the previously computed pieces $k-1$ and k will be used in computing $k+1$, but piece $k-2$ will no longer be used in factorization, so we can now save piece $k-2$ to the hard disk, and use node 3 to pre-fetch piece $k+2$. Fig. 4.11(b) shows this next step when piece $k+1$ is being computed. If we compare Fig. 4.11(b) with Fig. 4.11(a), we see that the network is like a "running wheel" rotating forward (clockwise) while it processes the matrix pieces sequentially. In order for a thread to hop to the right machine for a column, a map of a column number to a node number is kept on every node (*node*[.] in Fig. 4.9(b)). This map is a by-product of data distribution.

Two threads are employed in our implementation. The first one, named *Factor*, has its code (listed in Fig. 4.9(b)) augmented from the original Crout algorithm (Fig. 4.9(a)). Three *hop*()s (lines (1.1), (2.1), and (4.1)) and three *load*()/*unload*()'s (lines (1.6), (2.2), and (4.2)) are added. A *load*() statement copies data from a node variable to an agent variable, and a *unload*() statement does the opposite operation. The cost of the *hop*() statement is negligible if the destination node happens to be the one that the thread resides on. A second thread called *WR* (writer and reader) is injected (line (1.3)) to conduct post-writing and pre-fetching whenever *Factor* hops across node boundary (lines (1.1) and (1.2)). *WR*(j) would hop back to the node from which *Factor* came, write the factorized piece to disk,

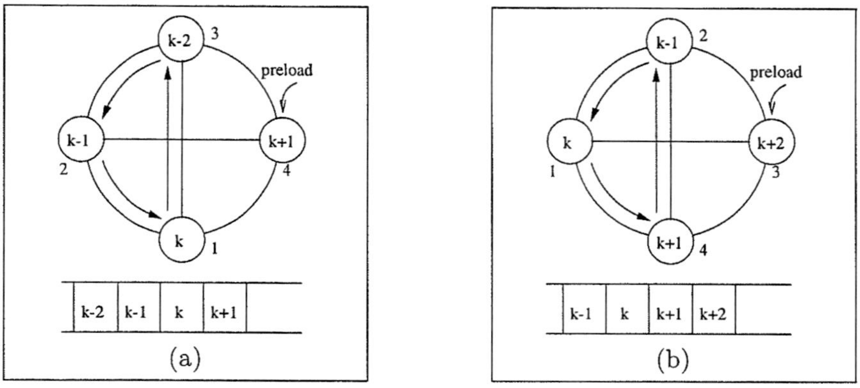

FIG. 4.11. *The network for Crout factorization. (a) currently computing piece k. (b) currently computing piece k + 1.*

read in the piece $b(j) + 1$, which is next to the one containing column j, and then signal an event $IO_{b(j)+1}$ that indicates that it has done the appropriate fetching. This event is caught by *Factor* at line (1.4), when it visits the node next time, to ensure correctness of the computation. The pseudocode for *WR* is similar to the one in Fig.4.1(c) and therefore not listed. We gain a huge advantage doing fetching not only from the pipelining of disk I/O, but also from the fact that now our program can solve problems that are many times (35 in our example) larger than the memory available on a single workstation with only few workstations (4 in our example). We would have had to use 35 machines had we not used fetching.

Fig. 4.12 shows the performance of Crout factorization. The K matrices used are banded, and their bandwidth is 10% of their dimensions. The numbers in parentheses by the MESSENGERS curve indicate the number of pieces into which the matrix K is subdivided. Total memory required is also marked for some problem sizes. One may notice that the gap between the two curves (excluding the segment corresponding to disk thrashing) now is larger than what's shown in Fig. 4.4 (matrix multiplication case). This is because the amount of communication through the network is larger. In fact, since almost all the columns (except for the columns in the very first piece) are carried around, the amount of communication is proportional to the size of the entire matrix ($\Theta(N^2)$). However, since the computational complexity of Crout factorization is $\Theta(N^3)$, our implementation is scalable. Also, with fast network (e.g., 100Mbps), our analysis and test show that the time for communication overhead can be reduced to about 5% of the total elapsed time.

Fig. 4.13 shows the pseudocode of Crout factorization using MP. Notice that in this pseudocode fetching is not considered at all, and some details, e.g., the boundary cases of k, are left out. Also, this code is written assuming that the matrix K is decomposed into P pieces with each working set decomposed into three pieces. More **Else If** constructs would be needed if working set is sliced into more pieces. In the pseudocode, μ is the process ID, which is defined as the index of a matrix piece that a processor owns. I_k is the index of the first column that piece k owns. And $\{K_{dd}\}$ is a vector of diagonal entries. If we compare the MP implementation shown in Fig. 4.13, with the original algorithm shown in Fig. 4.9(a), the differences are considerable. The **If/Else If** constructs artificially break the original code into blocks that will be executed on different nodes. In Fig. 4.13, code lines (6)–(8), (6')–(8'), and (6")–(8") used to be one loop in the original algorithm (lines (2)–(4) in Fig. 4.9(a)), or the NavP code (lines (2)–(4) in Fig. 4.9(b)), but they are broken up by MP into different sub-blocks. In contrast, NavP-based DSC implementation (Fig. 4.9(b)) keeps the original code structure unchanged.

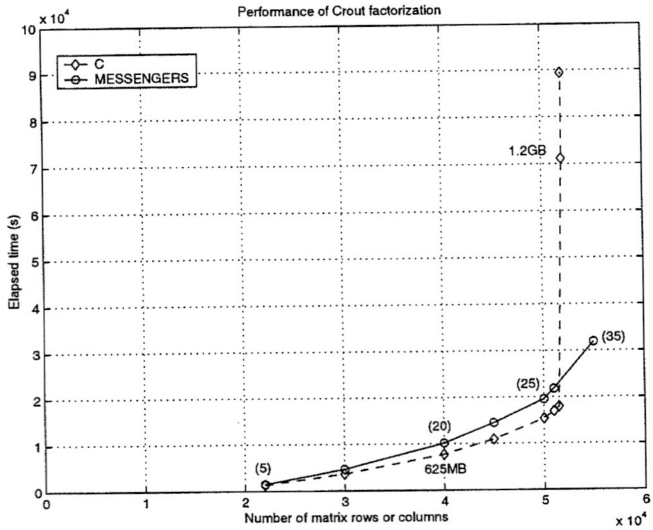

FIG. 4.12. *Performance of Crout factorization.*

```
(1)  For k = 1..P
(2)    If μ == k
(3)      For j = I_k .. I_{k+1} − 1
(4)        Send (col j, k − 2)
(5)        Recv (col j, {K_dd}, k − 1)
(6)        For i = I_k .. j − 1
(7)          K_ij ← K_ij − Σ_{l=1}^{i−1} K_li K_lj
(8)        End For
(9)        For i = 1 .. j − 1
(10)         T ← K_ij
(11)         K_ij ← T / K_ii
(12)         K_jj ← K_jj − T K_ij
(13)       End For
(14)     End For
(15)   Else If μ == k − 2
(16)     For m = I_k .. I_{k+1} − 1
(17)       Recv (col j, k)
(6')       For i = I_{k−2} .. I_{k−1} − 1
(7')         K_ij ← K_ij − Σ_{l=1}^{i−1} K_li K_lj
(8')       End For
(18)       Send (col j, {K_dd}, k − 1)
(19)     End For
(20)   Else If μ == k − 1
(21)     For m = I_k .. I_{k+1} − 1
(22)       Recv (col j, {K_dd}, k − 2)
(6")       For i = I_{k−1} .. I_k − 1
(7")         K_ij ← K_ij − Σ_{l=1}^{i−1} K_li K_lj
(8")       End For
(23)       Send (col j, {K_dd}, k)
(24)     End For
(25)   End If
(26) End For
```

FIG. 4.13. *Pseudocode for Crout factorization in MP (without fetching).*

5. Other Approaches. Using a network of workstations as a data paging farm is a promising notion because future improvements in the performance of disk paging appear to be limited by the inherent bottleneck of mechanical seek time, but there is no such limit on the speed and bandwidth of computer network. The "remote memory paging" approach [3, 4], as a special case of DSM, is based on the notion and is one way of doing DSC. In this approach, a stationary process runs on a single machine and accesses data remotely through the network. A major disadvantage of this approach is its non-scalability because the principle of pivot-computes is clearly violated. A positive feature of this approach is that it is a new paging scheme at operating system level which means it does not assume any knowledge of the specifics of any applications.

The approach of DSC using self-migrating threads distinguishes itself from remote memory paging in three ways. First, we do not move all data to one single machine; rather we move computation to large-sized data, which can significantly reduce communication overhead. Second, we use auxiliary threads (*WR* in two of our examples) with very simple behavior and synchronization to utilize the "spare" CPU cycles in the workstation farm to pipeline data I/O. This enables us to use only a few workstations to solve very large problems, with total data size much larger than the total amount of main memory available in the workstation farm. Third, we augment a sequential program to make it self-migrate in the network; this requires knowledge of data accessing pattern of the application.

The MP approach to DSC is scalable, but it achieves computation mobility by mimicing strong mobility manually. In contrast, the NavP approach passes the burden of code restructuring to a mobile agent compiler that supports strong mobility. Therefore, our approach is much easier than MP.

Another possible approach to DSC is the "remote procedure call," or RPC. Indeed, RPC can suggest pivot-computes too. Of course, pivot-computes requires that services are data-distribution driven, rather than being provided transparently by a middleware based on availability. But RPC and NavP approach use different metaphors. In fact, RPC is a special case of our approach. A remote procedure call will always have to return the control to the calling client, while a self-migrating thread does not have to return to the location where it is spawned. This could cause difficulties to RPC in handling certain applications (e.g., ones that have locus of computation move through a linear data structure like in Crout factorization). Although some RPC-based systems [9] have figured out ways to pass intermediate data from server to server directly without going through the client unnecessarily, method invocations will still have to be through the calling client. Rather than resolving these issues stemming from a metaphor that is improper for some applications, it is easier to directly embrace the NavP approach in general purpose distributed sequential programming.

6. Final Remarks. We have presented three case studies of distributed sequential computing on a network of workstations. In each case, the performance on a large problem, with a total size of data considerably larger than the memory of a single machine, is quite close to the performance that would be achieved if the data fit in memory. Scalability is achieved by following the principle of pivot-computes using computation mobility facilitated by self-migrating threads. In addition, through the use of a mobile agent compiler that supports strong mobility, our implementations preserve algorithmic integrity. The algorithms remain essentially unchanged: the main difference between our DSC implementation and the sequential algorithm is the addition of *hop*() statements to allow the computations to migrate in the distributed environment. Algorithmic integrity not only makes program development and maintenance easy, but also enables the DSC programs to be backward compatible with uni-processor architecture. Since the sequential code structure is unchanged in the NavP implementation, if the navigational statements are ignored, the NavP program runs correctly on a uni-processor machine. This is because data location information is referenced in the *hop*() statements (i.e., navigational statements), but not in any other statements. Backward compatibility to a uni-processor is more problematic in the case of MP code, since data location information is explicitly used in changing the code structure.

One may have noticed that in all our examples we use, as a starting point for the DSC implementation, a sequential algorithm with good locality of access. This makes it easy to insert *hop*() statements so that the resulting NavP program has relatively coarse granularity. While it might appear that this places special constraints on the NavP approach, we argue that this is not the case, for two different reasons. First, in most real-world situations, the sequential program will already have been written to take advantage of locality of access, so it will not be necessary to modify the sequential code before adding the navigational statements. Second, any fine-grained algorithm needs to be "coarsened" before it can be efficiently implemented in a distributed memory environment using any approach such as

MP. For example, in matrix algorithms, operations on scalars generally need to be replaced by operations on blocks in the matrix.

For programs that use large data sets, paging may become an impediment to scalability. NavP-based DSC provides a means of eliminating this paging overhead with only a minor amount of programming effort. Of course, further improvement can be usually gained from a parallel re-implementation. In some cases the parallel implementation is an easy modification of the sequential algorithm (e.g., the iterative method), while in other cases a parallel implementation may require significant rethinking and reworking of the sequential algorithm (e.g., Crout factorization). In any specific situation, the question of whether the additional improvement to be gained from a parallel re-implementation justifies what might be a major re-programming effort needs to be evaluated on a case-by-case basis. NavP-based DSC code provides a good starting point for incremental parallelization. Some preliminary work on using NavP-based DSC to facilitate distributed parallel programming is presented in [20, 21].

DSC frequently needs to perform fetching of data. This is seen in two of our examples. In DSC matrix multiplication, there are p^2 distinct sub-matrix pairs that must be multiplied. In DSC Crout factorization, total matrix size (e.g., 1.2GB) is much larger than the size of the working set (e.g., 64MB). In both cases, many more workstations would have been used had we not employed fetching. Fetching is quite easy in the NavP approach. Sequential NavP programs keep their original code structures, the threads doing fetching have very simple tasks, their code is separated from the code for real computations, and their synchronization with the main computation locus is straightforward. In contrast, with MP the code lines for computation and fetching are unavoidably tangled.

As described in this chapter, DSC using NavP requires inserting explicit navigational statements in the programs for computation to follow data. It would be useful if the navigational statements could be derived directly from data distribution and hence made implicit. This problem is related to recent research on thread migration in DSM [24, 12]. Some preliminary approaches to navigational programming in DSM are presented in [22].

REFERENCES

[1] J.-Y. Berthou and L. Colombet, *Which approach to parallelizing scientific codes—that is the question*, Parallel Computing, 23 (1997), pp. 165–179.

[2] W. L. Briggs, *A Multigrid Tutorial*, Society for Industrial and Applied Mathematics, Philadelphia, Pa., 1987.

[3] G. Dramimitnos and E. P. Markatos, *Adaptive and reliable paging to remote main memory*, Journal of Parallel and Distributed Computing, 58 (1999), pp. 357–388.

[4] S. Dwarkadas, N. Hardavellas, L. Kontothanassis, R. Nikhil, and R. Stets, *Cashmere-VLM: Remote memory paging for software distributed shared memory*, in Proceedings, 13th International Parallel Processing Symposium and 10th Symposium on Parallel and Distributed Processing, Los Alamitos, Calif., Apr. 1999, IEEE Computer Society, pp. 153–159.

[5] A. Fuggetta, G. P. Picco, and G. Vigna, *Understanding code mobility*, IEEE Transactions on Software Engineering, 24 (1998), pp. 342–361.

[6] M. Fukuda, L. F. Bic, and M. B. Dillencourt, *Messages versus messengers in distributed programming*, Journal of Parallel and Distributed Computing, 57 (1999), pp. 188–211.

[7] E. Gendelman, Messengers *User's Manual (version 2.1)*, Information & Computer Science, University of California, Irvine, 2001.

[8] E. Gendelman, L. F. Bic, and M. B. Dillencourt, *Fast file access for fast agents*, in Proceedings, 5th International Conference on Mobile Agents, MA 2001, G. P. Picco, ed., vol. 2240 of Lecture Notes in Computer Science, Berlin, Germany, Dec. 2001, Springer-Verlag, pp. 88–102.

[9] A. S. Grimshaw, *Object-oriented parallel processing with Mentat*, Information Sciences, 93 (1996), pp. 9–34.

[10] W. D. Gropp, *Learning from the success of MPI*, in Proceedings, 8th International Conference on High Performance Computing - HiPC 2001, B. Monien, V. K. Prasanna, and S. Vajapeyam, eds., vol. 2228 of Lecture Notes in Computer Science, Berlin, Germany, Dec. 2001, Springer-Verlag, pp. 81–92.

[11] T. J. R. Hughes, *The Finite Element Method : Linear Static and Dynamic Finite Element Analysis*, Prentice Hall, Englewood Cliffs, N.J., 1987.

[12] H. Jiang and V. Chaudary, *MigThread: Thread migration in DSM systems*, in Proceedings, International Conference on Parallel Processing Workshop on Compile/Runtime Techniques for Parallel Computing, Alamitos, Calif., Aug. 2002, IEEE Computer Society, pp. 581–588.

[13] D. Kotz, R. Gray, and D. Rus, *Future directions for mobile agent research*, IEEE Distributed Systems Online, 3 (2002).

[14] V. Kumar, A. Grama, A. Gupta, and G. Karypis, *Introduction to Parallel Computing: Design and Analysis of Algorithms*, Benjamin Cummings, Redwood City, Calif., 1994.

[15] D. B. Lange and M. Oshima, *Seven good reasons for mobile agents*, Communications of the ACM, 42 (1999), pp. 88–89.

[16] C. Leopold, *Parallel and Distributed Computing: A Survey of Models, Paradigms, and Approaches*, John Wiley & Sons, New York, 2001.

[17] D. Milojicic, *Trend wars: Mobile agent applications*, IEEE Concurency, 7(3) (1999), pp. 80–90.

[18] R. Morgan, *Building an Optimizing Compiler*, Butterworth-Heinemann, Boston, Mass., 1998.

[19] L. Pan, L. F. Bic, and M. B. Dillencourt, *Shared variable programming beyond shared memory: Bridging distributed memory with mobile agents*, in Proceedings of the 6th International Conference on Integrated Design & Process Technology (IDPT-2002), H. Ehrig, B. Kramer, and A. Ertas, eds., Grandview, Texas, June 2002, Society for Design & Process Science.

[20] L. Pan, L. F. Bic, M. B. Dillencourt, J. J. Huseynov, and M. K. Lai, *Distributed parallel computing using navigational programming: Orchestrating computations around data*, in Proceedings, 14th IASTED International Conference on Parallel and Distributed Computing and Systems (PDCS 2002), Calgary, AB, Canada, Nov. 2002, ACTA Press, pp. 458–463.

[21] L. Pan, L. F. Bic, M. B. Dillencourt, and M. K. Lai, *From distributed sequential computing to distributed parallel computing*, in Proceedings of the 2003 ICPP Workshop on High Performance Scientific and Engineering Computing with Applications (HPSECA-03), Los Alamitos, Calif., Oct. 2003, IEEE Computer Society.

[22] L. Pan, M. K. Lai, J. J. Huseynov, L. F. Bic, and M. B. Dillencourt, *Facilitating agent navigation using DSM – high level designs*, in Proceedings of the 7th International Conference on Integrated Design & Process Technology (IDPT-2003), A. Ertas, ed., Grandview, Texas, June 2003, Society for Design & Process Science.

[23] A. S. Tanenbaum and M. Van Steen, *Distributed Systems Principles and Paradigms*, Prentice Hall, Upper Saddle River, N.J., 2002.

[24] G. Vallée, C. Morin, J.-Y. Berthou, I. D. Malen, and R. Lottiaux, *Process migration based on Gobelins distributed shared memory*, in Proceedings of the 2nd IEEE/ACM International Symposium on Cluster Computing and the Grid CCGRID 2002, Alamitos, Calif., May 2002, IEEE Computer Society, pp. 301–306.

[25] C. Wicke, L. F. Bic, M. B. Dillencourt, and M. Fukuda, *Automatic state capture of self-migrating computations in* MESSENGERS, in Proceedings, Second International Conference on Mobile Agents, MA '98, K. Rothermel and F. Hohl, eds., vol. 1477 of Lecture Notes in Computer Science, Berlin, Germany, Sept. 1998, Springer-Verlag, pp. 68–79.

In: Applied Parallel and Distributed Computing
Editors: Yi Pan and Laurence T. Yang , pp. 21-37
ISBN 1-59454-174-4

Gled – AN IMPLEMENTATION OF A HIERARCHIC SERVER–CLIENT MODEL

MATEVŽ TADEL*

Abstract. GLED is an implementation of a hierarchic server–client model written in C++, having an outside form of an object oriented framework. Master server exposes its object space to its first-level clients which in turn provide mirroring facilities to second-level clients and also export their own object spaces. Each client therefore plays a role of a client, a proxy and a server. Infrastructure for propagation and broadcasting of method invocation requests is provided and is general enough to allow for an efficient access control. Synchronization of object spaces is achieved via streaming of object graphs and a time-ordered delivery of method invocation requests. Objects can acquire their own threads to perform different tasks such as computation, data acquisition & analysis or dynamic visualization. The obtained results can be pushed to other computing nodes or storage devices. As threads are spawned and controlled by standard method invocation requests, schedulers & job control mechanisms spawning across a whole GLED cluster can easily be implemented. On viewer level, GLED features automatically generated GUI widgets and a sophisticated 3D rendering infrastructure.

Key words. hierarchic server-client model for clusters, distributed computing, object-oriented framework/toolkit, remote procedure call implementation, data visualization & presentation

1. Introduction. The basic ideas of GLED are stemming from recent developments in high energy physics (HEP) computing as well as from modern information technologies (`web` & `grid`) and concepts of cyberspace (interactive computer graphics, virtual reality, multi-user online games). During the last ten years the paradigm of object oriented programming was making its way into HEP, both by migration of experiments from `fortran` to `C++` and appearance of ROOT data analysis framework [1]. The methodology of a typical physical analysis didn't change much though: it still consists of preparing the input, running the batch job(s) and post-processing & visualization of output. While ROOT simplifies transfer of data from batch job processing to analysis framework, the problem of unification of all the stages of analysis remains only partially addressed and requires, for its efficient solution, high computing skills on the part of a user. This is not a serious problem for a large, mature analysis which takes several days to complete but in early stages of analysis preparation users typically run many small jobs and thus aspire for a fast response of computing infrastructure with the least possible involvement in technicalities.

With the appearance of relatively cheap super-computers in form of computing clusters and powerful desktop computers the time spent maintaining the working environment is contrasted out far more than ever before. Large computing farms with modern schedulers can easily handle jobs with minimal time requirements to provide an unhindered analysis & algorithm prototyping while desktop computers can store data in an order of ~100Mb (as well as obtain it via its network connection) and provide enough computing power for its processing and visualization. One of the basic aims of the GLED project is to address these new possibilities and integrate algorithm development, input preparation, job execution, data visualization and user-to-user communication in a common environment.

Another element of modern computing that has likewise grown is the size of datasets and databases being processed, thus putting a heavy load on all data transport layers, from networks to permanent storage devices. For WAN-s and inter-cluster communication the problem has been effectively addressed with the introduction of `grid` technologies, while LAN-s within large computing clusters with centralized storage systems are still posing a challenge as many improvements minimizing the data transfers can be envisioned. A hierarchic structure of computing nodes interwoven with data storage and communication nodes seems an obvious solution and it provided one of the models for hierarchic server–client

* "Jožef Stefan Institute", Jamova 39, SI-1000 Ljubljana, Slovenia (`Matevz.Tadel@ijs.si`)

structure of GLED. By virtue of the hierarchic structure, the inner computing nodes do not need a direct WAN access. This architecture might also be of prime interest for distributed multi-user interactive environments where hierarchic structure allows for balancing of WAN traffic and local CPU usage.

1.1. The main design features of Gled. The GLED project aims at building of an object oriented framework/toolkit by extending the notion of a C++ class. It provides the following extensions to the C++ class paradigm:

1. **Serialization of objects.** ROOT's infrastructure for serialization of objects provides a firm base for storage of objects and their transmission over the network.
2. **Serialization of method calls** allows for a transparent implementation of remote method calls with objects acting as the natural elements that generate/process the requests.
3. **Automatic generation of GUI classes.** The auto-generated widgets always send serialized method calls to the central message processing unit and are therefore decoupled from the actual objects they are representing. The GUI classes are a convenient way for viewing and editing of objects.
4. **Rendering classes** coupled with GLED's rendering infrastructure provide an alternative representation of objects. It can be used to build advanced visualization systems or as a flexible method for representing and interacting with large object collections.

Furthermore, GLED has a low-level support for object aggregation (lists and smart pointers) allowing an easy construction of arbitrarily complex object structures (graphs). The object graphs can be shared across a cluster with the hierarchic server-client paradigm assuring a consistent object state and proper method call propagation.

From architectural point of view GLED is designed as a modular application with a minimal kernel, providing base classes and hierarchic server-client code. User classes/code can be imported into a running kernel by dynamic loading of appropriate shared libraries.

1.2. Development goals. The development of the GLED framework focuses on elements that allow for fast prototyping and implementation of:

- **class libraries** for scientific computation and visualization,
- **distributed applications** for scientific computing and collaborative object-space access/management,
- **intra/inter cluster** communication and data-transport & addressing protocols and
- **advanced visualization systems** for single and multi-user applications.

Object & method call serialization, hierarchic server-client architecture and GUI & data presentation elements of GLED also make it an interesting platform for projects seeking voluntarily contributed CPU power for CPU intensive distributed computations (e.g. SETI@Home [2] and Folding@Home [3]). The wide availability of broadband network access for home PCs is turning them into powerful computational and data analysis engines, suitable also for tasks with high demands on network throughput. The hierarchic server-client model can be effectively used to minimize the network traffic, provided that the topology of a cluster matches that of a network.

While the main development goal of GLED is to provide a generic platform for scientific computing and prototyping of `grid` protocols, many of its features might be of interest to a wider public. In particular, we see two possibilities for extending GLED in this direction.

1. Data-base interfaces coupled with GUI and rendering support of GLED would allow for an easy implementation of advanced information systems.
2. The hierarchic server-client model, object & method serialization and rendering capabilities make GLED an excellent platform for implementation of virtual reality

systems. In the extreme case GLED could even be used as a multi-player game engine.

Both of these extensions would further enhance GLED for its main purposes. It is our intention to attract open-source developers from external communities. Their contribution and wider interest for the project would also allow for an efficient dissemination of `grid` technologies to a wider public.

2. Overview and Terminology. The basic elements of GLED are objects, specializations of a class `ZGlass`, exported into a hierarchic server–client system. The common base class provides services for communication with the GLED system and, together with the PROJECT7 code-glue generator, enables its instances to be serialized in a context of an object graph as well as to send and execute *method invocation requests* (MIR). Compared to RPC [4], MIRs in GLED represent a distributed RPC implementation of a "call/no-wait" variety with internal rules that allow for propagation of MIRs through the hierarchy of a GLED cluster. ROOT's streaming mechanism guarantees interoperability of architectures and in this context corresponds to external data representation standard (XDR [5]) of RPC.

GLED objects are memory-resident and optimised for fast modification and immediate replication. Nodes in a GLED cluster share data and collectively modify it. If a given node desires access to some data it has to mirror it first and after that it receives and sends MIRs to keep the data in synchronization with the server. This is quite unlike LDAP [6] which is optimised for massive concurrent queries with slow modification and lazy replication. On the other hand, GLED objects can be imported from databases, either as static data, as query results or as dynamic data that can be changed and possibly reinserted into the database.

To be able to explain the details of functioning and habitat of GLED objects, an overview of the hierarchic server–client architecture and basic properties of the GLED system will first be made.

2.1. Towards a Hierarchic Server–Client Model. The basic idea of a hierarchic server-client model lies in extension of a simple server–client communication graph to a more general tree structure (Fig. 2.1). The most notable difference, beyond the appearance of multiple levels, is that each client becomes also a server for its clients and a proxy in respect to its server (as well as for all higher servers on the way to the master server). Separation of server spaces of clients belonging to one server is in fact the feature that makes the hierarchical model interesting: it allows nodes to share data selectively, making it visible only to the nodes that need access to it. The topology of a tree is arbitrary and can change dynamically. In practice it is dictated by the structure of the problem being addressed and should provide optimal functioning of the nodes while minimizing data transfers among different levels of the cluster hierarchy.

Another point to notice from the above figure is that a master server and pure-client nodes are just degenerate cases of the general node behaviour. This presents a drastic departure from the standard server-client model. To emphasize this difference and to avoid confusion, the term *Saturn* was chosen to signify an operational node in a GLED cluster. The naming is based on the analogy with planetary system and propagation of light: light emitted by the planet Saturn is partially the reflected light from the Sun and the rest is produced by the processes proceeding under the veil of the planet's atmosphere. The master server is called either a *zeroth-level Saturn* or *Sun Absolute*. Additionally, symbol $\mathcal{S}$ is used for any Saturn, $\mathcal{S}_0$ for the Sun Absolute and $\mathcal{S}_i$, $i > 0$ for an *i-th level* Saturn.

Since objects need to be uniquely identified across different nodes, they are numbered with positive integers spawning an *object ID space*. Intervals from the available set are claimed by Saturns in succession as they get attached into the system. Fig. 2.2 shows an example of object space partitioning for a chain of three Saturns. The linear partitioning with pre-reservation of desired ID-space interval minimizes efforts associated with routing

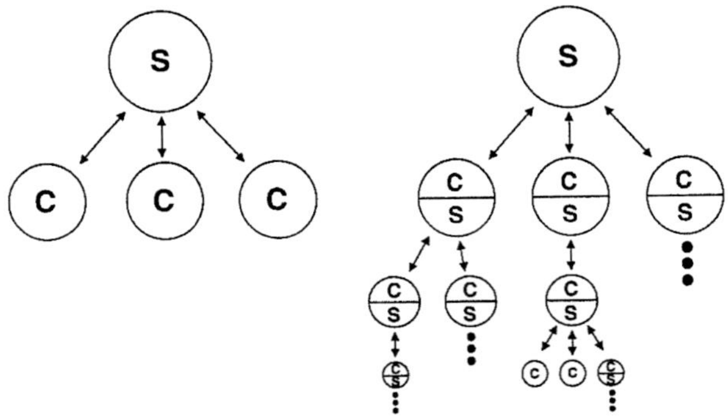

FIG. 2.1. *Comparison of standard (left) and hierarchic (right) server–client model. Circles represent computer nodes, while labels S and C stand for* server *and* client *respectively.*

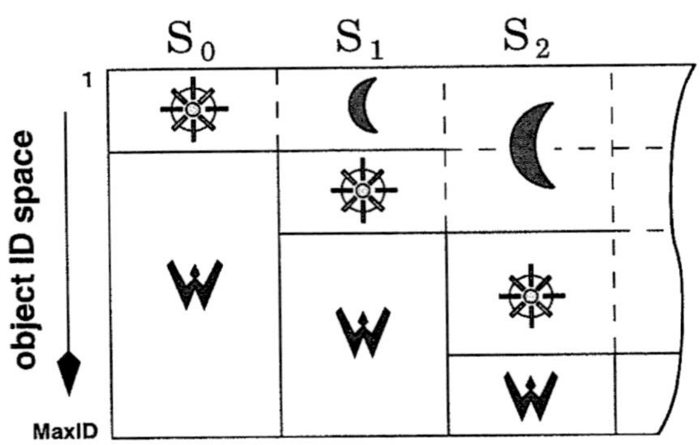

FIG. 2.2. *A scheme of object ID space partitioning. For each Saturn the sun symbol represents its server space, the moon symbol its proxy-client space and the fire symbol shows the local space of the Saturn.*

of MIRs without the loss of generality.

Objects in the server space (or *sun-space*) of $\mathcal{S}_0$ can be seen on all GLED nodes. MIRs directed at them from lower Saturns (or *moons*) are always routed up to $\mathcal{S}_0$ where the requests are checked and, if they are accepted, executed and broadcasted to $\mathcal{S}_1$ Saturns. They in turn execute the MIR and broadcast it further down the hierarchy. For a $\mathcal{S}_i$ Saturn, the object spaces of all higher Saturns are effectively merged into a common ID-space partition, called its *moon-space*, providing the proxy service. This furthers the light analogy: the light emitted by a Saturn on behalf of its higher Saturns is the reflected light, just as we see the Moon in the reflected light of our Sun. A Saturn has no executive power over its moon-space although operations (threads) issuing from it can perform tasks on behalf of other Saturns.

The same holds for each Saturn: it is the master of its sun-space and all MIRs affecting it must pass through its execution control prior to their execution and broadcasting.

Sun-space of each Saturn is further subdivided to allow for its partial exposure to lower Saturns. Migration of objects between different object-spaces is also possible. This features are discussed in section 4.

Another important feature of such partitioning is the natural arising of a *local object space* (or *fire-space*) on each Saturn (Fig. 2.2). It contains objects pertaining to local computation and viewing. Fire-space extends over the object-space following the Saturn's reserved sun-space. As the names suggest, objects belonging to fire-space are entirely local (light emitted by a simple fire can not reach other planets). Since global and local objects share the same ID-space, local objects can easily reference the global ones to modify their own behaviour. Also, a user is provided with the same interface in both cases.

2.2. The Main Aspects of Gled. GLED is built upon ROOT [1] and thus inherits its versatile I/O infrastructure (access of local and remote files with inner directory structure) and a rich set of data storage, analysis and presentation functions. CINT [7], a C/C++ interpreter, is also a part of ROOT's heritage and presently plays the role of a scripting language.[1]

As mentioned before, GLED-enabled classes stem from the common base `ZGlass`. Following the analogy with light any GLED class can be referred to as a *glass* (material, not a vessel) and any instance as a *lens*. Infrastructure enabling lenses to be fully operational is rather elaborate and could as such pose a heavy load on a programmer. To bypass this obstacle, definitions of glasses are preprocessed by two parsers/code generators:

- ROOTCINT (part of the ROOT system) produces a dictionary, serialization method and interpreter bindings;
- PROJECT7 (part of GLED) generates accessor methods, methods for streaming and processing of MIRs, connectivity introspection methods as well as GUI components for a given glass.

Both produce code that is in part included back into the class definition. Therefore some of the class semantics is implicit in data and function member declarations.

MIRs are always enclosed in a *context*, specifying the target lens, the identity of a caller and all lens-type arguments. This allows for authorization and dependency checking prior to complete unfolding of the request and provides a transparent way for creation of requests originating from a GUI.

To simplify the extension of the GLED system, build process and component deployment, glasses and their supporting structures are grouped into *library sets* which are dynamically loaded into a running system.

Viewing part of a library set is separated from its main part, following the general rule that the objects themselves should not know how and when they are being observed. Each Saturn can accept local viewers, or *Eyes*. They can be individually authenticated to allow different access privileges. Eyes instantiate lens-views, provide MIR sending facility, receive change notification messages and distribute them to targeted viewing fragments. Viewing classes have a read-only access to glass data and send MIRs to their Saturn to actualize the desired changes or to initiate actions.

3. The Data Model. In GLED the basic data element is an object of class derived from the common base class `ZGlass`, i.e. a lens. In any OO framework the functionality of a base class determines its programming paradigm: it imposes certain structure on programs by providing a means for static data structuring and models of algorithm invocation. In dynamic systems data can influence functioning of algorithms and algorithms can change data as well as its structuring, therefore making a distinct separation impossible in certain cases. GLED is rather permissive in this respect and does not enforce strict control over object access and method execution. Rather it provides infrastructure for object locking (each lens can be individually locked), setting & accessing of data and MIR processing and execution. This mechanisms must be used by the programmer to insure object graph consistency.

3.1. Data Members and Lens Aggregation Methods. The basic model for a glass is that of one automaton in a multi-cellular state-machine with dynamic topology. Data members of a glass represent its internal state. If they are declared as *exported* they are

[1]Currently CINT is not thread safe and therefore limits GLED's performance to a single scripting environment per Saturn. Usage of a loosely coupled scripting language (e.g. `perl6`) would allow several concurrent scripting sessions.

synchronized among GLED nodes that share an instance of this class. Non-exported members hold data that is local to each Saturn and they are not included in the data-stream created during object serialization. They can also serve for data that can be computed locally or as a storage for intermediate results and structures needed for visualization.

Data members can either be of simple types or they have to be descendants of ROOT's base class `TObject` which provides streaming facilities.[2] Data members that can be explicitly set by value must provide the interface in a form of an appropriate *set* method. Unless those methods have additional side effects they can be generated automatically by the PROJECT7 generator. Further, set methods must also be available in their streamed versions so that the elementary changes can propagate across the hierarchy of Saturns. They can always be generated automatically as they only produce a MIR containing the streamed value for the data member in question. This way the problem of setting the values of data members is directly mapped on the problem of method execution. Execution and propagation of MIRs is the subject of next subsection.

A special treatment is provided, on all levels of GLED, for an exported pointer to a *glass*, called a *link*. Links are the first option for aggregation of glasses and they extend a notion of object state into the realm of topological connectivity.

The second aggregation method is provided by a *glass* `ZList`. A list does not own its elements, it simply references existing lenses. The list interface is suitable for organization of ordered collections with frequent additions and removals of elements. It is flexible enough and can easily be extended over the same basic interface.[3]

Using both aggregation methods arbitrarily complex object graphs can be constructed. Also, these graphs need to be synchronized over the GLED cluster, often in a form of sub-graphs connected to an already existing object system. Therefore a versatile interface is provided for marking of sub-graphs, their streaming and rebuilding. Structures encapsulating a sub-graph are called *comets* to be reminiscent of celestial objects that traverse a planetary system or even leave it altogether. Comets can be stored into files or sent to another GLED node for implantation in one of its object spaces. Advanced deep-copying can also be achieved using the comet mechanism.

The base class includes reference counting facilities, mandatory for streaming and management of multiply connected graphs. Methods for modification of links and lists take care of that automatically.

3.2. Data Manipulation & Method Execution. A fair number of methods of any class usually provides a means for changing the static data (either in an object itself or in an object that is accessible from it). In GLED, special care must be paid to methods that change the *exported* data of a glass. Such methods must be executed on all Saturns holding a copy of the lens in question in order to retain consistency of object-spaces. This effectively means that the method call needs to be serialized and delivered to all nodes that must execute it.

Serialization operators for basic types are provided by ROOT and streamers for user-defined classes (as well as for glasses) are automatically generated by ROOTCINT. PROJECT7, in turn, generates wrappers for creation and execution of MIRs. Its operation is guided by instructions encapsulated in comments following the declarations of methods. This provides a natural extension of C++ semantics without affecting its syntax. ROOT in itself already uses such comments for control of streaming.

3.2.1. Set methods. The *set* methods for exported glass members fall directly into this category. To minimize the amount of typed code these methods as well as methods for

---

[2]ROOT provides a rich set of classes for data storage, among others also matrix and vector classes. Creation of custom classes is trivial and is supported by the GLED build process.

[3]Implementation of `ZList` is based on STL `list` container and can be used with STL algorithms.

```
class ZGlass  : public TObject {
  ...
  TString    mName;       //  Xport{GS} 7 Textor()
  TString    mTitle;      //  Xport{GS} 7 Textor()
  Bool_t     bActive;     //  Xport{GS} 7 BoolOut()
  Short_t    mRefCount;   //! Xport{G}  7 ValOut(-width=>4)
  ...
};

class ZList  : public ZGlass {
  ...
  virtual void Add(ZGlass* g);                          // Xport{E} Ctx{1}
  virtual void AddBefore(ZGlass* g, ZGlass* before);    // Xport{E} Ctx{2}
};

class ZNode  : public ZList {
  ...
  ZNode*  mParent;                      // Xport{GS} Link{} Structural parent
  ...
  Int_t MoveLF(Int_t axis, Real_t amount);              // Xport{E}
  ...
};
```

FIG. 3.1. *Code snippets from* GLED *base classes. C++ comments following the declarations contain instructions for further handling by the* GLED *system. The //! syntax prevents streaming of that member and thus declares it un-exported (this syntax is inherited from ROOT). Comments of the form* `Instruction`*{args} are instructions for the* PROJECT7 *parser/code generator and fully specify which methods will be auto generated for the data member. Constructs following 7 in comments fields are constructors for* `perl` *classes that generate code for GUI widgets.*

generation of their MIR-producing counterparts can be generated automatically. Examples of instructions for PROJECT7 parser are shown in Fig. 3.1, top part. E.g. a name of a lens is stored in a member `mName` and the `Xport{GS}` declaration (`Xport` ∼ *eXport*) in the comment field following it induces the generation of methods `GetName()`, `SetName()` and MIR-producing `S_SetName()`. Links as rather special members have to be declared as such (e.g. `Link{}` for member `ZNode::mParent`). The generated code is shown in Fig. 3.2.

3.2.2. Ordinary methods. For other methods only their MIR counterpart needs to be generated (declaration `Xport{E}`; `E` ∼ *Exec*). MIRs contain a method context intended to hold glass-type arguments for the call. A good example of methods that use this facility are list modification methods (e.g. Fig. 3.1: `ZList`). Declaration `Ctx`$\{n\}$ instructs PROJECT7 to store the first n arguments into the context part of the MIR while retaining the same function call signature.

3.2.3. MIRs and their Routing. A MIR is just a buffer containing a streamed context and identification of the method to be executed followed by its arguments (and possibly by some custom data). A MIR contains all the information needed to execute the method and can be created at any point in the code that has access to the lens. Then the MIR must be passed to local Saturn either via a socket or directly from the calling thread. Each Saturn provides sophisticated routing services and an execution enviroment to assure that MIRs are properly processed (routed and executed) by the Saturn hierarchy.

There are two types of MIRs, handled differently by the Saturn's routing code and serving different purposes.

Flares. Flares cause a synchronized change of a lens on all Saturns possessing it. Imagine a lens in a sun-space of Saturn $\mathcal{S}_i$. Flares targeted at the lens must originate from $\mathcal{S}_i$ or from any of its moons. If a flare originates from a moon it is first routed, level by level, up to the $\mathcal{S}_i$, where the context check is performed. Then the MIR is passed to $\mathcal{S}_{i+1}$ Saturns and executed on the $\mathcal{S}_i$ Saturn. The $\mathcal{S}_{i+1}$ Saturns, upon receiving a flare from above, pass it on to $\mathcal{S}_{i+2}$ Saturns and execute it themselves with no further checking: the context check is only done on the top Saturn. *Flares* are shot into the system and then their light is scattered among the Saturns.

Beams. Beams invoke a method in a lens on a single Saturn, without passing the request to lower Saturns. A beam is routed via common parent of the sender and the receiver. At the destination the checks are performed and the MIR is executed. Methods invoked by beams often start a new thread or serve as a source of new beams or flares. *Beams* cut through the Saturn structure without effecting any other hierarchy node than the receiver.

The type of MIR can be set after a MIR has been created so a common interface can be used for production of both kinds of MIRs.

3.2.4. Execution. Execution of a MIR proceeds on three levels:

1. first the appropriate *library set* handler is selected and a lens is locked for the execution,
2. the library set handler (auto-generated) determines the class that will provide the actual execution method,
3. the `E_Exec` method (auto-generated, e.g. Fig. 3.2) of a glass determines the method, de-serializes the arguments and makes the actual method call.

During the method execution a lens has access to MIR data, including the message buffer. This information can be used to determine the type of MIR that invoked the call. Further, the message can be followed by any amount of custom data which is thus made available to the lens-method processing the MIR.

3.2.5. Updating of lens-views. At this point it is appropriate to explain the functioning of a view-update mechanism. Its cycle is initiated from a lens itself by calling its *stamping* method (e.g. Fig. 3.2, in method `ZGlass::SetName()`). This in turn instructs Saturn to notify its Eyes that the object has changed. Each Eye then performs an update of corresponding views.[4] Viewer updates are, as demonstrated, largely arbitrary. Further, they can be blocked for any lens or a group of lenses belonging to a common chunk of object-space. The auto-generated *set* methods adhere to stamping and relieve the programmer of this duty.

Fig. 3.3 shows a schematic representation of a flare execution on a Saturn.

3.3. MIR Processing Performance Measurements. To benchmark the performance of the MIR processing mechanisms several simple tests have been performed. The goal was to determine the performance of the infrastructure itself and none of the tests does anything useful: they simply invoke the relevant mechanisms of GLED.

The benchmarking code was implemented within the GLED framework itself. The tests used thread execution environment of GLED (described in more detail in Sec. 6) The execution performance of an empty thread loop is shown in *"Thread Loops"* column of Tab. 3.1.

Methods invoked in a context of a Saturn can optionally emit viewer update requests or *stamps* (see Sec. 3.2.5). As stamping presents an execution penalty (serialization of the stamp, broadcasting to viewers and processing of the stamp by viewers) the two modes have been tested separately. In Tab. 3.1 they are represented by column groups (a) *"Method call"* (thread calls an empty method in a lens) and (b) *"Method call & Stamp"* (the method also performs stamping). Furthermore, as streaming and emitting of the stamp does not occur unless viewers are connected to a Saturn, we have made two sets of measurements on each machine: one with pure server and another with a single connected viewer. For pure servers there is a minimal performance penalty associated with stamping. In case (b) it is interesting to note the performance benefits of a two-processor machine where server and viewer threads can run in parallel.

[4]Presently the update is sub-optimal in a sense that all members of a lens declared in a given class are refreshed. There are special notifications for *link* and *list* changes as well as the possibility of user-specified notifications.

```
// Get/Set methods for ZGlass::mName
const Text_t* ZGlass::GetName() const {return mName.Data();}
void ZGlass::SetName(const Text_t* s) {
  mExecMutex.Lock(); mName = s; mExecMutex.Unlock();
  Stamp(LibID(), ClassID());
}

// Method to create MIR for calling ZGlass::SetName()
ZContext* ZGlass::S_SetName(const Text_t* s) {
  ZContext* _ctx = new ZContext(mSaturnID);
  *_ctx->Message << (LID_t)1 << (CID_t)1 << (MID_t)101;
  _ctx->Message->WriteArray(s, strlen(s)+1);
  return _ctx;
}
// and its execution part.
Int_t ZGlass::E_Exec(TBuffer* buf) {
  MID_t methId; *buf >> methId;
  switch(methId) { ...
  case 101: {
    Text_t* s; s=0; buf->ReadArray(s);
    SetName(s); delete s; return 0;
  } ...
}

// Method to create a MIR for calling ZList::AddBefore()
ZContext* ZList::S_AddBefore(ZGlass* g, ZGlass* before) {
  ZContext* _ctx = new ZContext(mSaturnID,
    (g ? g->GetSaturnID() : 0),
    (before ? before->GetSaturnID() : 0));
  *_ctx->Message << (LID_t)1 << (CID_t)2 << (MID_t)1001;
  return _ctx;
}
// and its execution part.
Int_t ZList::E_Exec(TBuffer* buf) { ...
  case 1001: {
    ZGlass* g = dynamic_cast<ZGlass*>(mCtx->Beta);
    ZGlass* before = dynamic_cast<ZGlass*>(mCtx->Gamma);
    AddBefore(g, before); return 0;
  } ...
}
```

FIG. 3.2. *Snippets of code produced by the* PROJECT7 *code generator.*

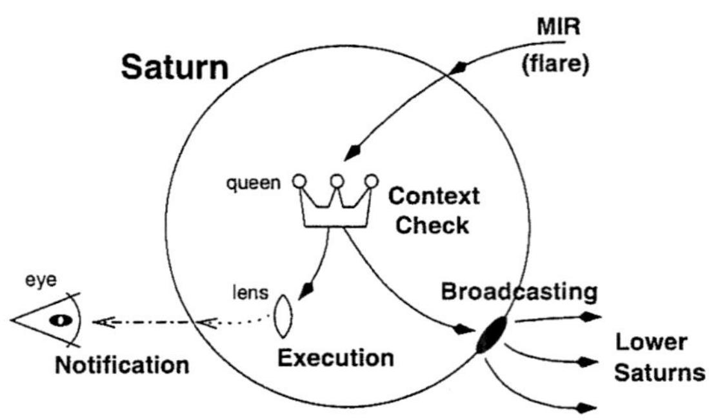

FIG. 3.3. *Execution of a* flare *on a Saturn. In case of a* beam *the broadcasting of MIR is not performed.*

For both methods types three different modes of method invocation have been tested:

1. **Direct:** A direct method call. For empty method calls the cost is equvalent to the cost of a function call, while for methods with stamping the stamping procedure is also performed (note the drastic performance drop when a viewer is connected). These measurements also represent reference values for MIR-based invocation schemes described below.
2. **MIR:** MIR is created within the main thread and posted directly to the Saturn for processing and execution. All MIR processing proceeds within the same thread.

3. **Beamed MIR:** MIR is created on a client machine and sent to the server in *beam* mode. Saturn's thread listening to client sockets receives the MIR, unpacks it and processes it as in the above case.
It is important to note that the limiting factor was the processing speed of the server and not the available network bandwidth.

Machine	Thread Loops	Method call			Method call & Stamp		
		Direct	MIR	Beam	Direct	MIR	Beam
AMD-2600 Dual	245.6	244.9	78.6	54.6	234.5	75.1	52.9
as above + viewer	243.0	242.6	79.2	51.4	87.6	28.4	22.4
AMD-2600 Single	237.9	237.3	76.4	53.1	226.8	72.8	51.4
as above + viewer	235.1	234.6	78.2	47.3	64.4	21.8	17.9
P3-1000 Dual	123.8	123.0	35.8	27.2	111.6	34.6	26.6
as above + viewer	123.9	123.2	35.6	26.4	54.5	18.1	15.0

TABLE 3.1

Results of execution performance measurements for different machine configurations expressed in thousands of executions per second. AMD stands for AMD Athlon *and P3 for* Pentium III *processor. See Sec. 3.3.*

The presented results show the execution penalties for different elements of the GLED infrastructure. It is interesting to observe that the measured performance spawns over one order of magnitude. In real-life uses of GLED the very basic mechanisms would be used for data transport and only a few specialized objects would emit viewer update requests. By allowing a programmer to use an arbitrary combination of framework elements, GLED can serve to implement a wide range of advanced RPC techniques with optional continuous updating of connected viewers. But as we have demonstrated that comes at a cost.

4. Management of Saturn's Object-Spaces. A sun-space and a fire-space of each Saturn are both managed (or *ruled*) by its *king* lens. A king has purely administrative duties: it holds its reserved object-space and delegates *queens* to actually rule upon their entrusted ID-space chunks (*queen-spaces*). Queens can be serialized to, or resurrected from, comets (see Sec. 3.1) and they are the smallest object-space elements that can be mirrored by lower Saturns.

Upon connection, a new Saturn only receives serialized kings and queens without the actual contents of their object spaces. The mirroring of each queen-space is performed separately and can be dynamically controlled. Request for mirroring of a queen on a given Saturn (this request is also a MIR) can originate from any of the Saturns that know about the existence of a given queen. A queen can be marked as *mandatory*: in this case all new Saturns are requested to pull it into its moon-space.

Further, queens provide lens instantiation facilities: a lens can be created and attached into the existing lens-graph by sending the queen a single MIR. Lenses can be created as default objects (by sending library set and class IDs of desired glass) or from an existing serialized lens.

Another very important role of queens is *blessing* of MIRs directed at their subjects. A Saturn performs rudimentary context checking to provide error trapping, while queens can offer extensive dependency and access control.[5] By sub-classing the `ZQueen` class, a programmer can gain a complete control over creation of lenses and their access in respective queen-spaces.

[5]The basic queen implementation of MIR blessing checks that all context arguments belong to the queen or to its dependencies. As all arguments of link and list modifications enter into the context part of a MIR, the consistency of object-spaces with respect to dependencies is guaranteed.

Kings and queens are *lenses* and they are placed in the first available address of the ID object-space they are ruling. Each *ruler* also manages itself and can be accessed using the standard GLED mechanisms (MIRs, GUI control).

A queen can depend on other queens in the same sun-space or in the moon-space of a given Saturn. When a queen $\mathcal{Q}$ depends on a queen $\mathcal{Q}'$, subjects of $\mathcal{Q}$ can reference subjects of $\mathcal{Q}'$ by either aggregation method (link to them or hold them as list members). This means that $\mathcal{Q}'$ must be mirrored by a Saturn prior to mirroring of $\mathcal{Q}$. Otherwise the reconstruction of $\mathcal{Q}$'s queen-space would result in unresolved references.

Queens can migrate to other kings, either to higher or lower levels in Saturn hierarchy. This is facilitated by the ability of queens to create comets. Saving them to disk, for permanent storage or swapping purposes, is thus also possible.

Queen Types: Ordinary queens are created with no subjects and later instantiate them into their queen-spaces. When a lower level Saturn requests mirroring of a queen-space, it has to be serialized and sent to the moon. This is reasonable for dynamic data that is constantly changing. But often one needs a static library of lenses that can be referenced from other dependent queens. One such service is provided by the `IceQueen` class. Ice queens are instantiated from a comet and block all incoming MIRs. Lower Saturns can instantiate them in the same manner, by loading the comets from a permanent media, thus saving the network bandwidth. Another option, semi-statical in nature, is given by the `FileQueen` class. File queens are spawned over a ROOT file and provide a mapping from a full pathname to a lens identifier. When sending such queens to a moon it is enough to stream this mapping and the moon can instantiate the objects from the local storage devices. A similar concept could be used for connecting GLED's object-spaces to a database system.

5. Representation and Management of a Gled Cluster. A GLED cluster is composed of Saturns organized in a tree structure. Inside GLED each Saturn is represented by a lens of glass `SaturnInfo`. It provides the network identity of a given node and is also the natural place to store access privileges and other static or dynamic properties of a node.[6] Further, `SaturnInfo` has three links: one to its master Saturn (for SunAbsolute this is link is `null`) and two to lists holding its direct client Saturns and connected Eyes (viewers). Representants of all Saturns are instantiated and maintained under a special queen, called the *sun-queen.* It is the first queen of the sun-king of Sun Absolute and is pushed down to all connecting Saturns. This means thateach node in a GLED cluster is always aware of the whole cluster structure. Furthermore, this structure is rooted in the object-space itself and directly accessible using the standard mechanisms of the GLED paradigm.

A Saturn can accept connections from any number of Eyes. They also have a corresponding `EyeInfo` structure allowing each viewer to have its own access privileges. Various messages can be sent directly to an Eye, thus providing an efficient way for delivery of messages, warnings and errors resulting from execution of MIRs originating from the Eye in question.

Structure of a GLED cluster is therefore exported to all Saturns but is managed centrally at the Sun Absolute. Any lens can get information about any Saturn or Eye in the cluster and send it requests or messages. A direct bridge can be opened between any two Saturns to allow for node-to-node data transmissions.

The `SaturnInfo` structure also holds unique identifications of both sun-king and fire-king of its Saturn. By combining these IDs with MIRs directed at the Saturn in question, kings can create queens in their object-spaces on request from any Saturn in the cluster (although the requesting Saturn might not be able to *see* this queen). These queens can then perform

[6] E.g. node architecture, amount of RAM, CPU speed, load averages and other monitoring data. Fig. 7.1 shows all GUI enabled data members of the `SaturnInfo` glass.

some computation on behalf of the caller, either locally or by spreading it further down to lower level Saturns.

In a similar manner connections between several GLED clusters could be implemented.

6. Operators & Threads. Each Saturn can run many threads simultaneously. A glass that needs to acquire its own thread for a certain task or computation must be subclassed from the `Eventor` glass. The common base provides mechanisms for thread control and identification. Each `Eventor` contains a directory-like structure of `Operators` (also glasses) representing the actual algorithmic elements of a thread. The operators can be traversed once or several times until some exit condition is met. All thread operations are therefore encapsulated in the framework and can be controlled with MIRs as well as from GLED GUI.

Execution of and descending into individual operators can be controlled at run-time, so the operator graph traversal is determined by the state of its elements. Thread methods are exception throwing to provide error recovery and thread state management facilities.

When a thread is created, its owner becomes the sender of the MIR that triggered thread's execution. This is rather important as threads can create MIRs and post them directly into a Saturn's routing system. By accessing this information the Saturn can determine the owner of the thread and set the caller ID of MIR accordingly.

Any method can be called from a thread (there is no built-in restriction mechanism) and it is rather easy to spoil the consistency of object-spaces by direct modification of lenses when a MIR should have been used. Also, locks must be used when accessing data of lenses which are not guaranteed to remain constant. Threads are no toys: they are high-speed execution agents that would, if limited in their execution power, hinder the computational performance of GLED.

Threads can be used to perform computations, certain periodical tasks (such as monitoring of the node activity) or can be input-driven if they perform I/O operations. They can also spawn new processes and act as their supervisors, faithfully representing their state and monitoring the output.

7. Viewing & Rendering Infrastructure. GUI elements provided by an application framework/toolkit should be general enough to allow implementation of a wide range of user interfaces. GLED GUI, as the rest of the system, is based on the notion of extended `C++` class: its main purpose is to allow users to manipulate object-data and to invoke object-methods. This implies that the application front-end has to be representable by a collection of classes that hold the relevant configuration data and implement the desired functionality.[7] As a default GUI is provided for all classes the prototype application GUI is readily available.

The GUI architecture is modular and extensible. Each library set can, besides the autogenerated widgets for glasses, define their own GUI elements. This, in principle, allows for construction of custom, hand-made GUI front-ends and restricted user interfaces.

7.1. Standard GUI elements. Viewing objects are completely decoupled from the core of the GLED system. They are managed by the `Eye` class which serves as a router between the local Saturn and actual viewing elements. Towards the Saturn it transmits MIRs generated by lens-views in their GUI callback functions. From Saturn it receives change notifications objects (or `Rays`) containing, among other things, the lens identity and type of change that occurred (change of member data, links, list contents, etc.). As each Eye holds a mapping from viewed lenses to list of their lens-views, it can efficiently update all views of the changed lens. This also implies that each lens can have an arbitrary number of GUI representations.

[7] In OO applications this is always the case, anyway.

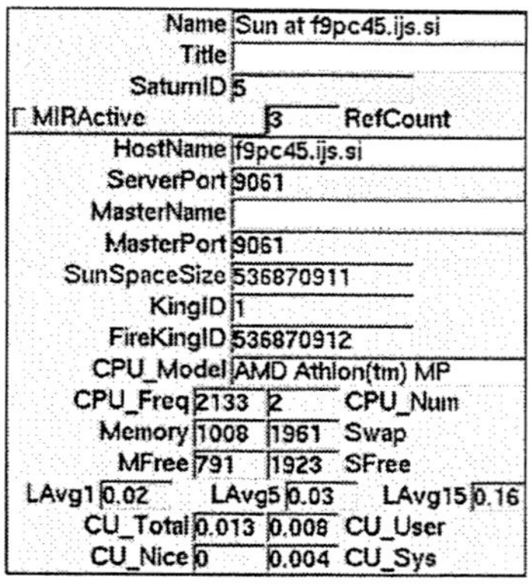

FIG. 7.1. *A* full-lens-view *for the SaturnInfo glass.*

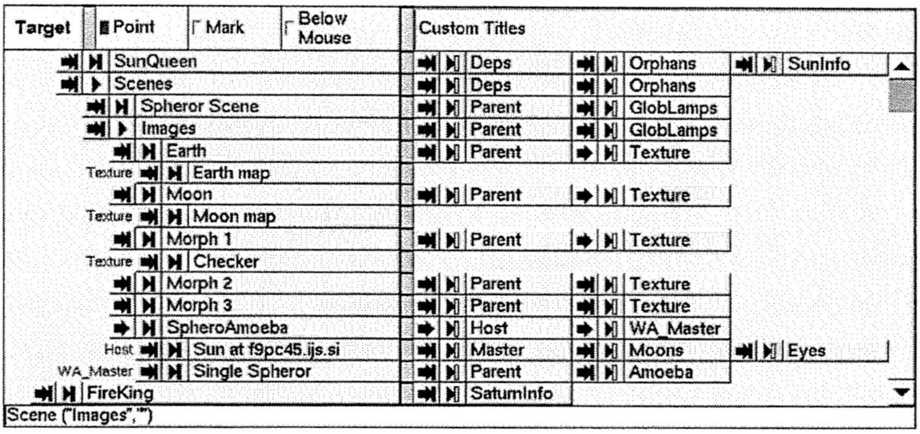

FIG. 7.2. *A lens browser displaying a lens graph. Each entry has two collapsing buttons: one for links and the other for list members. Links of each lens are displayed on the right part of the browser.*

The base class for lens-views (A_View) contains a minimal representation of the observed lens and some abstract methods for handling of change notifications. Further base classes are provided for representations of links and lists. Automatically generated widgets for lenses as well as the hand-made GUI front-end are all built upon these base classes. As details of the implementation are beyond the scope of this article, the emphasis will be put on features of the GUI (implemented using the FLTK widget library [8]).

For each lens a window containing a collection of all automatically generated widgets for a given lens can be created (e.g. Fig. 7.1). It includes widgets for all parent classes, ordered by the class hierarchy.

An important feature of the GLED GUI is a generalized structure browser (*lens-browser*). It displays lenses together with their list members and links. The list members are shown in a collapsible vertical structure (as in most standard file/object browsers) while links are represented in a horizontal structure, allowing more compact views of selected lenses (e.g. Fig. 7.2). The lens-browser provides a means for manipulation of links, modification of list contents and instantiation of new lenses. Lenses can also be exported into the C++ interpreter shell for manual operations.

The lens-browser has another mode in which its right part contains a custom set of widgets for each lens (sub-selection of those from a full-lens-view). The desired glasses and their members can be specified using a simple syntax. A specialized parser then creates the

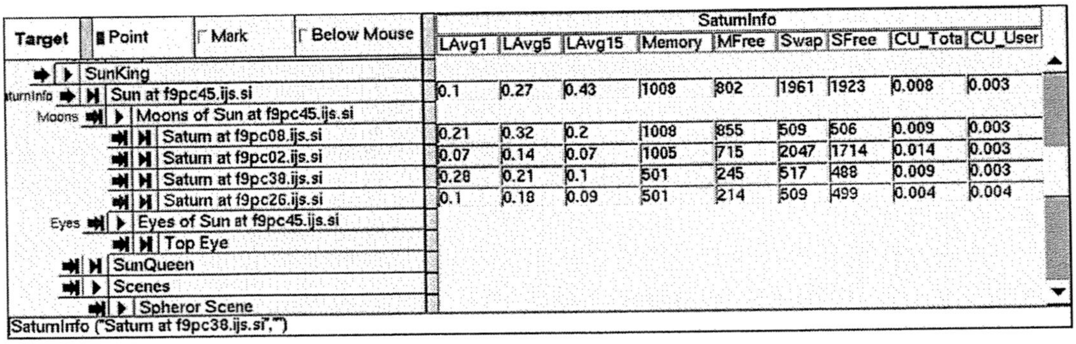

FIG. 7.3. *A set of custom-generated widgets inside a lens browser showing* `SaturnInfo` *structures for a* GLED *cluster composed of five nodes.*

appropriate widgets for each lens (Fig. 7.3). Such views provide an efficient way for viewing and editing of a large number of lenses.

7.2. Rendering. The rendering infrastructure offers the representation of lenses and lens-graphs in 3D space. Actual rendering of lenses is done by a parallel class structure that has to be coded manually for each rendering device.[8] It is not mandatory for glasses to have a corresponding rendering class: they can use the renderer of any of their base classes. Rendering classes for each device and each library set are produced as independent libraries and can be dynamically loaded into a running GLED system.

A high level of flexibility is achieved by actual rendering of each lens being split into three functions: `PreDraw()`, `Draw()` and `PostDraw()`. Further, rendering is proceeding on an arbitrary number of levels allowing the draw methods of the lens, its links and list members to be called in any order. This provides a versatile infrastructure for traversal of lens-graphs as well as for management of renderer state (lighting, polygon mode, material properties, texturing, etc.).

More examples of GLED's GUI and can be found at the project's homepage [9].

8. Applications of the Gled system. We have presented the core functionality of the GLED system which, from this perspective, offers an OO framework. However, if one is interested in building a distributed application, the base classes of GLED can be seen as elements of a toolkit. Future work will, among other things, focus on development of library sets (offering particular implementations for selected areas of interest) and preparation of corresponding demonstration programs. Based on these, GLED will also become a toolkit for respective development areas.

To conclude this paper the GLED system will be discussed from the point of view of four different usage modes. This will serve to recapitulate the main ideas, to merge the presented details into a coherent whole and to discuss future extensions of GLED.

8.1. Single machine, single user usage. GLED classes can serve as an interface to configuration and execution of user algorithms as well as for visualization of resulting data. Persistency of configuration data and results of algorithms is achieved by using ROOT's object serialization and I/O infrastructure (ROOT files and trees).

Glass member functions can hold the implementation of the algorithms or can serve as a wrapper layer for a specialized (numerical) library which can be implemented in any language linkable with `C++`. By sub-classing the base thread glass (`Eventor`) finer control over operation and configuration of algorithms can be achieved.

[8]OpenGL is used as the standard real-time renderer, others can be added using a common render-driver API.

As GUI classes are automatically generated for all glasses, they can immediately serve for composition of object graphs, for configuration and editing of member data and for algorithm control via management of threads. CINT, the `C/C++` interpreter, offers a general scripting interface to all GLED's functionality and thus complements the GUI functionality for complex and repetitive tasks.

Standard data presentation services, such as histograms and graphs, are offered by the ROOT system. Further, ROOT has a rich set of tools and algorithms for statistical analysis, minimization and spectral analysis.

Dynamic real-time 3D visualization can easily be programmed by providing the rendering classes and using the `Eventor`-thread infrastructure. As rendering crucially depends on the underlying data-structures it is hard, if not impossible, to provide a generic and efficient set of rendering atoms. However, for some specific cases the renderers are already available. E.g. a representation of a 2D function on a rectangular mesh (using ROOT's `TMatrix` class) and 3D triangulated surfaces (wrapper over GTS library [10]). Further rendering elements will become available with appearance of new library sets and with their proper structuring GLED will offer a generic multi-purpose rendering toolkit.

8.2. Distributed and `grid` computing. The GLED framework enables prototyping and control of algorithms performing computation or dynamic visualization within a hierarchic server-client-viewer model. As topology of the cluster is not limited and can also change dynamically, sophisticated problem solving strategies can be implemented over heterogenous clusters (MIRs and streamed data are architecture independent).

A particularly interesting feature of GLED is that the cluster structure itself is directly accessible to algorithms using the standard framework mechanisms. On one hand this provides a means for cluster monitoring and visualization while on the other it allows for dynamic optimization of the cluster structure.

Currently there are no central mechanisms for node allocation and acquisition. Such mechanisms will be implemented as daemons or network services with a top-level node manager. Another option is to adopt `grid` resource allocation services when they become standardized. Until then standard remote command execution mechanisms can be used (e.g. `rsh` or `ssh`).

Each node in a distributed cluster and each thread within a node analyses and/or produces data. Based on the nature of the problem, different solutions for emitting the resulting data may be applied.

- If the data is segmented into many relatively small fragments or is needed for continuation of computation on some other node, then it can be sent encapsulated into a MIR. The object that receives the MIR can properly place the data into a larger structure or further propagate it to relevant algorithms. Arguments of the MIR can serve as instructions for management of the subsequent data. This way MIRs can serve as carriers for a sophisticated data exchange protocol.
- If the data is produced in large fragments and is not instantly needed for further computation then it can be emitted via standard data-exchange mechanisms, e.g. `ftp`, `rootd` (remote access to ROOT files) or distributed file-systems (nfs, afs). The data can also be cached in the vicinity of the local node and transmitted on request upon completion of the computation on a larger scale. This allows minimal network connection duration and provides means for shaping of the network traffic.

Similar problems arise when algorithms need read access to shared data. Further development of GLED will also address various data exchange mechanisms and will offer some concrete implementations of data traffic structuring and `grid`-aware data addressing protocols.

8.3. Multi-user information systems. Hierarchic structure of the GLED cluster makes it an interesting platform for implementation of collaborative tools and VR systems. Intermediate proxy nodes can provide an effective reduction of network traffic when several nodes from several organizations are connected into a common information system.

The concurrent access of several user requires an elaborate authentication & access control mechanism. Implementation of such infrastructure is under way. Authorization is performed during MIR processing stage (as a part of blessing of a MIR by a `Queen`) and further infrastructure is being implemented that allows individual lenses and `Queens` to specify access policy. At first GLED will use internal user and group databases and in due time interfaces to appropriate LDAP and `grid` services will be created.

As GLED offers a direct correspondence between lenses and their 3D representations, advanced VR systems with immersive control over object graphs can be implemented. This requires further work on UI infrastructure, which has to provide mechanisms for creation of complex object contexts with transparent access to available member functions and their arguments. However, the infrastructure for emitting MIRs from UI and receiving update requests is implemented as a part of the core system. The available GUI elements (full-lens-views, lens-browser and GL rendering window) provide a general interface to mechanisms of the GLED system and offer an example of complexity that can be achieved by indirect mapping of lenses to GUI structures.

8.4. Encapsulated network services. By encapsulating network services within a sub-class of the `Eventor` glass, threads from within the Saturn can offer any kind of service to outside clients, for example:

- Provide information about local Saturn and local computing node (status, monitoring data, catalog of locally available data and availability of other services).
- Export its object-spaces and local data to consumers by using any desired protocol. For example, lens graphs and lens data could be exported via `http` protocol in `html` or `xml` format.
- Serve as entry point for computation or service instantiation requests. After a successful authentication such request can result in creation of a thread that will provide the required service.
- Serve as entry point for data coming from external sources, such as other processes or sensors connected to the node.

In this respect GLED offers monitoring and replication facilities for such services as well as infrastructure for following and reporting the usage patterns (ROOT trees, histograms and graphs). It is also an advantage that multiple services can be spawned from within the same process: it allows for easier load balancing between different services and allows implementation of advanced strategies for resolving complex queries (e.g. `grid` resource allocation requests) or providing parallel file I/O operations.

9. Conclusion. The GLED system brings together a colorful collection of modern computing techniques and binds them within a fairly general implementation of a hierarchic server–client model. By merging cluster creation and configuration tools, object-based RPC, threaded exectuion environment, automatically generated GUI widgets and sophisticated 3D rendering infrastructure, GLED has been shown to represent a useful OO framework/toolkit for development of a number of distinctly different applications that can take advantage of distributed computing environment, object serialization, cooperative multi-user GUI and rich data presentation & visualization infrastructure. In GLED these complex techniques are represented at a fairly abstract level but at the same time a low-level interface is available to allow for further extensions and more specialized implementations.

We hope that GLED addresses the demands and possibilities of modern computing in a fashion that is both interesting as a research project and usable as a concrete framework implementation.

Availability. The implementation of the described framework is publicly available [9]. While GLED is constantly developing, its core functionality is stable and suitable for implementation of production systems. As it is with any open-source project, the future development of GLED largely depends on interests and contributions from users of outside communities.

Acknowledgments. I am infinitely indebted to my friend J. J. Javoršek for his support and enthusiasm for the GLED project. Without his willingness to spend countless hours discussing the arising problems and ideas GLED, most probably, would not exist at all.

Many thanks go to teams developing ROOT, `perl`, FLTK and GNU development tools for excellent packages that make the burdens of software development bearable.

REFERENCES

[1] R. Brun and F. Rademakers, *ROOT - An Object Oriented Data Analysis Framework*, Proceedings AIHENP'96 Workshop, Lausanne, Sep. 1996, Nucl. Inst. & Meth. in Phys. Res. A 389 (1997) 81-86. See also `http://root.cern.ch/`.

[2] SETI@home, *The Search for Extraterrestrial Intelligence*, `http://setiathome.ssl.berkeley.edu/`.

[3] Folding@home, *Distributed protein folding simulations*, `http://folding.stanford.edu/`.

[4] A.D. Birrell and B.J. Nelson, *Implementing Remote Procedure Calls*, XEROX CSL-83-7, October 1983.

[5] R. Srinivasan, *XDR: External Data Representation Standard*, RFC 1832, Sun Microsystems, Inc., August 1995.

[6] W. Yeong, T. Howes and S. Kille, *Lightweight Directory Access Protocol*, RFC 1777, Performance Systems International, University of Michigan, ISODE Consortium, March 1995.

[7] M. Goto, *C++ Interpreter - CINT*, CQ publishing, ISBN4-789-3085-3 (Japanese).

[8] B. Spitzak, et al, *FLTK - A Fast Light ToolKit*, `http://www.fltk.org/`.

[9] The GLED project homepage: `http://www.gled.org/`.

[10] *GTS - GNU Triangulated Surface Library*, `http://gts.sourceforge.net/`.

In: Applied Parallel and Distributed Computing
Editors: Yi Pan and Laurence T. Yang , pp. 39-52

ISBN 1-59454-174-4

TOWARD AUTOMATIC POLICY MANAGEMENT IN DISTRIBUTED SECURITY INFRASTRUCTURES*

VALENTINA CASOLA†, NICOLA MAZZOCCA† , ANTONINO MAZZEO‡ , AND VALERIA VITTORINI‡

Abstract. In the recent years, the need of Policies to dynamically face security problems has grown in all computer system areas, especially in distributed and heterogeneous systems where security is a strong requirement, and in Security Infrastructures, in particular in Public Key Infrastructures on which our attention is focused. Policies assist systems administrators in specifying rules for the management of resources and members, they are usually very complex object and there is a strong need for unifying frameworks and automated tools to help administrators in the management of a policy in its all life cycle. In this paper, we first present the results of our analysis on policies and policy languages used to formally express security statements in distributed systems; then we will illustrate our framework for a certificate policy formalization and finally a policy-based approach to solve security interoperability problems that arise in un-trusted distributed domains is proposed.

Key words. Distributed infrastructure, Public key infrastructure, Policy frameworks, Policy-based security

1. Introduction. Information security is growing in importance in all organizations in which there is a need to integrate diverse systems as part of a broader environment, allowing the rapid integration of disparate platforms and legacy systems, applications and information. Furthermore, the continuous development of Distributed Architectures and Systems offers the opportunity to have a wide number of resources that are geographically distributed. Such resources and, at the same time, the easiness with which they can be created and placed at disposal of those who can access the system, causes several problems especially related to their integration. Distributed Systems and wide Infrastructures have reached a very high complexity; they manage a big amount of functions and data in multiple formats and they allow to exchange information in many formats, too. Such complexity not only makes them vulnerable to attacks but, if not well managed, it seriously risks to compromise the performances of the system.

Our research field copes interoperability problems of heterogeneous components and especially the security problems involved in their integration. An heterogeneous distributed architecture presents several security requirements, the main problem is that the final system is composed by several sub-systems each one characterized by different security policies and their integration involves heavy security management problems which could make the whole system weak. Heterogeneous security environment are characterized by some internal nodes on internal networks, protected from the Internet by firewalls and with encrypted internal communications; other nodes may be out in the open network, they require network, transport or application-level mechanisms to protect the confidentiality and integrity of communications. Traditional distributed applications may have their own security mechanisms that companies can manage on individual basis. But, maintaining different security mechanisms and protocols for each module will make managing overall system security impossible. The security policies applied within such environments must specify protection of individual object, resources and control access, but such policies have to be able to include

*This work is part of a wider research project in the field of security management by the University of Naples Federico II and by the Second University of Naples; it is partially supported by Consorzio Interuniversitario Nazionale per l'Informatica (CINI) and by the National Research Council (CNR).

†Department of Computer Science, Second University of Naples, (valentina.casola@unina2.it,nicola.mazzocca@unina2.it).

‡Department of Computer Science and System Analysis, University of Naples Federico II, (mazzeo@unina.it,vittorin@unina.it)

the integration of all security services. We are seeing a substantial growth in the number of policy engine and policy-enabled services and applications. Interoperability problems are directly associated to incompatible security policies, looking forward end-users and systems-administrators will need to have a unified, conceptually "centralized view" of the policies that they have specified and a unified understanding of how the policies will play out the underlying infrastructure. At this aim, we have focused our attention on policy formalization, since the definition of a common policy framework could be explicitly used to trust other domains and extend security mechanisms. The use of a common policy language, that is a language suitable for all system components, to efficiently model the security critical aspects, looks like very promising if we think of flexible and efficient functionality of policy-based security technology applied not only to manage the resource of a system, both locally and via-Web (access management), but also to configure each system component, guarantying its security and integrity.

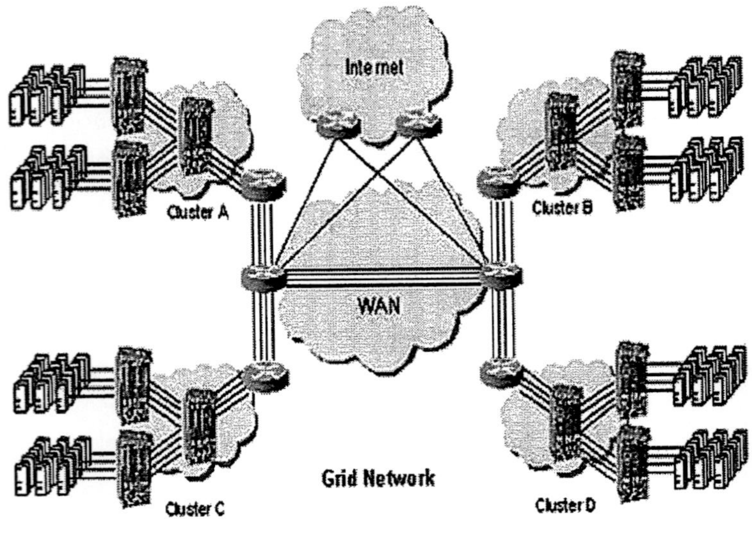

FIG. 1.1. *The layered model of a Distributed Architecture*

This research field is very interesting because actually there are a lot of policies to manage security protocols and applications and this represents a grave lack to inter-domain interoperability. There is a wide number of private structures and languages in which the policies are expressed, and the lack of a common language to express them is an open problem for the whole community.

So, we have decided to face interoperability problems starting from the definition of common languages; we first illustrate our analysis on some proposals available in literature, then we will describe our framework. the first result of our work is the capability of establish a "network of trust" in an heterogeneous environment between distributed infrastructures on the basis of their single policies without the help of external Third Parties or pre-defined hierarchical structures. At this aim we are evaluating the potentialities of polices in the Access Control and Authentication management with a special focus on a trusted authentication of users of different domains by means of automated policy-mapping. In particular, we will illustrate how our approach could be helpful in automating policy management and comparison in wide distributed architectures, especially to authenticate and trust users certified in un-trusted domains by un-trusted Public Key Infrastructures (PKIs).

This paper is an extension of a precedent work, it is organized as follow: in Section 2 we will illustrate the analysis of some existing policies expressed in "proprietary" languages; in Section 3 there is a depth-in introduction on policies for Virtual Organizations and on Policy Languages; in Section 4 we will illustrate how we were able to translate a particular class of policies (Certificate policy for Public Key Infrastructure), according to the defined formalization, in a suitable language, and we will illustrate some examples and a case study. Finally in Section 5 there is a wide description of Future works.

2. Security Policies. In the recent years, the need of Policy to dynamically face security problems has grown in all computer system areas, especially in distributed and heterogeneous systems where security is a strong requirement, and in Security Infrastructures (PKI) on which our attention is focused. These infrastructure present peculiar characteristics, such as: decentralization in architecture and in administration, heterogeneity in implementation technologies, distribution across multiple departments, peer-based architecture, open to the public Internet. Any of these characteristics present challenges to the overall security of the system, for example there is the need to:

- enforce a security policy across an entire environment with multiple heterogeneous systems;
- ensure that security policies are enforced by special users, as "desktop administrators";
- be able to work with an outside vendor that is weak in security or with legacy systems;
- monitor and audit activities and administrate access across multiple heterogeneous systems.

In the following subsections we first present the requirements a policy must meet and then a number of policies languages available in literature. According to us, they could be very suitable for our purposes, looking for methods and mechanisms to express the security policy of a system combining together the policies at the base of the single components and managing all the conflicts that could arise in managing shared resources.

2.1. Policy requirements. In literature we have found a lot of policy languages, they all present security models or mechanisms trying to define logical languages for expressing Policies and, in general, security constraints. We have tried to extract from the existing approaches the main features and requirements a policy must meet. What it is emerged is not the syntactical or semantical approach of each proposal (almost all of them define policies and their provisions as sets of couples (provisions-type, value-of-provision)), but the way they define a logical structure of the security provisions (Graphs, hierarchical structures, Knowledge-based representations, XML-based and RDF approach), trying how to:

- express a policy in a domain-independent way;
- build flexible language;
- extend trust to domain with different policies.

It is in fact on the chosen structure that they are able to impose constraints (both domain dependent and independent) and verify properties to guarantee security requirements. In this subsection we want to illustrate the main features of the languages analyzed. Among the wide number of languages available in literature, we have looked for proposal in which users could be able in separating policy from system mechanisms (that is its implementations details), allowing behavior of the system and its management strategy to be changed by changing the policy without affect the implementations. It is in fact on such policies languages that we could address feasible solutions for interoperability problems. According to this research, we have located some requirements a policy model must satisfy:

1. *Composition*, which allows to enforce several policies on the same environment

grouping both basic security policies and management policies relating to roles, to organizational units or to specific applications;

2. *Extensibility*, which is needed to cater for new types of policy and security statements that may arise in future;
3. The model must be *comprehensible* and *easy* to use by policy users.

Moreover, there is the need of "structuring techniques" to facilitate the specification of policies relating to large systems; and it must be possible to "analyze policies" for conflicts and inconsistencies resolution, both in static and dynamic ways.

2.2. Policy languages. In this subsection we describe some policy language available in literature, trying to underline their capability to meet the illustrated requirements, since they could help in system security integration. We are going to consider the following languages:

1. Ponder;
2. SPL;
3. ASL;
4. Rei.

We have chosen these languages for their capability in solving conflict resolution because interoperability problems often arise from a wrong conflict resolution management when addressing to heterogeneous systems which share common resources.

2.2.1. Ponder. Ponder [1] allows general security policies to be specified. A policy is made up of a set of rules that define a choice in the behavior of a system, separating policy from mechanisms. Ponder is a declarative, strongly typed and object-oriented language for specifying both security and management policies. An important element of each policy is the set of conditions under which the policy is valid; these conditions could depend on other policies active in the domain; Ponder divide constraints into two categories: "single policy constraints" (based on temporal and state conditions and which can be resolved at compile time) and constraints for groups of policies, called meta-policies (to express constraints which bound the permitted policies in the system, or don't allow the simultaneous execution of conflicting policies). This second category is a very important feature of Ponder, it represents the possibility to structure policy by groups, roles, types or relations; this is very important for the policy management in large, complex enterprizes (scalability feature) and, from our point of view, scalability is very important in all that distributed systems with nodes that share common security policies.

2.2.2. SOL. SPL [2] is a security language that is flexible enough to express simultaneously several types of complex authorization policies. One of the problems of putting together several policies on the same environment is the conflict that arises from contradictory decisions produced by the different policies. SPL solves this problem by forcing security administrators to take priority decisions on every policy composition. SPL is a policy-oriented constraint-based language. It is composed of four basic blocks: entities, sets, rules and policies. The fundamental block of the language is the rule. Rules express constraints in terms of relations between entities and sets. Policies are complex constraints that result from the composition of rules and sets into logical units; they can also be composed into more complex policies until they form a global and single policy. Policies provide the structure needed to build complex access control mode, it is model-independent but not model-less. A rule can be composed of other rules through a specific tri-value algebra with three logic operators: conjunction ('AND'); disjunction ('OR'); and negation ('NOT'). In order to increase the flexibility of composition, SPL defines universal and existential quantifiers over rules. Moreover, it's possible to apply constraints on rules written by different authors in different domains (polymorphic restriction operator). So this language seems very suitable to integrate different policies.

2.2.3. ASL. ASL [3] describes the specifications of a language based on logic that tries to support different access control policies. ASL allows users to not only specify authorization policies, but also specify the way the decisions over these policies are made. The language comprises different kinds of rules, among these we find resolution rules, which regulate how conflicts between authorizations must be resolved and integrity rules, which are used to express different kinds of constraints on the specification and use of authorizations. Using these rules, it is possible to describe different access control policies. This language requires proper skills to be used because it consists of inter-dependent rules that the user has to fully understand; the formal mathematical approach is not intuitive and does not easily map onto implementation mechanisms. ASL does not make provisions for domain dependent information even if it includes a form of meta-policy called "integrity rules" to specify application-dependent rules that bound the range of acceptable policies, and insists on a restricted set of conditions.

2.2.4. Rei. Rei [4] is a general policy language with an associated policy engine that interprets policies written in this language. The language is modelled on deontic logic. Rei policy language provides constructs based on deontic concepts. These constructs are extremely flexible and allow different kinds of policies to be stated. This simple policy language is not tied to any specific application and allows domain dependent information to be added without any modification. The policy engine associated with Rei accepts policies in first order logic and in Resource Description Framework [5]. By separating policies from mechanisms, it is possible to change the behavior of entities dynamically without changing the implementation. Systems are viewed as divided into overlapping domains, each domain is either a physical or a virtual domain. It should be able to express security policies and management policies.

The languages illustrated in this section are very suitable to express security statements, especially the ones related to access control and authorization; furthermore, they are very helpful in understanding how we could use a language to solve conflicts and other interoperability problems that arise in distributed systems. Starting from these approaches, in the next sections we will illustrate a specific language for express security provisions and procedures for a Public Key Infrastructure.

3. Policies in Virtual Organization. As distributed and parallel computing evolves, Virtual Organization (VO) will become more important, they have a lot of resources and members and it will become very difficult to administrate them. VO policies assist the creators and administrators of Vo by allowing them to specify a set of rules that govern the virtual community, an important issue is how any of the VO system services can ensure the integrity of the messages they receive and how they can authenticate the senders.

Users, hosts and services need to be able to authenticate themselves in a distributed environment. Basically, authentication between two entities on remote nodes means that each party establishes a level of trust in the identity of the other party.

In practical use an authentication protocol sets up a secure communication channel between the authenticated parties, so that subsequent messages can be sent without repeated authentication steps, although it is possible to authenticate every message. Solution available in literature [14] make use of digital signature on messages exchanged between services. For example the WS-Security specification [15] defines a standard technique for signing XML messages, PKI cryptography and X.509 certificates can be used to generate signatures or to encrypt only a part of the message. The identity of an user and in general of an entity is typically represented by a token or a name that uniquely identifies that entity. One commonly used identity token is provided by an X.509 public key certificate. In order for a relying party to trust identity certificates signed by a given CA, it must trust that only the CA has access to the CA's private key, so that no other entity can sign certificates with that key, trust that the CA always associates each Distinguished Name (DN) and public key with the same individual or entity. i.e., the DN and the public key are permanently assigned to this entity (even after revocation or expiration, they cannot be reused by another entity),trust that the CA did acceptable job of verifying that the holder of the certificate is the individual named by the DN. All these aspects must be carefully defined by a policy. How these objectives are going to be achieved should be defined in the Certification Policy (CP) and Certification Practice Statement (CPS) documents of each CA. The CP should spell out the obligations of a certificate holder, to keep the private key secure, but both the CA and the relying party must trust the user to follow the procedures. If each of these assertions is true then the relying party can trust that the person or other entity connected via a secure protocol is the unique entity that is named in the X.509 certificate. Thus the certificate can be used to make a secure and authenticated connection. Some persons are members of more than one VO and they would end up with a certificate from each VO. This could be seen as a good thing, since it would allow a user to act in different capacities (or roles) by using different identity certificates. However, managing different certificates is also a burden on the user, especially in view of the primitive tools available for certificate handling. A more serious objection was the merging of authorization into the concept of identity and authentication. The general consensus was that we should remain with the principle of using X.509 certificates purely for authentication of identity and handle authorization as a separate problem (for example with X.509 Attribute Certificate).

3.1. Certificate policy. Public key certificates can be characterized by a number of different aspects including the nature of the registration process that preceded their issuance, how active is their life cycle management, and the level of protection afforded to the associated private key. The relevance of a particular certificate to a given application may depend on these characteristics, as they will together determine the level of assurance that a relying party can place in that certificate. Other factors that may impact whether or not a certificate is appropriate to a given application include: the level of liability the issuing Certification Authority (CA) is willing to assume if the certificate is shown to be fraudulent and the obligations of entities (subjects and relying parties) who may use that certificate. RFC-2527 [6] defines a framework for expressing this information in two related but separate documents - the Certificate Policy (CP) and Certificate Practices Statement (CPS)[9] a common (but not universally accepted) distinction is that the CP contains what is to be adhered to, while the CPS states how it is adhered to. In this interpretation then, the CP is thus seen as more fundamental; a Relying Party decision to trust a particular certificate is ultimately determined by the assertions that the CA makes with respect to the CP requirements, the Relying Party could choose not to concern itself with the details of how the CA meets these requirements. The legal complexity and size (sometime on the order of 100 pages) of CPs and CPS prevent them from being readily read and understood; consequently they may not adequately support the necessary legal concept of clear disclosure to be legally meaningful.

4. Cross Certification in a Distributed Infrastructure. In this section we are going to show how we were able to solve interoperability problems by using security policies in a distributed environment such Public Key Infrastructures (PKI). PKIs suffer of the same problems as distributed systems and there must be a way to combine separate infrastructures into a larger distributed "network of trust" [16]. The most basic PKI architecture contains a single Certification Authorities (CA) that provides the PKI services (certificates, certificate status information, etc.). All the users of the PKI place their trust in the only CA of the architecture, that is, the architecture has a single user trust point. This kind of architectures are not very scalable and a natural extension is to connect CAs that support different communities to create a larger PKI. In Figure 4-1 signer and verifier belong to two different CAs, if trust has not been established between the two domains prior the transaction (transaction between "strangers"), the verifier could not accept and trust the digital signature of a user whose Public Key Certificate (PKC) was issued in the domain A. An user who wants to verify a signature must verify the PKC first and then he must be sure that certificate has been issued by a trusted Certification Authority whose security procedures are expressed in a trusted security policy.

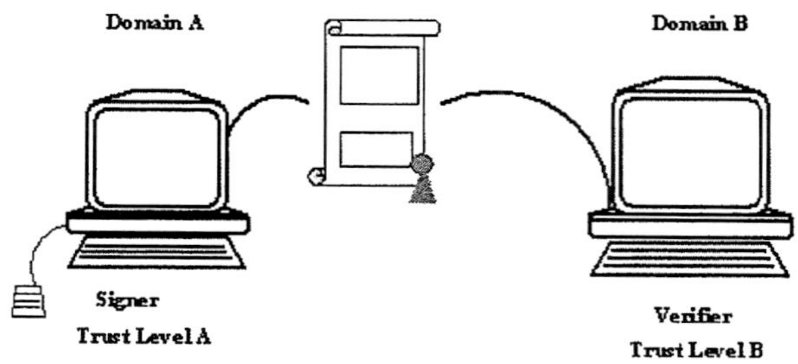

FIG. 4.1. *Verification of a digital signature*

A relying party may want to evaluate independently each CA that it is going to trust before installing its certificate. However, an alternative trust model exists where a CA will sign another CA certificate once it has verified that the other CA enforces policies that are as secure as its own (e.g. with an equivalent trust level). A subordinate CA is similar except that it only has a CA certificate signed by the parent CA, where a cross-signed CA has either a self-signed CA certificate or a CA certificate signed by a parent CA. The advantage of this model is that a relying party can accept subscribers from more CAs without having to individually evaluate and install all the CA certificates. However, it is important for a relying party to know if a trusted CA signs for other CA's certificates. Otherwise the relying party may be unexpectedly widening its trust domain. Note that not all path validation software recognizes CA chains, but may insist on having the certificates for every trusted CA.

Our target would be to realize an automatic method to verify a certificate issued by a different PKI without any common trusted point, helping CAs to decide which certificate policies from other security domains can be considered equivalent. To do this, each component within the larger network of PKIs needs a way to reliably recognize and trust digital certificates generated by the other domains, solving all involved security and interoperability problems. It's important to underline that PKI interoperability will be reached not just by technical specification interoperability or ciphering algorithms interoperability. Really, the international standards such as X.509 [6] [7]technically solve PKIs interoperability problems but they present great applicability problems. A PKI involves several "system, environments, policies, people and tools" and it becomes a tricky job to decide to trust other domains certifying them [8].

At this aim, several conceptual models are actually utilized [10][12][13]; they are all based on the definition of trusted common points:

- hierarchical model;
- bridge Certification Authority architecture;
- mesh architecture.

In Figure 4-2 there is an example of mesh architecture; in it you could see all the subject of a typical distributed PKI: the circles represent CAs, the little squares represent the issued certificates, a double sided arrow between CAs states that the CAs are mutually trusted (thanks to previous cross-certification) and finally the gray areas represent trusted domains.

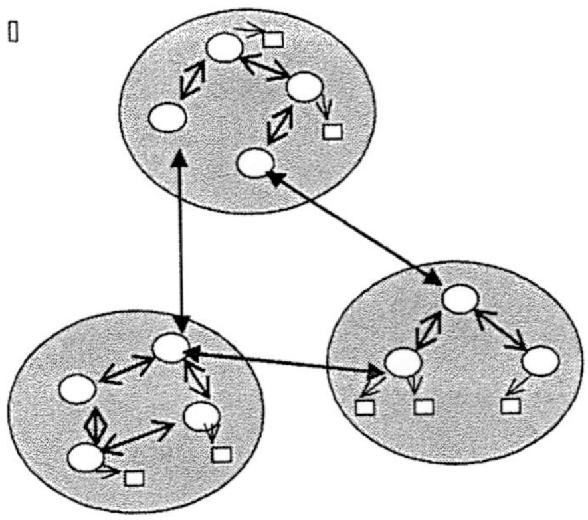

FIG. 4.2. *Mesh Architecture: Interoperability among PKIs with previous Cross Certifications*

Basically, isolated CAs are combined to form larger PKIs using superior subordinate relationships, or peer-to-peer relationships [16][17]. Each model has strengths and weaknesses and a clearly superior method has yet to emerge, nevertheless, all trust models have a common point: the policy mapping, that is a previous agreement between the Authorities based on the provisions described in their policies. Such activity is called "Cross-Certification"; it consists of a mutual agreement between the infrastructures; both technical and organizational teams are involved in deciding if the provisions described in the security policies and the trust level associated to them are equivalent.

After a Cross Certification, if the external CA is trusted, the verifier of Figure 4-1 could accept the signature of an external user simply verifying if the certificate and its corresponding key pair are valid. Actually the policy mapping is completely per-formed "by hand" and this represent one of the "open problems" in the practice of the Digital Signature in a distributed environment.

Until now there have not been automatic processes to verify and accept a certificate issued in an un-trusted domain. We think that a formalized certification policy could represent a very interesting solution to face this problem, at least in a well-defined operative context. A certificate policy standard doesn't exist yet, according to the assumptions of the first sections, if it had existed, an automatic policy mapping would have been possible and considerably simplified. The approach of following the same template would have the advantage of making easy the comparison of different policies and the identification of their similarities and differences.

4.1. Policy-based security interoperability: the proposed solution. We have focused our attention to the formalization of certificate policy, since they could be explicitly used to trust the information embedded in a PKC. As mentioned before, there is no standard format or standard list of topics for a policy which could be potentially very complex. Furthermore, because the provisions of different policies need to be compared, it would be beneficial if there were a commonly agreed approach to structure policy content. We would realize an automatic method to verify a certificate issued by a different PKI; our approach is not based on the availability of a trusted common point, as in the mentioned models, but on an automatic policy mapping, by means of a formalized security policy. To internationally recognize which are the guidelines to develop a policy is certainly a first footstep toward the formalization of the problem in the optics of the interoperability but, until now, these guidelines represent just a valid tool (or better, an outline) for those people who are about to write their organization policies. Some proposals of policy formalization have been made to develop Policy Framework or template; in literature, some examples of formalization of general security policies and Certificate Policies are available [18][19][20]. Probably, the most detailed and relevant suggestion for the formal presentation of Certificate Policies was described in the RFC2527. In all examined frameworks, high-level provisions which need to be part of a certificate policy were identified, but not in a formalized way, that is, even if there is a structure, policies are still supposed to be written in a natural and ambiguous language which represent one of the major problems for the automation of the cross certification process.

Starting from existing approaches [21] and guidelines [22], we propose a fine-grain formalization for a policy template; the obtained framework is structured by means of XML obtaining an extensible language to express potentially all security provisions and procedures of a PKI.

In particular the methodology we have developed, is made up of the following steps:

- analysis and formalization of PKI certificate policies;
- definition of a grammar of elements to specify an extensible policy language, by which all CAs could express their provisions and procedures.

In the first steps of our work, analyzing several policy, we have found all main provisions which could be represented in a parametric form, so, we were able to formalize all procedures and protocols described in the policy, and, where possible, to structure the textual provisions in a very fine-grain [11]. We have confirmed a hierarchical structure of the provisions as in other formalization attempts and we have confirmed the choice of main-topics, too, but what we have done is to refine the grain of fundamental provisions and procedures. Some of them primarily correspond to quantifiable parameters (key length, CRL publication period, etc) and they are usually used in available literature when comparing policies; other elements have a more complex and structured representation and the applicability of our method to those elements is the true innovation of our work. For all critical fields we have structured the data until we have obtained "leaves" representing the definition of new atomic or enumerative types. Following, there are examples of such structures implemented by XML; we first present the DTD for the definition of provision-types formalization, then the resulting XML is showed.

DTD of some Technical Security Provisions:

```
<!ELEMENT KeyPairGenerationInstallation (KeyPairGeneration,
PrivateKeyDeliveryEntity, PublicKeyDeliveryCertificateIssuer,
CAPublicKeyDeliveryUsers, KeySizes, PublicKeyParametersGeneration,
ParametersQualityChecking, HardwareSoftwareKeyGeneration,
KeyUsagePurposes)> ..
<!ELEMENT KeySizes
(Alghorithm,BitLenght)>

<!ELEMENT PrivateKeyProtection (StandardsCryptographicModule,
PrivateKeyMultiPersonControl, PrivateKeyProtectionBOX,
PrivateKeyEscrow, PrivateKeyBackup, PrivateKeyArchival,
PrivateKeyEntryCryptogrphicModule, MethodActivatingPrivateKey,
MethodDeactivatingPrivateKey,  MethodDestroingPrivateKey)> ..
<!ELEMENT PrivateKeyProtectionBOX (PrivateKeyNoProtection,
```

```
PrivateKeyOnLocalPC, PrivateKeyOnFloppy, PrivateKeyOnSmartCard,
PrivateKeyOnSmartCardWithBiometricSensor)>
```

XML implementation of some Technical Security Provisions:

```
<TechnicalSecurityControls> .....
        <KeyPairGenerationInstallation>

            <KeySizes>
                <Alghorithm>..... </ Algorithm >
                <BitLenght>..... </ BitLenght >
            </KeySizes> .................
        </KeyPairGenerationInstallation>
        ........
    <PrivateKeyProtection>
        <PrivateKeyProtectionBOX>
                <PrivateKeyNoProtection>..</PrivateKeyNoProtection>
                <PrivateKeyOnLocalPC>..</PrivateKeyOnLocalPC>
                <PrivateKeyOnFloppy>..</PrivateKeyOnFloppy>
                <PrivateKeyOnSmartCard>..</PrivateKeyOnSmartCard>
                <PrivateKeyOnSmartCardWithBiometricSensor>..
                </PrivateKeyOnSmartCardWithBiometricSensor>
        </PrivateKeyProtectionBOX
        ..
        <PrivateKeyEscrow>..</PrivateKeyEscrow>
        <PrivateKeyBackup>.</PrivateKeyBackup>

    </PrivateKeyProtection>
    ..........
</TechnicalSecurityControls>
```

DTD of some Publication Repository Provisions:

```
<!ELEMENT PublicationRepository (PublicationCAInformation,
FrequencyPublication, AccessControls, Repositories)>
<!ELEMENT FrequencyPublication (PolicyIssuanceFrequency,
PublishedCertificateIssuanceFrequency, CRLIssuanceFrequency)>
<!ELEMENT CRLIssuanceFrequency (FrequencyDays, FrequencyHours,
FrequencyMinutes, FrequencySeconds
```

XML implementation of some Publication Repository Provisions:

```
<PublicationRepository>
  <PublicationCAInformation>......</PublicationCAInformation>
  <FrequencyPublication>
    < PolicyIssuanceFrequency>.....</ PolicyIssuanceFrequency>
    < PublishedCertificateIssuanceFrequency>...
    </ PublishedCertificateIssuanceFrequency>
    < CRLIssuanceFrequency>.....</ CRLIssuanceFrequency>
  < FrequencyDay>.....</ FrequencyDay >
```

```
  < FrequencyHours>.....</FrequencyHours >
  < FrequencyMinutes>.....</ FrequencyMinutes >
  < FrequencySeconds>.....</ FrequencySeconds >
</FrequencyPublication> ........
</PublicationRepository>
```

All the provisions values are "parametric" so they allow CAs to solve the ambiguity tied to a personal interpretation of textual provisions. A simple XML parser could be used to extract from the proposed structure the information needed to automatically evaluate the value associated to each provision. Such formal structure helps during a cross certification, for example when:

1. The relying parties want to find specific provisions of the policy to trust, for a more accurate analysis.
2. The relying parties want to fix the conditions which trustworthy policy provisions have to match with.

We are already working on tools to manage in the appropriate way the parametric values extracted by the parser. In Figure 4-3 and 4-4 we show how a typical policy appear and how it has been transformed after our formalization. In Figure 4-3 there is part of the full original text (translated in English) of the Policy of Centro Tecnico, an Italian CA (Sections 10.2 and 10.3 of Centro Tecnico Policy)[23], while in Figure 4-4 there is the formalization corresponding to the policy of Figure 4-3.

```
A CA must ensure that the keys for digital signature operations
must be 1024 bit; for digital signature generation and
verification, the following algorithm must be used:  RSA.
Key pairs for all entities may be generated in a software or hardware
cryptographic module.
```

FIG. 4.3. *Example of Policy written in a natural language*

```
<KeyPairGenerationInstallation>
    <KeySizes>
            <Algorithm> RSA  </ Algorithm >
            <BitLenght> 1024 </ BitLenght >
    </KeySizes>
</KeyPairGenerationInstallation>

<PrivateKeyProtectionBOX>
    <PrivateKeyOnLocalPC>
        <cryptographic_module> software </cryptographic_module>
    </PrivateKeyOnLocalPC>
    <PrivateKeyOnSmartCard>
        <cryptographic_module> hardware </cryptographic_module>
    </PrivateKeyOnSmartCard>
</PrivateKeyProtectionBOX>
```

FIG. 4.4. *XML description of some Technical Security Provisions*

With this structure and with the language chosen (XML-based) it is in fact very simple for the relying parties find specific provisions of the policy to trust or investigate accurately specific procedures.

This XML could be machine-queried (searching to determine if the maximum liability is acceptable) as well as rendered for human consumption in a variety ways (e.g. through an XSLT conversion to HTML). We have used this approach to easily compare statements; in Figure 4-5 the Policy of Centro Tecnico and the Policy of the Government of Canada [24] are compared. It is plain that also a simple parser could be used to extract from the proposed structure the information needed to automatically perform a policy mapping; it is still semi-automated but it is suitable to develop fully automated methodologies and tools to manage policies of different security levels in all their life cycles.

		Gov of Canada	Centro Tecnico
Provision 1	Plain Text	Asymmetric Key Size = A CA must ensure that the key pairs for all PKI entities must be 2048 bit RSA (From Section 6.1.5)	Asymmetric Key Size = A CA must ensure that the keys for digital signature operations must be 1024 bit Algorithm = for digital signature generation and verification, the following algorithm must be used: RSA (From Section 10.2 and 10.3)
	XML formalization	<KeyPairGenerationInstallation > .... <KeySizes> <Algorithm> RSA </Alghorithm > <BitLenght>2048 </ BitLenght > </KeySizes> .... </KeyPairGenerationInstallation >	<KeyPairGenerationInstallation > .... <KeySizes> <Algorithm> RSA </ Algorithm > <BitLenght>1024 </ BitLenght > </KeySizes> .... </KeyPairGenerationInstallation >
Provision 2	Plain text	Hardware\Software key generation= Key pairs for all entities may be generated in a software or hardware cryptographic module (From Section 6.1.8)	Digital Signature Token for key generation = Key pairs may be generated and protected in the digital signature token (Smart Card); private key escrow is denied. (From Section 10.2)
	XML formalization	<PrivateKeyProtectionBOX > <PrivateKeyOnLocalPC> software cryptographic module </PrivateKeyOnLocalPC> <PrivateKeyOnSmartCard > hardware cryptographic module </PrivateKeyOnSmartCard > </PrivateKeyProtectionBOX >	<PrivateKeyProtectionBOX > <PrivateKeyOnSmartCard > hardware cryptographic module </PrivateKeyOnSmartCard > </PrivateKeyProtectionBOX >

FIG. 4.5. *Example of direct policy mapping*

5. Future works. We have already said that a policy is a very complex object; we think that only a formalized framework could help users and administrators to manage a policy in its life cycle. In particular, we are very interested in those aspects of the formalization which could help us in the comparison of policies to extend the trust to other domains governed by different policies. The first step in this direction is the formal definition of different security policy levels associated to the global system (usually represented by the security level associated to the applicability of the issued certificates), but also of the security level associated to the individual provisions since they usually bring very complex information which could be very critical for the overall security and that need to be taken in count with the appropriate weight. At this aim, starting from our formalization, we have imposed an order relation on each provision-type; such relation could be:

- explicit, if the element type is quantifiable or numeric;
- dependent by criteria established by the user or by PKI "experts" [25];

The aim of this step is the definition of a metric space with a distance criterium which could help us in the definition of a more sophisticated comparison criterium for policies. There are several ways to build a metric space, in particular, we are investigating techniques based on the definition of proper "security levels" which consider combinations of simple provisions. We think that this approach could represent a valid support to manage a policy in a not ambiguous way. The management of a policy is a very critical aspect of an Infrastructure and the solution based on common languages preserve the flexibility of the policy based approach and, at the same time, provide a valid tool for the management phases: from the editing to the analysis phase, from the validation to the comparison phase. So, we are now working on the integration of our approach with the definition of proper security metrics to evaluate a PKI trust level and to implement fully automated techniques.

6. Conclusion. The need of Policy to dynamically face security problems has grown in all computer system areas, especially in distributed and heterogeneous systems where security is a strong requirement, and in Security Infrastructures (PKI). After an introduction on security policies and on policy languages available in literature to formally express security statements, we have illustrate our policy-based method to solve interoperability problems between un-trusted PKIs. The solutions available in literature are able to guarantee a strong interoperability due to their hierarchical architecture or to trusted third parties who had already verified the policy mapping and had cross-certified other domains. In this paper we have proposed an approach which is not based on the availability of a trusted common point but on an automatic policy mapping, thanks to a previous policy formalization. We would like to integrate our approach with the definition of proper security metrics to evaluate a PKI trust level and to implement fully automated techniques to efficiently manage a certificate policy in its all life cycle.

REFERENCES

[1] DAMIANOU, N., DULAY, N., LUPU, E., SLOMAN M., *The Ponder policy specification language*, In Morris Sloman, editor, Proc. of Policy Worshop 2001, Bristol UK

[2] RIBEIRO, C., ZUQUETE, A., FERREIRA, P., GUEDES, *SPL: An access control language for security policies with complex constraints*, Proceedings of Network and Distributed System Security Symposium (NDSS) 2001 , San Diego, California.

[3] JAJODIA, S., SAMARATI, P., SUBRAHMANIAN, V.S, *A Logical Language for Expressing Authorizations*, Proc. IEEE Symp. on Research in Security and Privacy: 31-42, Oakland, California,

[4] KAGAL L., FININ T., JOSHI A.,*A Policy Language for a Pervasive Computing Environment*, Proceedings of the 4th Workshop on Policies for Distributed Systems and Networks (Policy 2003)

[5] *RDF: Resource Description Framework (RDF) Schema Specification 1999*

[6] S. CHOKHANI, W. FORD , *RFC: 2527 Internet X.509 Public Key Infrastructure Certificate Policy and Certification Practices Framework*, March 1999

[7] *RFC 2459: Internet X.509 Public Key Infrastructure Certificate and CRL Profile*, January 1999;

[8] W. FORD, M. S. BAUM, *Secure Electronic Commerce*, Prentice Hall Inc., Upper Saddle River (1997).

[9] S. BOEYEN, *Certificate Policies and Certification Practice Statements*, Version 1.0, February 1997, Entrust Technologies www.entrust.com

[10] W.POLK, N. HASTINGS, *Bridge Certification Authorities: Connecting B2B Public Key Infrastractures*,September 2000

[11] V. CASOLA, A. MAZZEO, N. MAZZOCCA, V. VITTORINI, *Policy Formalization to combine separate systems into larger connected networks of trust*, Proceedings of Net-Con'2002 Conference, October 2002, Paris, France.

[12] DR. S. BERKOVITS, DR. S. CHOKHANI, J. A. FURLONG,J. A. GEITER, J. C. GUILD , *Public Key Infrastructure Study, Final Report* , April, 1994 National Institute of Standards and Technology, Gaithersburg,

[13] *Report of Federal Bridge Certification Authority Initiative and Demonstration*, NIST 2001.

[14] G. WASSON, M. HUMPHREY, *Towards explicit policy management for virtual organizations* ,Proceedings of the 4th Workshop on Policies for Distributed Systems and Networks (Policy 2003)

[15] B. ATKINSON, *Web Services Security* , http:77msdn.microsoft.com7library7default.asp?url = /library/en-us/dnglobspec/html/ws-security.asp

[16] IAN CURRY, *Trusted Public-Key Infrastructures*, Version: 1.2, August 2000 , Entrust Technologies www.entrust.com

[17] JIM TURNBULL, *Cross-Certification and PKI Policy Networking*, Version: 1.0, August, 2000 Entrust Technologies www.entrust.com

[18] T. KLOBUCAR, B. JERMAN-BLAZIC , *A Formalization and evaluation of certificate policies*, Computer Communication 22 (1999), 1104-1110

[19] R. GRIMM, T.HETSCHOLD, *Security Policies in OSI management: experiences from the DeTeBerkom Project BMSec*, Proceedings of the JENC6,1995.

[20] MENDES, S.; HUITEMA, C., *A new approach to the X.509 framework: allowing a global authentication infrastructure without a global trust model*, Proceedings of the 1995 Symposium on Network and Distributed System Security (SNDSS'95)

[21] S. GRILL, *An Approach to Formally Compare and Query Certification Practice Statements*, Published on Informatik GI Workshop 2000 Berlin.

[22] *American Bar Association, Information Security Committee, Section of Science and Technology, Digital Signature Guidelines*, (1996) www.abanet.org/scitech/home.html

[23] *Centro Tecnico per la Rete Unitaria, Sezione Sicurezza: Manuale operativo per il servizio di certificazione di chiavi pubbliche per la rete unitaria della pubblica amministrazione*, Versione 1.1 , 4 Maggio 2001.

[24] *Digital Signature and Confidentiality, Certificate Policies for the Government of Canada Public Key Infrastructure*, version 3.02 , April 1999.

[25] S.A. KOKOLAKIS, E.A. KIOUNTOUZIS , *Achieving Interoperability in a Multiple-Security- Policies Environment*, Computers and Security 19, Issue 3, 1 March 2000

In: Applied Parallel and Distributed Computing
Editors: Yi Pan and Laurence T. Yang , pp. 53-61 ISBN 1-59454-174-4

INTEGRATION OF SEMANTIC AND CLUSTERING TECHNIQUES FOR WEB INFORMATION RETRIEVAL *

BENIAMINO DI MARTINO†, ANTONINO MAZZEO‡, AND NICOLA MAZZOCCA§

Abstract. In this paper we describe an hybrid semantic and statistical technique, and its prototypical implementation, for Information Retrieval of text documents and Web pages and sites. We have integrated a semantic based query definition technique, based on production rule expert systems technology and semantic networks representing semantical relationships among terms and hierarchical relationships among their constituents, with an automatic document classification method, more precisely an unsupervised and hierarchical clustering one. The defined technique produces a hierarchical classification tree from the set of analyzed documents, and therefore classifies them with respect to paradigmatic similarity relationships. This technique has been implemented and a prototype tool has been produced, completely realized in Java and Prolog. This prototype provides the user with information retrieval functionalities, by means of a search document map based graphic interface.

Key words. Information Retrieval, Clustering, Semantic query definition, Semantic Networks

1. Introduction. The explosive increase of information available on the Web, in form of digital unstructured *documents* [1], has made evident the problem of *Information Retrieval* or *Information Extraction.* In order to extract information from a document, its global comprehension at semantic level, though possible, is considered as unrealistic, given the complexity of the comprehension techniques, coupled to the huge sizes of the document corpora involved. Usually the document analysis has to be limited to lexical and structural levels. The result of such analysis produces the document *indexing* with a set of normalized keywords.

Different is the case with the *Query Definition.* The limited complexity involved with the query definition phase motivates the use of sophisticated techniques aimed at assigning semantic meaning to the query, by defining concepts and composing them in a suitable way, thus improving precision and recall. In this area techniques range from the traditional, purely syntactically based boolean composition of keywords, to natural language processing, to query expansion by means of *Thesauri.* This technique is adopted for instance in *WordNet*[14].

Another promising methodology to support Information Retrieval is the *Automatic Classification* of documents. Techniques for automatic classification are generally based on the association of a set of descriptors said *features* to the documents, which represent the relevant information they embed. This set of descriptors is then utilized to group (cluster) documents "similar" with respect to a given metric [2]. Clustering techniques, which ranges from statistical techniques [13] to genetic algorithms [6] to neural networks [5], can be generally distinguished in *supervised* and *unsupervised* ones [8]. In the first case the classification is driven by a set of documents already classified (*training set*), in the latter case the classification is performed without any example or knowledge external to the set of documents

*This work has been supported by the CNR - Consiglio Nazionale delle Ricerche, Italy (Agenzia 2000 Project *ALCOR* - n. CNRG00A41A), and by the Campania Reg. government (Projects "L41/96 Smart ISDN" and "Regional Competence Center on Information and Communication Technologies").

†Dipartimento di Ingegneria dell'Informazione, Second University of Naples, Italy, Email: beniamino.dimartino@unina2.it

‡Dipartimento di Informatica e Sistemistica, University "Federico II" of Naples, Italy

§Dipartimento di Ingegneria dell'Informazione, Second University of Naples, Italy

[1]With the word document we refer in the following to text documents written in natural language, even though the problem here dealt with is common to other kind of information media, such as images, movies, multimedia

[2]A metric distance formula is defined to quantitatively determine the degree of similarity among documents

to be classified.

In this paper we describe a technique, and its prototypical implementation, for Information Retrieval of text documents and Web pages and sites, based on integration of two techniques:

- a semantic based query definition and expansion technique, based on production rule expert systems technology and semantic networks representing semantical relationships among terms (such as synonymy, omonymy, polysemy and hyponymy) and hierarchical relationships among their constituents (*seeds*);
- an automatic classification method, more precisely an unsupervised and *hierarchical* clustering method, known in literature as *Neighbor Joining*.

The defined technique produces a hierarchical classification tree from the set of analyzed documents, and therefore classifies them with respect to paradigmatic similarity relationships. This technique has been implemented and a prototype tool has been produced, completely realized in Java. This prototype provides the user with information retrieval functionalities, by means of a graphic interface based on the concept of "document maps". The functionalities offered by the tool can be applied to three different kind of document bases: local text bases, Web pages obtained by a propaedeutic search with a classical search engine, and entire Web sites. In fact the tool can interact with the search engine Google, in order to apply the classification to a set of web document retrieved by the search engine on the basis of an user query; in addition, it's possible to download from the Web pages of an entire site. Retrieved documents are saved on disk and the defined technique is applied in local.

The paper is structured as follows. Section 2 describes the procedure defined for document retrieval, lexical analysis, classification based on unsupervised clustering and query analysis. Section 3 describes the implemented prototype functionalities and utilization cycle, by means of an example. Section 4 describes the most well known models for I.R. and automatic classification applied to the I.R. systems.

2. The Procedure for Document Classification and Retrieval. The procedure we have defined for document classification and retrieval is composed of the following steps:

- Lexical analysis and Inverted Index extraction
- Unsupervised Clustering
- Categories labelling
- Semantic Query definition
- Matching between query and categories and graphical provision of results

2.1. Lexical analysis. The first phase is performed in order to index each document (*Indexing*), that is to represent each document with a set of keywords. Each document is firstly pruned from *empty words* and *empty syntagma*. When the commonly occurring syntagma are full, or rather meaningful, they are replaced with compound words. Subsequently the documents are *normalized* with respect to syntactic variations, like gender variations, singular/plural variations, moods and tenses of verbs, through the replacement of the words with their *stems*[3]. It has to be noted that the procedure for document normalization is defined for the italian language. For each normalized document j a set W_j of occurring words is obtained; each word is weighted with the *Salton's weight function*[11]; this weight relates the frequency of occurrence of the word in the document, with the biggest of such frequencies in the document. In this way the weight of each word is independent from the length of the document, as shown in the following formula:

$$f_{ij} = 0.5 + 0.5(\frac{freq_{ij}}{max_l freq_{lj}})$$

[3]With *stem* we refer in the following to the common root of the words.

where $freq_{ij}$ is the frequency of occurrence of the word i in the document j. Therefore each document is represented in the n-dimensional space by its *feature vector*

$$\vec{w_j} = (f_{1j}, \ldots, f_{tj})$$

consisting of the weight of all of its keywords. The feature vectors are used to calculate the *similarity matrix* of documents through an opportune metric, for instance the Euclidean or Scalar product one. The Euclidean distance is defined by the following formula:

$$d = \sqrt{(w_i(1) - w_j(1))^2 + \ldots + (w_i(n) - w_j(n))^2}$$

instead the Scalar product metric is represented by:

$$d = (\vec{w_i} \cdot \vec{w_j})$$

From geometric considerations it's clear that the first is a dissimilarity measure between documents, the second is a similarity one. Both have been implemented in the tool. This defined technique belongs to the I.R. model said *Vectorial model* (see section 4).

2.2. Unsupervised clustering. The clustering algorithm considered, and implemented in the tool, is the Saitou and Nei's method, known in literature as *Neighbor Joining algorithm*[16] which is a hierarchical unsupervised clustering method. The clustering obtained model is characterized by a hierarchical binary tree, in which the nodes are clusters (*grouping*) and leaves are classified events. The *Neighbor Joining* algorithm calculates repeatedly the distance between documents and identifies at each step the two more similar documents. The algorithm has complexity in the order of $O(n^3)$, at least in the revision presented by *Studier* and *Keppler* [18]. We give a summary description of the algorithm: being $r[]$ the sum of distances from node i to other nodes, recalculation of $r[]$ is optimized by using the following shortcuts, which come from the definitions of $r[]$ and the new node distances. Suppose nodes i and j have just merged to form node u, and let k be any other node. There are N nodes, counting i and j but not u. Then:

$$r[u] = (r[i] + r[j] - N * d(i,j)) \div 2$$

and

$$r'[k] = r[k] - d(i,k) - d(j,k) + d(k,u)$$

where $r'[]$ is the set of new divergences for nodes other than i, j, and u. These formulas don't improve the ordering, because we still search over all $j < i < N$ for the minimum value of the similarity matrix $M_{i,j}$, but the constant factor multiplying N^3 is reduced. The algorithm can be made slightly more elegant by running through N-2 iterations, rather than N-3.

2.3. Categories labelling. Once obtained the hierarchical tree of categories and subcategories, we describe the step devoted to categories labelling. We have assign a label to each obtained cluster or sub-cluster. This one is characterized by the three most meaningful words of the documents belonging to the cluster. Categories labelling is obtained by associating a feature vector to each cluster and sub-cluster, given by the average of feature vectors of documents belonged to them. From this one, the three words, corresponded to the its most weighted component, are obtained.

2.4. Semantic query definition. A sophisticated query definition needs a representation of relationships usually occurring among words and terms composing the documents. Such a representation is usually named *Thesaurus*. A thesaurus provides a representation of several kinds of relationships among the words of the language, such as relationships of similarity and opposition, and including more specifical relationships such as synonymy, omonymy, polisemy and iponymy. Some of the relationships refer to the lexical or syntactical characteristics of the language (*lexical* relationships) while other relationships relate the meanings or *concepts* expressed by the words (*semantical* relationships). Special representations are used for semantical relationships, including *semantic networks*.

We have defined a semantic based query definition and expansion technique, based on production rule expert systems technology and semantic networks representing semantical relationships among terms (such as synonymy, omonymy, polysemy and hyponymy) and hierarchical relationships among their constituents (*seeds*).

The knowledge base represents the meaning of generic and application domain oriented terms, in a hierarchical and recursive way, with utilization of other terms, which represent their *semantic constituents*. The semantic description of each term is thus a *composition* relationship which is recursive (thus can represent generalization / specialization hierarchies) and can represent alternatives in the composition. Base terms (whose meaning cannot be described with other terms) are called *seeds*.

An example with use of Prolog facts, and `and / or` predicates to represent composition of meaning or alternative, is presented in the following:

```
composed(circuito,or(frode,insidia)).
composed(circuito,and(circolarit,strada)).
composed(circuito,and(unione,conduttura,elettricit)).
composed(circuito,movimento). composed(frode,and(errore,insidia)).
pk(circolarita). pk(unione). pk(insidia).
```

The inference rules of the inferential engine act on the knowledge base in order to identify paradigmatic relationships of similarity, opposition, hyponimy-hyperonimy (generalization-specialization), antinomy etc [4, 7] among terms.

An example of Prolog rule identifying synonimi of a given word is the following:

```
synonimi(Word,SynList) :-
  seed(Word,WordSeedList),
  findall(Syn,
          ( word_seed(Syn,SynSeedList),
            member(ElWordSeedList,WordSeedList),
            member(ElSynSeedList,SynSeedList),
            ( subset(ElWordSeedList,ElSynSeedList) ;
              subset(ElSynSeedList,ElWordSeedList)
            )
          ),
          SynList1),
          list_to_set(SynList1,SynList).
```

The user specifies the query by means of a graphical user interface, where she/he can selectively browse the semantic network from typed search terms, and in particular the semantic constituents of terms with their hierarchical relationships. The user can select constituents of a typed term, and compose terms and constituents. The query such defined

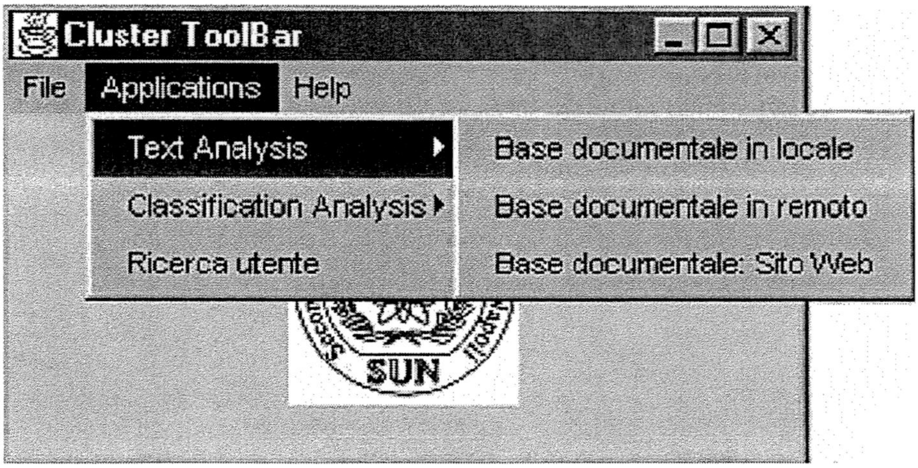

FIG. 3.1. *The tools' main panel.*

is then expanded by the inference engine by means of properties which can be selected by the user, or automatically applied. The user can browse the result of the expansion and possibly add or delete terms.

2.5. Matching of query and categories. The retrieval of the information related to desired query, is obtained through the *matching* between the feature vectors associated to the query and clusters' ones.

Matching between the query's feature vector and clusters ones is obtained through the calculation of the similarity between vectors used an opportune metric, or other Euclidean or Scalar product one.

3. The Prototype Description. The prototype implemented supports Information Retrieval on a local or distributed document base such as the Web. In fact the developed software allows to recover either the pages of a Web site, or the documents distributed on the Web, preselected with a desired query through the search engine Google. We're using Prolog (SWI Prolog ver. 3.3) to represent the knowledge base and to implement the Semantic Network Extractor engine. We are using Java to implement the Graphical User Interface; the Java module directly drives the firing of Prolog rules, and interfaces with the Google search engine through the protocol Xml and Soap, in particular by using the api Java of the package googleapi.jar.

In the following the graphic interface of the defined prototype is described. In figure 3.1 is shown the Graphic Interface of the tool, with menus showing the three available functionalities: Lexical Analysis, Cluster Analysis and Information retrieval related to the desired query. These phases should be performed sequentially, but they can be executed asynchronously, because their results can be saved on disk. The document corpus can be a local document base, a set of documents distributed on the Web, or pages of an entire Web site, as shown in figure 3.1.

In figure 3.2 it is shown the panel of the *Semantic query definition.*

As shown in figure 3.2, the user can selectively browse the semantic network from typed search terms, and in particular can browse the tree-like structures representing the semantic constituents of terms with their hierarchical relationships (where a black node represent a composition of meanings, while a yellow node represents an alternative. The user can select constituents of a typed term, and compose terms and constituents, by building a tree-like structure with connectives from the displayed ones. The query such defined is then

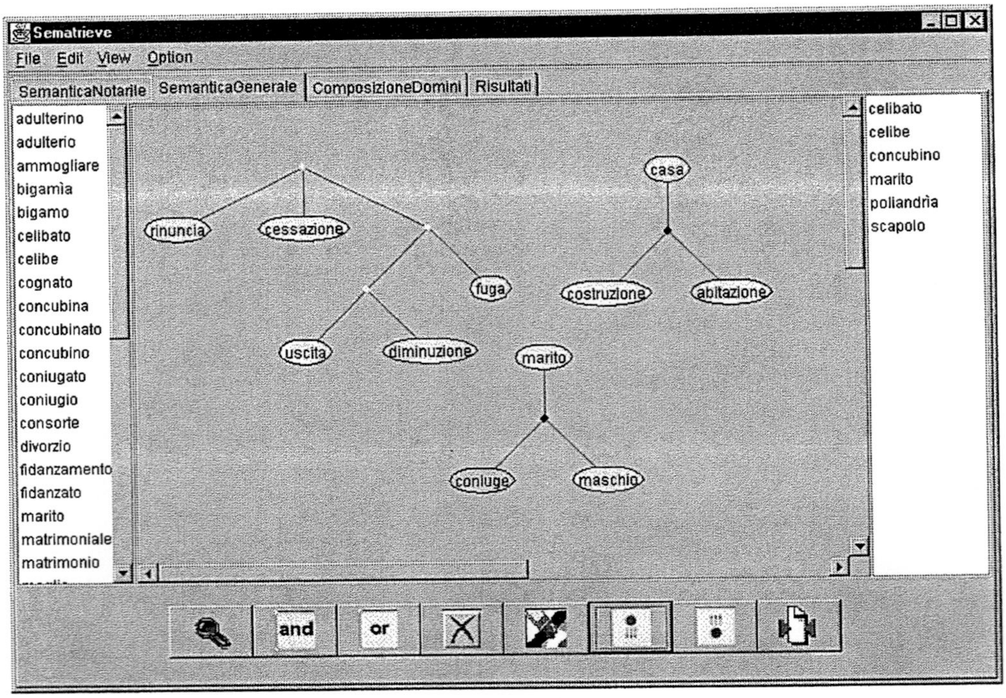

FIG. 3.2. *Semantic query definition.*

expanded by the inference engine by means of properties which can be selected by the user, or automatically applied. In figure 3.2 are shown the synonimi (left) and hyponimi (right). The user can browse the result of the expansion and possibly add or delete terms, before finalizing and normalizing the query.

The n-dimensional representation of documents and query, obtained through feature vectors, is mapped into a bi-dimensional space, and depicted as a so called "search map". The graphic panel for the visualization of the search map is shown in figure 3.3. This panel is divided in two parts. On the left the hierarchical tree of the documental classification, related to the second application's phase, is represented. On the right it is shown the desired string, visualized in red, written at the bottom, and the most similar cluster, visualized as pink rectangles, and documents belonged to it, visualized as black points, put to given distance with respect to the query. This distance is calculated using a similarity metric; users can chose between Euclidean or Scalar product one.

On the right of the graphic panel, it's possible to visualize documents by double clicking on the corresponding point.

4. Related Work. In I.R.'s system, the efficient retrieval of the information is due to two important aspects:

- *query must be expressed in a clean semantical way*
- *documents must be expressed in a logic view.*

The tree classical models of Information Retrieval are:

- *Boolean*
- *Vectorial*
- *Probabilistic*

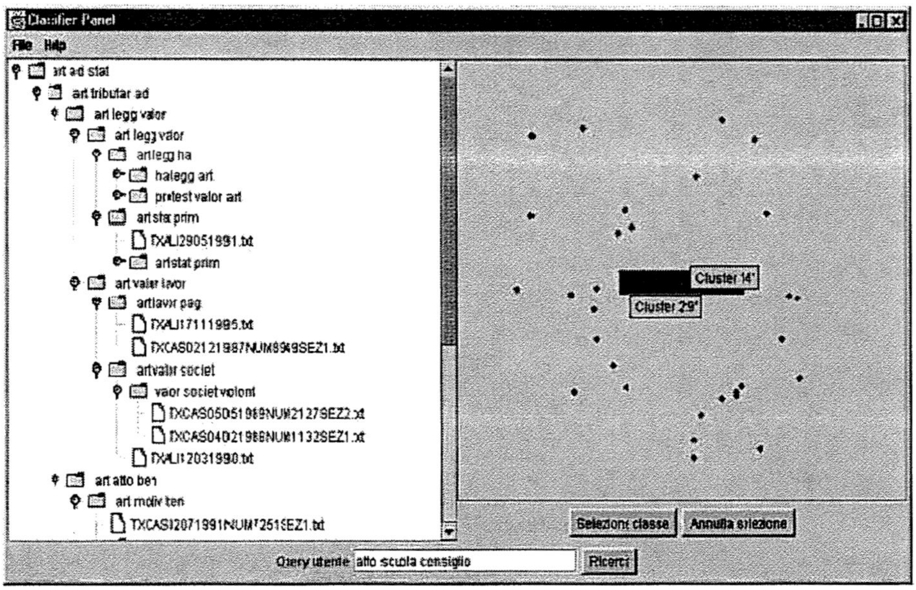

FIG. 3.3. *Graphic representation of the results related to the desired query.*

In the first, documents and query are represented as *keywords set*, so that this model is said *set theoretic*; the representative analytical formula for this model is:

$$sim(d_j, q) = \{1se\exists\overrightarrow{q_{cc}}|(\overrightarrow{q_{cc}} \in \overrightarrow{q_{dnf}}) \bigwedge(k_i : g_i(\overrightarrow{d_j}) = g_i(\overrightarrow{q_{cc}})$$

in which d_j is the document, q_{dnf} is the disjunctive form of the query q, q_{cc} is the conjunctiva component of q_{dnf}. If $sim(d_j, q)$ is 1,d_j is a relevant document with respect to the query q.

In the second model, documents and query are represented by vectors, so that this model is said *algebraic*; the representative analytical formula for this model is:

$$sim(d_j, q) = \frac{\overrightarrow{d_j} \cdot \overrightarrow{q}}{|\overrightarrow{d_j}||\overrightarrow{q}} = \frac{\sum_{i=1}^{t} w_{i,j} w_{i,q}}{\sqrt{\sum_{i=1}^{t} w_{i,j}^2}\sqrt{\sum_{j=1}^{t} w_{j,q}^2}}$$

In the latter the model of reference for the representation of documents and query, is the probability theory, so that this technique is said probabilistic one.

With respect to the automatic classification, the principal supervised approaches are:

- Bayes probability
- Decisional or Inductive trees
- Neural net as Back Propagation.

The principal algorithms belonged to the technique of machine learning are *vector support machines*, *naive Bayes classifier*, *k-nearest neighbor classifier*, *induction of rules and trees*. With respect to the unsupervised learning methods, the principal approaches are:

- Partitioning algorithms
- Hierarchical algorithms
- Density based algorithms.

The first ones operate iteratively as shown int the following steps:

- Arbitrary choice of k centers as initial solution;

- Calculation of the cluster of affiliation of every patterns with respect to the actual choice of k centers;
- Re-calculation of the centers of the clusters;
- Iteration returning to the point 2 if it isn't satisfied the convergence's criterion.

Between such algorithms we mention CLARA and CLARANS [2].
The second ones,hierarchical algorithm, individualize a set of groupings organized in increasing sense. It is said *hierarchical classification* if:

- all the levels of distance are considered
- The groups gotten to a certain level of distance include all those gotten to a level of inferior distance.

The hierarchical analysis technique is distinguished in:

- *Divisive* in which the set of the unities is left again in groups so that, to every stage of analysis, the groups that form are subset of the group that related to the preceding stage up to come to the extreme case in which each unity is a group.
- *Agglomerative* in which initially each unity constitutes a group , and to every stage of analysis it admits groups of the preceding stage,up to comes to the situation limit in which all the unities belong to one group only.

Between such algorithms we mention AGNES, DIANA, CURE [2].
The density based algorithms identify clusters as regions of the dense space, separated from zones to more scarce density, that represent therefore noise. These algorithms possess therefore the intrinsic ability to notice clusters of arbitrary form and to filter noise identifying the outliers. The principal algorithms density based used are DBSCAN [9], OPTICS, DENCLUE.

REFERENCES

[1] Google api java. *www.google.com/apis/*, *www.elgoog.nl/tools.html*.
[2] Survey of the state of the art in human language technology. Sito Web:*cslu.cse.ogi.edu/HLTsurvey/*.
[3] Vivisimo. *vivisimo.com/demo/Clustering$_E$ngine$_D$emos/Web.html*.
[4] Berruto. *La Semantica*. Zanichelli (Bologna, Italy), second edition, 1976.
[5] J. P. Bigus. *Data Mining with Neural Networks*. McGraw-Hill, 1996.
[6] Chen. Machine learning for information retrieval: neural networks, symbolic learning and genetic algorithms. *Journal of the American Society for Information Science*, pages 46(3) pp. 194–216, Apr. 1995.
[7] Dorr. Machine translation, 1993. Solving thematic divergencies in machine translation. 7(3) pp.135-193.
[8] R. Duda and P. Hart. *Pattern Classification and Scene Analysis*. Wiley (New York, NY), 1973.
[9] Sander Xu Ester, Kriegel. Density based spazial clustering of application with noise, 1996.
[10] C. Fellbaum D. Gross G.A. Miller, R. Beckwith and K. Miller. Five papers on wordnet. Technical report, Princeton University's Cognitive Science Laboratory, 1993. Technical Report.
[11] G.Salton and Chris Buckley. Term weighting approaches in automatic text retrieval. Technical report, Cornell University, November 1987. Technical Report TR 87-881.
[12] J. Kittler and D. Pairman. Pattern recognition, 1989. Optimality of reassignement rules in dynamical clustering. pp.169-173. vol. 21(2).
[13] P. Michaud. *Recent advances in Automatic Classification*, volume vol. 7. Wiley, 1992. Stochastic Models and Data Analysis. Applied.pp. 167-182.
[14] G. A. Miller. *WordNet, A Lexical Database for English*. In CACM, 1995. pg. 38.
[15] H. Uszkoreit G. Varile A. Zaenen A. Zampolli R. Cole, J. Mariani and V. Zue. Survey of the state of the art in human language technology. Cambridge University,Press and Giardini.
[16] N. Saitou and M. Nei. *The neighbor-joining method: a new method for reconstructing phylogenetic trees*. Mol.Biol.Evol., 1987. pg. 4, 406- 425.
[17] G. Salton and M.J. McGill. *Introduction to Modern Information Retrieval*. McGraw-Hill, 1983.
[18] J.A. Studier and K.J. Keppler. *A note on the neighbor-joining algorithm of Saitou and Nei*. Mol.Biol.Evol., 1988. pg. 5:729-731.

[19] H.P. Zipf. *Human Behaviour and the Principle of Least Effort.* Addison-Wesley, Cambridge, Massachusetts, 1949.

In: Applied Parallel and Distributed Computing
Editors: Yi Pan and Laurence T. Yang , pp. 63-72

ISBN 1-59454-174-4

DISTRIBUTED SYSTEMS FOR TELECOMMUNICATION APPLICATIONS: FROM CORBA TO WEB SERVICES TECHNOLOGY

ANNA BONIFACIO AND GIACINTO SPINILLO *

Abstract. This article describes architectures and solutions for the accessibility of telecommunications networks from external client applications, and the fast implementation of telecom enabled applications. While standardization efforts were driven by CORBA technology, a paradigm shift is in progress from CORBA to Web services architectures. In this article the two different approaches are compared.

Key words. Web Services, CORBA, Distributed systems for telecommunication, SOAP, UDDI

1. Introduction. During the past few years, much effort has been spent in the aim of defining architectures and software solutions for opening up telecommunications network in order to provide access to the network from external systems, providing multi-vendor and multi environment interoperability. Standards committees (3GPP, ETSI, etc) are working on the definition of public interfaces and frameworks for the realization of multi-vendor distributed telecommunications applications. The final goal is to achieve the possibility of integration and seamless compatibility of commercial development environments with proprietary, carrier grade existing legacy systems and integration between different hardware vendors and portability between different low level protocols. Past standardization efforts led to a well defined set of standard CORBA interfaces and classes for the telecommunication industry (Parlay Gateway definition), which are currently implemented by a number of telecommunications hardware vendors. Even if there are several implementations of the Parlay framework around the world, and the number of Parlay client applications is increasing, the development and usage of Parlay frameworks from third parties software vendors did not reach though the expected diffusion. The number of Parlay enabled applications deployed in the real network is still limited and the community of software developers seems to prefer more web oriented technologies. As a matter of fact the CORBA programming paradigm may result cumbersome and difficult to use, and not so easy to learn, compared to web protocols. As a result of these practical considerations, a paradigm shift is foreseen, from CORBA technology towards webservices/SOAP middleware usage. Even if the two technologies cannot be considered completely equivalent since they are based on different programming paradigms and offer different functionality at different levels, there are ongoing activities for the adaptation of CORBA software frameworks to the Web service architecture. This article briefly summarizes the two competing technology (CORBA and Web services), giving a short overview of the basic concepts of the two technologies, the pros and cons of each approach and the existing telecommunication standards.

2. CORBA (Common Object Request Broker Architecture). CORBA is an object oriented middleware standard defined by the OMG (Object Management Group)[1], a consortium which includes over 700 information technology industries. CORBA defines specifications to have distributed objects located in different network nodes, developed using different programming languages on different hardware/software machines, seamless interoperating. In order to achieve this goal the following key concepts are defined:

- IDL Language - Objects interfaces are defined using a neutral IDL language interface, which defines the "contract" between a client and the object implementing the interface.
- CORBA IDL provides operating systems and programming language independent interfaces. It allows client and server written using different programming languages

*Covansys - Rome - Italy

[1]Common Object Request Broker Architecture, OMG

to interoperate.

- Object Request Broker (ORB) - The interactions between a client application and the server object is obtained via the ORB, which mediates communications between the client and the server. It lets objects transparently make requests to remote objects and receives responses back. A CORBA ORB provides also a variety of distributed middleware services, such as:
  1. Static and dynamic methods invocations -A client application can use a known server IDL interface or discover it at runtime.
  2. Multi Language Support -Possibility of mapping IDL interfaces to any implementation language
  3. Security and Transactions Support
  4. Local - Remote Transparency

2.1. Parlay interfaces. Parlay/OSA (Open Service Access) [2] is a set of API enabling operators and 3rd party applications to make use of telecommunication network functionality through a set of open, standardized interfaces. Traditional applications deployed for telecommunications operators were usually developed using proprietary environments SCE (Service Creation Environment) and running on legacy systems; this implies that each time an operator wanted to develop a new application, the time needed to implement it were very long and there were few chances to have these applications integrated with different systems, such as with pure information technology application; moreover the change of a low level protocol interfaces had severe impacts on the whole telecommunication application. As a matter of fact, new applications had a very high time to market and poor integrations with non legacy systems. Moreover, the solutions were completely defined by the network operator, allowing poor configuration capability to the end user, a big difficulty on achieving time to market, a slow penetration of new technology and incompatibility issues when trying to integrate different technologies, mobile and fixed lines, multiple vendor networks. A challenge faced by the network operators now is how to attract third party application developers by providing a process for the fast development of applications. In fact innovative applications and services are the key to future growth, and generation of revenues for both application developers and network operators. Scope of Parlay interfaces is enabling the access to telecommunications networks via standardized CORBA interfaces. The Parlay Group is a multi-vendor consortium, started in March 98 to develop open, technology-independent application programming interfaces (APIs) that enable the development of applications that operate across multiple, networking-platform environments. The logical architecture of the Parlay API involves the following entities:

- Client Applications
- Applications Servers
- Service Capabilities Servers (SCS)
- Framework.

Client Applications running on application servers wants to use telecommunication functionality; they will use the API exposed by the SCSs to invoke specific SCSs methods, but only via the mediation of the Framework, which authenticates the client application and checks the service level agreement and rights associated to it. The Parlay/OSA Gateway consists of several Service Capability Servers (SCS): functional entities that provide Parlay/OSA interfaces towards applications. Each SCS is seen by applications as one or more Service Capability Features (SCF): abstractions of the functionality offered by the network, accessible via the Parlay/OSA API. Sometimes they are also called services. The OSA Parlay Framework acts as a mediator between the external applications and the functionality provided by the network via the SCSs. It provides the following functionality :

[2] CopyRight 2002 The Parlay Group, Inc All Rights Reserved

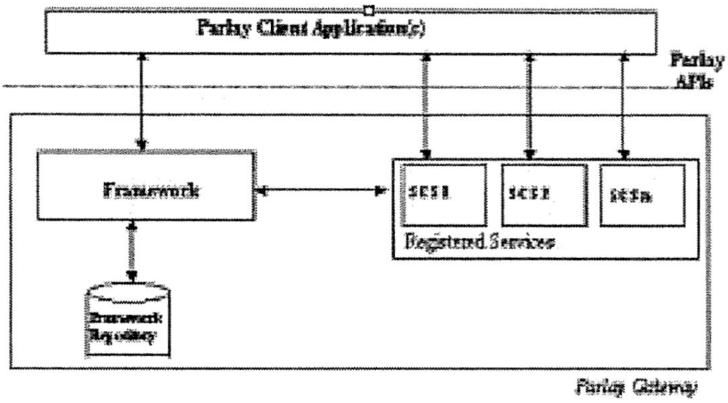

FIG. 2.1. *The Parlay Framework Model*

- Application Authentication
- Load Management and Integrity management
- Service Level Agreement Repository

The functionality of the OSA Framework is grouped in two main sets of interfaces:

- Interfaces to the 3rd Party Applications, which provide mechanisms for controlling their access to the network (Authentication and Authorization), for ensuring the integrity of the network (e.g. Load and Fault Management), and for the Applications to Discover the functionality that the operator's network exports via the OSA API.
- Interfaces to the other Service Capability Servers, which provide mechanisms for registration in the Framework of their Service Capability Features so that the Applications may discover them; they also provide the necessary access control mechanisms to allow the Framework functionality to be provided by an independent business entity (multi- domain).

The different phases required to make available a new SCS in the framework, enabling its usage by client applications are:

- **Registration of a new SCS** Before a service can be brokered (discovered, subscribed, accessed, etc.), it has to be registered with the Framework. The Service Supplier first must be authenticated by the framework and has to establish an access session with the framework. Then, the framework checks the supplier permissions and in case of a successful registration it updates its repository adding the SCS to the list of supported service types and declared service properties. After the service has been registered with the framework, the service supplier announces the availability of the service, basically making available to the framework the SCS service manager interface. At this time, the service is discoverable by clients and service sessions can be created.
- **Application's Service Agreement Setup** Each application that wants to use the framework capabilities has to be configured in the framework repository, configuring a service level agreement. This agreement specifies the SCSs each application is enabled to use, eventually specifying also the quality of service to be provided.
- **Run time Usage of an SCS** The client application must first authenticate itself with the Framework. As preliminary steps, the framework must authenticate the client application using a prescribed encryption method and challenge/response protocol previously negotiated between the Enterprize Operator and the Framework Operator. Once the client application has been authenticated with the Framework, it can gain access to other framework interfaces, as an example the one that lists

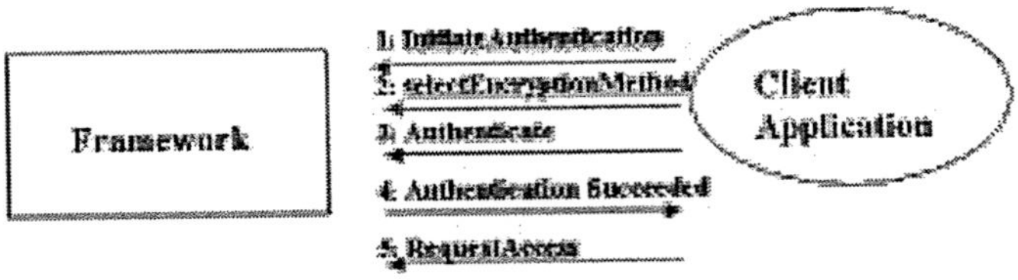

FIG. 2.2. *Client Application Authentication*

all of the SCS registered to the framework. The client identifies the SCS it has decided to use and selects it via the framework's service agreement interface. The Framework checks the application's service agreement in its internal repository and verifies if the application is authorized to use the selected service; in the positive case, the Framework will request the specific SCS to create a specific instance for the client application, tuning also the run- time SCS behavior according to the service level agreement stored in the repository (quality of service, maximum usage time, guaranteeing a maximum number of sessions, etc).

The interfaces already defined by the OSA/Parlay API include the following ones:

- Call Control - Management of calls, multimedia calls, conferencing
- User Interaction -Management of calls, multimedia calls, conferencing
- PAM Presence and Availability management
- Content Based Charging, Charging based on application usage
- Account Management User's account management
- Data Session Control Control of data sessions
- Terminal Capabilities Capabilities of the end user terminal
- User Location Mobility - User Location
- User Status Mobility - User Status

While the SCS classes define a generic interface, the implementations will map the abstract high level SCS interface to specific networks protocols; as an example, the methods defined for the Call Control SCS interface may be implemented for each of the following south bound interfaces: INAP, Camel, SIP. In this way, a client application using multiple Call Control SCSs may interact at the same way with fixed line phone subscribers (INAP), with mobile users (Camel) and with Voice Over IP (VOIP), abstracting in this way the application from the low level network interfaces. The benefits of this type of architecture consist in the possibility of reusing services across different types of accesses, reducing the cost of complex interfaces development and support. Moreover, the application developer is not supposed to be expert in telecommunication networks functionality, he has to know CORBA programming. The network provider can give access to a subset of the telecommunication network functionality, and in a controlled way since the client application has to be authorized by the framework and can access only the services listed in the service agreement.

3. SOAP and Web Services.

3.1. SOAP (Simple Object Access Protocol). SOAP is a protocol for the exchange of information; it provides a simple and lightweight mechanism for exchanging structured and typed information between peers in a decentralized, distributed environment using XML. A SOAP message is an XML document that consists of:

- a mandatory SOAP envelope

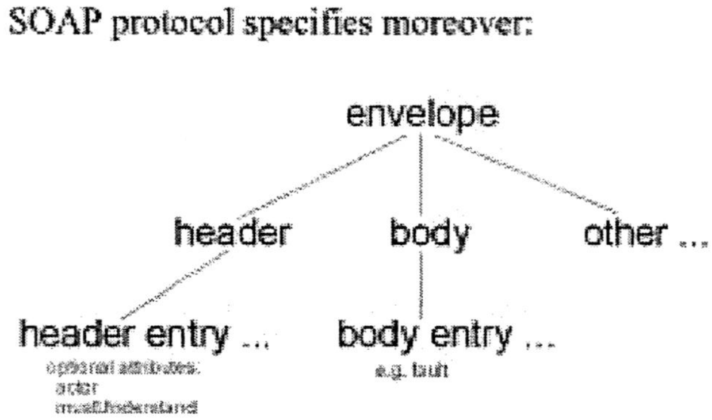

FIG. 3.1. *SOAP Message*

- an optional SOAP header
- a mandatory SOAP body

This XML document is referred to as a SOAP message. The SOAP envelope defines a framework for describing the content of a message and the way to process it. The **Body** element is a generic container in that it can contain any number of elements from any namespace. This is the container of the data, which is ultimately exchanged.

The **Envelope** is the top element of the XML document representing the message. The **Header** is a generic mechanism for adding features to a SOAP message in a decentralized manner without prior agreement between the communicating parties; as an example, inside an header it is possible to put commands to be interpreted by the SOAP processor that will receive the message. Higher level protocols, such as eBXML Message Service, have defined specific elements which are included in the SOAP header, such as the From, To, MessageID elements, while the actual message content is contained inside the SOAP Body.

SOAP protocol specifies moreover:

- A set of encoding rules for expressing instances of application-defined datatypes; the SOAP encoding rules defines a serialization mechanism that can be used to exchange instances of application-defined datatypes
- A convention for representing remote procedure calls and responses; the SOAP RPC representation defines a convention that can be used to represent remote procedure calls and responses.

SOAP can potentially be used in combination with a variety of other protocols; however, the most common binding is SOAP in combination with HTTP and HTTP Extension Framework. The base interaction between a client and server is via the exchange of SOAP messages between the two entities. While all of the other RPC mechanisms have problems in the connection between peer entities which are separated by a firewall, this problem does not come with SOAP, when using as a transport layer HTTP. SOAP is currently the de facto standard for XML messaging for a number of reasons, first of all it is a relatively simple layer on top of existing network technologies such as HTTP that are already broadly implemented, then SOAP is flexible and extensible it provides an extensible, composable framework that allows solutions to be incrementally applied as needed. SOAP is based on XML. Finally, SOAP enjoys broad industry and developer community support

Two applications, can communicate via SOAP messages, if they are able to:

- exchange data across networks via either HTTP or SMTP
- parse and construct XML documents

- understand MIME
- perform an action, if required by the protocol

SOAP business model is based on a synchronous one way transmission from the sender to the receiver, even if SOAP messages can be combined to implement a request/response model over HTTP.

3.2. Web services. According to the W3C specifications, a web service is: *" is a software system identified by a URI, whose public interfaces and bindings are defined and described using XML. Its definition can be discovered by other software systems. These systems may then interact with the Web service in a manner prescribed by its definition, using XML based messages conveyed by internet protocols"* .

The basic Web service architecture models the interactions between three roles i.e. the service provider, service discovery agency, and service requestor:

- **service provider** - hosts a network accessible software module (an implementation of a web service). The service provider defines a service description for the web service and publishes it to a requestor or service discovery agency.
- **service requestor** -uses a find operation to retrieve the service description locally or from the discovery agency (i.e. a registry or repository) and uses the service description to bind with the service provider and invoke or interact with the web service implementation.
- **discovery agency** (i.e. a registry or repository) a storage of web services descriptions and bindings, which publishes services descriptions, making them remotely accessible. A web service is described using a standard, formal XML notion, called its service description, that provides all of the details necessary to interact with the service, including message formats (that detail the operations), transport protocols, and location.

The operations which are applicable to these roles are:

- publish a web service description
- find a web service description
- bind operation

The nature of the interface hides the implementation details of the service, so that it can be used independently of the hardware or software platform on which it is implemented and independently of the programming language in which it is written. The Web services architecture uses WSDL (Web Services Definition Language) as a web service description language. WSDL has been submitted to the W3C and is being actively developed by the W3C Web Services Description WG. WSDL is an XML document format for describing Web services as a set of endpoints operating on messages containing either document-oriented or procedure-oriented (RPC) messages. WSDL describes Web services starting with the messages that are exchanged between the service provider and requestor. The messages themselves are described abstractly and then bound to a concrete network protocol and message format. A message consists of a collection of typed data items. An exchange of messages between the service provider and requestor are described as an operation. A collection of operations is called a port type. A service contains a collection of ports, where each port is an implementation of a portType, which includes all the concrete details needed to interact with the service.

The operations and messages are described abstractly, and then bound to a concrete network protocol and message format to define an endpoint. Related concrete endpoints may be combined into services. WSDL is sufficiently extensible to allow description of endpoints and their messages regardless of what message formats or network protocols are used to communicate. WSDL1.1 describes bindings for SOAP1.1, HTTP POST, and MIME. WSDL1.2 adds binding support for SOAP1.2.

FIG. 3.2. *Web Services*

The **UDDI (Universal Description, Discovery, and Integration)** protocol defines standardized procedures in order to publish and find information defining a web service. UDDI is a single conceptual registry distributed among several nodes; the UDDI Business Registry is a distributed repository of web service descriptions. The UBR can be accessed by the client applications to make queries against the repository, while only authorized applications can add entries to the registry. In this way a sort of white pages for web services is public and available for discovery. Once the Web service interface is known by the client application, (either directly or via a query the UDDI Registry), there are different business models that can be applicable to the dialog between the client application and the service provider:

- **Request/Response Model** - This model supports clients that are not addressable, allowing many existing client devices to interact with the web services, thus providing a simple programming model. In this model the client initiates the web service and the web service executes synchronously.
- **One Way Model** -It is similar to the Request/Response model, with the difference that the client will not wait for the Web service operation to complete, so no result will be returned back to the client.
- **Notification Model** It provides the Request/Response mode and one way models from the server side. The notification model relies on the device to be addressable, and to support a stack capable of processing a received Web service invocation, for this reason is applicable to smart phones or PDA but not yet to existing mobile phones.

The web services model is suitable in order to achieve a highly distributed, service oriented architecture. A web service can be published, found and invoked in a transparent way, if it is running inside the enterprize network or outside in the internet.

A brief summary of the Web Service characteristics in the table below:

Interface	XML/WSDL
Network Protocols	SOAP, HTTP, MIME
Registry	UDDI
Security	HTTP/SSL
Firewall	Port 80 HTTP

For distributed software architectures, one of the problems to be solved is the firewall traversal, the easiest choice so far seems to be SOAP and Web services, mainly for the fact that HTTP is the preferred network transport for SOAP. HTTP is associated with a well defined port, so most firewalls have been configured to accept HTTP traffic. SOAP messages can traverse on HTTP messages, and can hence can tunnel through firewalls. These are the pros of a web services approach:

- No need to conform to rigid API
- Send XML message and let the receiver parse it
- Contracts published in a standard format (WSDL)
- Easily passes through firewalls

On the other way round, the weakness of the web service model is:

- Performances
- Security
- Integrity

3.3. Parlay X working group. The objective of the Parlay X Working Group is to define a set of powerful yet simple, highly abstracted, imaginative, building blocks of telecom capabilities that developers and the IT community can both quickly comprehend and use to generate new, innovative applications.

- Each building block will be abstracted from the set of telecom capabilities exposed by the Parlay APIs.
- The Parlay X Web services are intended to stimulate the development of next generation network applications by IT developers who have a limited knowledge of telecommunications.
- The capabilities offered by a building block may be homogeneous (e.g. Call Control only) or heterogeneous (e.g. Mobility and Presence and Availability Management).
- The interaction between the application and the building block (i.e. a Parlay X API) will be realized by a simple Extensible Markup Language (XML)-based message exchange.

The addition of Web Services provides an alternate development and deployment choice, which can be easier integration and reduces costs by using the existing HTTP infrastructure and reusing existing skills. Parlay X Web services represent an abstraction and a Within the standardization efforts, two different deployment models may be used :

- The Gateway exports just the web service interface. - The Parlay X Web Service directly maps SOAP messages to the underlying network protocol. In this case the Parlay X server will implement the Web service via a direct connection to the network element.
- The Parlay gateway supports both a standard CORBA API interface and a Web Service interface. In this case the gateway supports remote method invocation using SOAP based on the concept of a XML Gateway (XGW), which translates each request to the framework from SOAP to IIOP, and viceversa for responses returned from the Framework. The interaction between a client application and the server incorporating the web service will be achieved via SOAP messages, while internally CORBA methods invocations will be achieved.

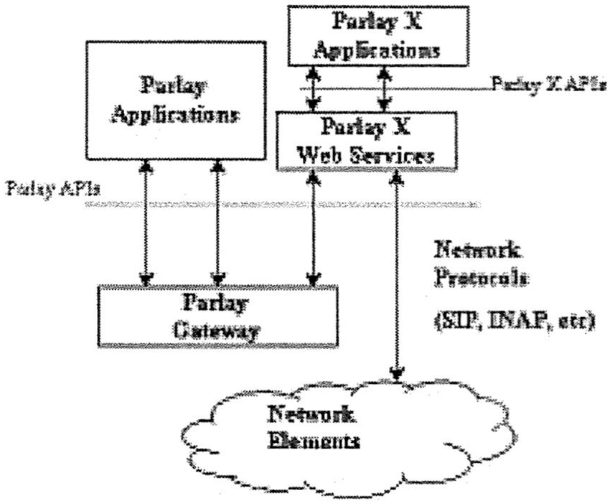

FIG. 3.3. *Parlay X Interface*

As you may see from the picture 3.3, Parlay X Web Services Interface represents an abstraction and a simplification of the CORBA Parlay API; it is anticipated that most Parlay X Web Services will be implemented by invoking functionality on a Parlay Gateway, however there will also be cases where the Parlay X interfaces will be directly mapped to network functionality. In this way, a Parlay X application can be written in any language, using any development environment, once the appropriate invocation is done. As an example, a client application wishing to send a SMS message to a mobile phone using the Parlay X interface will just send a SOAP message to the Parlay X Gateway, of this type (without namespaces and binding descriptors):

```
<sendSMS>

<destAddressSet> tel:01234567</destAddressSet\>

<senderAddressSet> tel:0111111</senderAddressSet>

<message> Hello World </message>

</sendSMS>
```

In the table below, a comparison between the functionality exported by the CORBA API and the ones exposed via the Web service interface:

Function	Parlay Environment	Web Services Environment
Service Registration	Framework (Service Registration)	Web Service Registry (Publish)
Service Discovery	Framework (Service Discovery)	Web Service Registry (Find)
Service Parameter Negotiation	Framework (Service Selection)	Not yet defined
Service Interface Repository	Framework (Service Registration and Discovery)	Web Service Registry
Service Interface Publication	Direct Publication of Service Interface	Web Service Registry
Service Binding	Framework (Service LifeCycle)	Service Interface Definition
Authentication	Framework (Initial Access and Authentication)	Not yet defined
Authorization	Framework (Service Discovery and selection)	Not yet defined

4. Conclusions. Some industry analysts think that the web service paradigm will be the solution to all the interoperability problems between different enterprizes and different companies, changing the way distributing computing is conceived. It is too early to draw conclusions; though the model seems to provide a solution to interoperability problems and multi-language development, it is better not to forget that back in 1997 CORBA was designed in order to provide the solution to the same problems. CORBA needed vendor supplied middleware installed in each node of the system, thus preventing a wide diffusion of CORBA enabled applications (it is a big issue compelling the business partners to install specific middleware in their nodes in order to access the service implemented by the enterprize system). The other issue about CORBA was the way of crossing corporate boundaries in a secure way; while the IIOP protocol was proposed for this, it has never achieved a widespread diffusion in firewall implementations. Will Web service technology solve all the problems faced by other technologies? SOAP, WSDL and UDDI are not seem to promise interoperability and platform independence. The minimum requirement to have two applications inter-operate is being able to construct and destruct SOAP messages on top of HTTP. The success of the technology will depend on how the major vendors and the players in the service arena will be able to propose solutions and development platforms truly open and standard, without implementing each one a specific Web service flavor.

REFERENCES

[1] D. Chapell and Tyler Jewell, *Java Web Services*, O' Reilly.
[2] The Parlay Group Inc, *Parlay Web Services Architecture Comparison*, (2002), Parlay Standard.
[3] The Parlay Group Inc, *Parlay Web Services Business Models*, (2002), Parlay Standard.
[4] The Parlay Group Inc, *Parlay Web Services Overview*, (2002), Parlay Standard.
[5] The Parlay Group Inc, *Parlay Web Services WSDL Style Guide*, (2002), Parlay Standard.
[6] The Parlay Group Inc, *Parlay X Web Services Interfaces*, (2002), Parlay Standard.
[7] W3C, *Web services description language*, http://www.w3.org/TR/wsdl/.
[8] W3C, *Simple object access protocol*, http://www.w3.org/2000/xp/.
[9] Object Management Group (OMG), The Common Object Request Broker: Architecture and Specification, 2.5 edition, September 2001.

SECTION 2: NUMERICAL APPLICATIONS

In: Applied Parallel and Distributed Computing ISBN 1-59454-174-4
Editors: Yi Pan and Laurence T. Yang , pp. 75-88

PARALLELIZATION OF THE THREE-DIMENSIONAL TRANSPORT EQUATION FOR BORON NEUTRON CAPTURE THERAPY

ERIC E. AUBANEL* AND FAYSAL EL KHETTABI†

Abstract. We propose an asynchronous parallel algorithm for the linear Boltzmann transport equation in three dimensions, for Boron Neutron Capture Therapy (BNCT) radiation therapy planning, which can be implemented efficiently on shared memory parallel computers. The three-dimensional multigroup discrete ordinates transport equation is cast into a set of coupled two-dimensional equations, and discretization is accomplished on a grid of arbitrarily-shaped prismatic cells. This allows the 3D multigroup discrete ordinates transport equation to be solved using spatial parallel techniques originally developed in a recent work for the 2D discrete ordinates transport equation by using domain decomposition techniques on an unstructured triangular mesh. We use the Single Program Multiple Data approach to formulate a shared memory parallel numerical implementation with OpenMP. Our results demonstrate that the parallel version of the 3D deterministic algorithm yields good parallel efficiency.

Key words. Neutron transport equation, Boron Neutron Capture Therapy, Parallel algorithms, OpenMP

1. Introduction. The Boltzmann transport equation is the most comprehensive mathematical model, and also the most complicated and computationally intensive, for performing calculations in the radiation engineering field and in many areas of science and engineering [2]. For instance, the planning of the radiation treatment of a tumor begins with the creation of a three-dimensional image of the tumor and surrounding healthy tissue, using techniques such as computed tomography or MRI. The treatment planning occurs after the imaging is completed and involves substantial computations using the Boltzmann transport equation to study the radiation penetration in a portion of a patient's body and to derive the dose calculations as a result of excitation and ionization events in tumor and surrounding healthy tissue [1].

The current practice in radiation therapy planning is to use the Monte Carlo method for these calculations [4]. Deterministic methods offer the promise that high order approximation of the solution over the volume of an element could provide high accuracy without the statistical error of Monte Carlo methods, but they are difficult to apply in complex geometries [5, 6, 7, 8]. These methods must be implemented on parallel computers, since clinical use requires turnaround times in minutes.

Discretization of the Boltzmann equation is typically done using the discrete ordinates method for the angular variable, characteristic or discontinous finite element methods for the space variable, and the multigroup method for the energy variable [4]. Several studies on parallelization have been performed for deterministic transport calculations by applying angular and spatial domain decomposition [11]-[15]. Since the transport sweeps over discrete ordinate directions are independent of each other, parallelization over these discrete ordinate directions is trivial. This approach may not be ideal, since the number of the discrete ordinate directions is much less than the number of finite elements, and may be less than the number of processors available. An asynchronous iteration scheme based on parallelization of energy groups was proposed ten years ago [16], but to our knowledge this approach has not been adopted, primarily for reasons of efficiency [14]. An additional rationale for spatial parallelization is that the quality of the mesh is the most critical factor determining the accuracy of the results, which can lead to domains with millions of elements. Partitioning of the discrete ordinate directions or energies requires duplication of the entire mesh on each

*Faculty of Computer Science University of New Brunswick, Fredericton, New Brunswick, E3B 5A3, Canada, aubanel@unb.ca

†Laboratory for Threat Material Detection University of New Brunswick, Fredericton, New Brunswick, E3B 5A3, Canada, faysalek@unb.ca

processor, which may not be possible and is certainly not efficient. Spatial partitioning can lead to a better memory access pattern and even superlinear speedups [9]. Until recently, parallelization based on spatial domain decomposition has been restricted to rectangular meshes. In the past few years there have been several applications to unstructured meshes: Nowak and Nemanick [14] used a Hybrid MPI/OpenMP implementation of a method using Jacobi iteration, Plimpton *et al.* [15] developed an asynchronous message passing algorithm, and the present authors extended the ideas of Yavuz and Larson [11] to unstructured triangular meshes together with a shared memory SPMD implementation using OpenMP [9]. In the present work, we extend the latter work to three dimensions with multiple energy groups.

The organization of this paper is as follows. In Section 2, we review the multigroup neutron discrete ordinates transport equation for Boron Neutron Capture Therapy (BNCT) and formulate our spatial numerical solution for the three-dimensional transport equation. In Section 3, we discuss our asynchronous parallel algorithm and present results of an implementation with OpenMP in Section 4. Finally, we close with a summary and some conclusions in section 5.

2. Neutron Transport Equation. The neutron transport equation is a special case of the Boltzmann equation, whereby the highly unlikely collisions among neutrons are ignored, thus rendering the resulting integro-differential equation linear [2]. The multigroup discrete ordinates approximation for G groups and M discrete ordinate directions can be written as [4]:

$$\begin{aligned}\Omega_m \cdot \nabla\psi_m^g(\mathbf{r}) + \sigma^g(\mathbf{r})\psi_m^g(\mathbf{r}) &= \sum_{g'=g}^{G} \sigma^{s,g'\to g}(\mathbf{r})\phi^{g'}(\mathbf{r}) \\ &+ Q_{es,m}^g(\mathbf{r}), \quad m = 1,...,M, \quad g = 1,...,G,\end{aligned} \tag{2.1}$$

where $\mathbf{r} = (x, y, z), \Omega_m = (\mu_m, \nu_m, \xi_m)$ is the unit vector along the discrete ordinate direction m having the corresponding weight ω_m, Q_{es} is an external source of neutrons, ψ is the angular neutron flux, σ^g and $\sigma^{s,g'\to g}$ are group constants(cross-sections) and ϕ^g is the scalar flux at energy group g:

$$\phi^g(\mathbf{r}) = \sum_{m=1}^{M} \omega_m\psi_m^g(\mathbf{r}). \tag{2.2}$$

To model neutron transport for BNCT we place the source of neutrons only in the highest energy group. The dose deposited to the material can be computed from the scalar flux ϕ^g.

In this work we use the same multigroup method as in [3], where the energy partition into G groups was defined by:

$$\{\mathbf{E}_0, \frac{\mathbf{E}_0}{\alpha_{max}}, \frac{\mathbf{E}_0}{\alpha_{max}^2}, ..., \frac{\mathbf{E}_0}{\alpha_{max}^G}\}, \tag{2.3}$$

where α_{max} is a positive constant less than one which is related to the atomic mass number of the material and $\mathbf{E}_0$ is a given energy. Equation 2.1 can be solved by using back substitution, beginning with the highest energy of the energy partition $\mathbf{E}_0/\alpha_{max}^G$.

For the purpose of spatial discretization we assume that the domain $\mathbf{D}$ has the form

$$\mathbf{D} = \mathbf{D}_{x,y} \times (\mathbf{a}, \mathbf{b}),$$

where $\mathbf{D}_{x,y}$ is a two dimensional polygonal domain. Let $\mathbf{a} = z_0 < z_1 < z_2 < ... < z_N = \mathbf{b}$ be a subdivision of $(\mathbf{a}, \mathbf{b})$ and $\Delta z_i = z_{i+1} - z_i$. After an integration on the interval (z_i, z_{i+1})

and specification of boundary conditions, equation 2.1 can then be written for positive ξ_m (indices and constants can be adjusted for negative ξ_m) as:

$$\mu_m \frac{\partial \psi^g_{i+\frac{1}{2},m}}{\partial x}(x,y) + \nu_m \frac{\partial \psi^g_{i+\frac{1}{2},m}}{\partial y}(x,y) + (\sigma^g_{i+\frac{1}{2}}(x,y) + \frac{\xi_m}{\mathbf{c}\Delta z_i})\psi^g_{i+\frac{1}{2},m}(x,y)$$

$$= \sigma^{s,g\to g}_{i+\frac{1}{2}}(x,y)\phi^g_{i+\frac{1}{2}}(x,y) + Q^g_{i+\frac{1}{2},m}(x,y) + \frac{\xi_m}{\mathbf{c}\Delta z_i}\psi^g_m(x,y,z_i), \tag{2.4}$$

$$\psi^g_{i+\frac{1}{2},m}(x,y) = \psi^g_{in,i+\frac{1}{2},m}(x,y), \quad \mu_m n_x(x,y) + \nu_m n_y(x,y) < 0, i = 0,1,...,N_z-1,$$

the notation $f_{i+\frac{1}{2}}$ refers to

$$f_{i+\frac{1}{2}}(x,y) = \frac{1}{\Delta z_i}\int_{z_i}^{z_{i+1}} f(x,y,z)dz, \tag{2.5}$$

and we have supplemented the system by assuming for the flux ψ^g_m the following relation,

$$\psi^g_{i+\frac{1}{2},m}(x,y) \approx \mathbf{c}\psi^g_m(x,y,z_{i+1}) + (1-\mathbf{c})\psi^g_m(x,y,z_i), \tag{2.6}$$

where the quadrature formula coefficient $\mathbf{c}$ is a real in $(0,1)$, the function ψ_{in} is a given function on the boundary of $\mathbf{D}$, and $n(x,y)$ is the outer unit normal on $\partial\mathbf{D}_{xy}$ at (x,y). Equation 2.4 can be solved by the source iteration scheme, in which one iterates on the scattering source ϕ^g [9]. Note that the term Q in equation 2.4, for non fission multigroup computation can be split into two terms, an external source Q_{es} and the source due to scattering from higher energies to lower energies:

$$Q^g_{i+\frac{1}{2},m}(x,y) = Q^g_{es,i+\frac{1}{2},m}(x,y) + \sum_{g'=g+1}^{G} \sigma^{s,g'\to g}(x,y)\phi^{g'}_{i+\frac{1}{2}}(x,y), \tag{2.7}$$

where $\phi^{g'}_{i+\frac{1}{2}}(x,y)$ is the scalar flux at energy g'.

2.1. BNCT model problem. As epithermal neutron beams can come only from an exterior source such as nuclear reactors or charged particle accelerators, the given epithermal neutron source function is on the surface of the domain. The spatial domain is a cylindrical phantom-like head that models the brain only. We triangulate $\mathbf{D}_{x,y}$ by means of a uniform set of x triangles and $x^{1/2}$ subdivisions of $(\mathbf{a},\mathbf{b})$. An S_8 angular quadrature approximation, which spans 40 angles in the plane, is used for the angular variable. We use the step discontinuous finite element method for the spatial flux evaluations with 0.5 as value for quadrature formula coefficient $\mathbf{c}$.

As we assume that the most abundant elements in the head are Hydrogen, Oxygen, Carbon and Nitrogen, the value of α_{max} is that of Oxygen (0.78). This gives 36 energy groups (see equation 2.3) to simulate the distribution of neutrons between the epithermal (10 kev) and thermal (1 ev) energies. Epithermal neutrons easily penetrate tissue and in so doing slow down and become thermal neutrons, as shown in figures 2.1 and 2.2 for results from the numerical solution of equation 2.4.

Execution time was more than 13 hours on a 400 MHz MIPS R12000 processor using a mesh of 15,580 triangles for the $\mathbf{D}_{x,y}$ domain. Reducing this to under a few minutes to make it feasible for use in BNCT treatment planning can only be done with implementation on a parallel computer. We present in the following section a parallel algorithm and implementation.

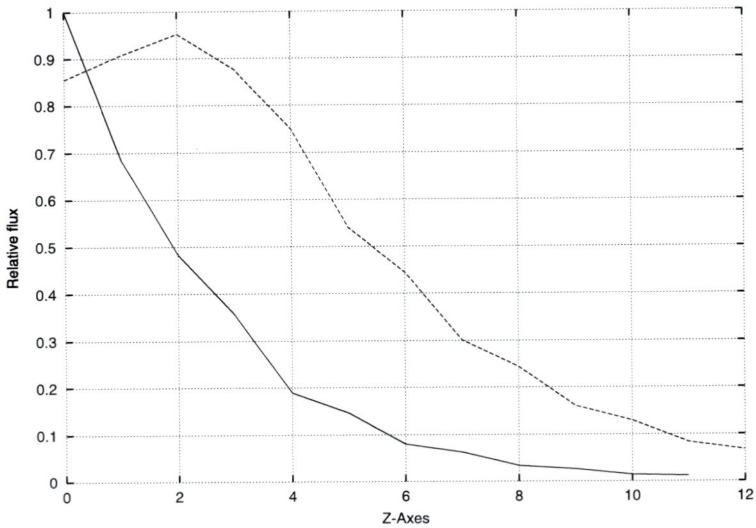

FIG. 2.1. *Relative epithermal (solid line) and relative thermal (dashed line) total neutron scalar flux along z axis with a source along z axis*

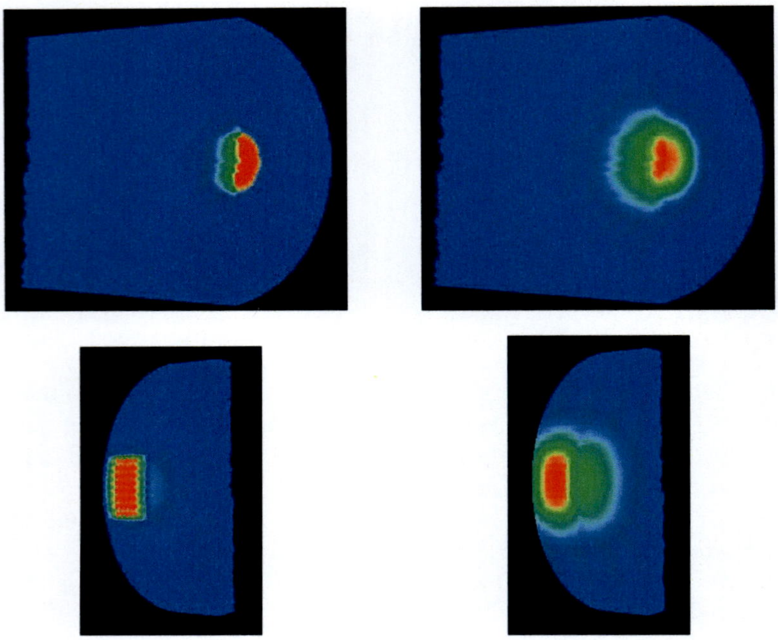

FIG. 2.2. *Epithermal (left) and thermal (right) total neutron scalar flux, with a horizontal source (bottom; horizontal slab of cylinder shown) and with a vertial source (top; half of cylinder cut away)*

3. Parallel Source Iteration. We introduce an asynchronous parallel algorithm and an implementation on a shared memory parallel computer.

The source iteration method to resolve the three-dimensional multigroup discrete ordinates transport equation requires transport sweeps across the z-axis and in the domain $\mathbf{D}_{x,y}$ for each discrete angular direction $(\mu_m, \nu_m, \xi_m = \pm\sqrt{1-\mu_m^2-\nu_m^2})$ (see equation 2.4).

The sweep along the z-axis depends on the sign of ξ_m. When ξ_m is negative, the sweep is from the top to the bottom otherwise the sweep is from the bottom to the top. If ξ_m is positive (and if not, the system indices and constants are adjusted accordingly), the inflow flux $\psi^g_m(x, y, z_{i+1})$ for slice z_{i+1} is computed by using

$$\psi^g_m(x, y, z_{i+1}) = \frac{1}{c}\psi^g_{i+\frac{1}{2},m}(x, y) - \frac{(1-c)}{c}\psi^g_m(x, y, z_i), \tag{3.1}$$

where the flux $\psi^g_{i+\frac{1}{2},m}$ between the slice z_i and slice z_{i+1} is calculated by solving equation 2.4. This requires transport sweeps over the domain $\mathbf{D}_{x,y}$ in the M discrete ordinate directions.

A triangulation $\mathcal{T}_h$ is established over the domain $\mathbf{D}_{x,y}$, i.e, the set $\mathbf{D}_{x,y}$ is subdivided into a finite number of triangles T of dimension h. For each direction (μ_m, ν_m), we partition the mesh into layers $S^m_0, S^m_1, ..., S^m_{end}$:

$$S^m_0 \equiv \{T \in \mathcal{T}_h : \partial^m_{\text{in}} T \subset \partial^m_{\text{in}} \mathbf{D}_{x,y}\}, \tag{3.2}$$

$$S^m_{i+1} \equiv \{T \in \mathcal{T}_h : \partial^m_{\text{in}} T \subset \partial^m_{\text{in}} (\mathbf{D}_{x,y} - \bigcup_{j\leq i} S^m_j)\}, i = 0, 1, ..., end, \tag{3.3}$$

where $\partial^m_{in}\mathbf{D}_{x,y}$ is the inflow boundary of $\mathbf{D}_{x,y}$ and $\partial^m_{in}T$ is the inflow boundary of the triangle T.

With this partition of $\mathcal{T}_h$, the approximate solution may be obtained in an explicit manner, first in S^m_0, then in S^m_1, etc. The updated exiting fluxes in S^m_i are transferred to the neighboring layer S^m_{i+1} for use as updated incident fluxes.

Within each spatial cell, the approximate solution can only be computed from the incident flux on the inflow boundary and the source of the cell. The updated exiting fluxes are transferred to neighboring spatial cells for use as updated incident fluxes. Thus, the calculation for any given spatial cell depends on the calculations in all "upwind" cells. This approach represents an inherently sequential procedure which can only be parallelized at the cost of slower convergence of the solution. In order to overcome this obstacle, we extend our previous work on the two-dimensional neutron transport problem [9]. The domain $\mathbf{D}_{x,y}$ is decomposed into P subdomains $\mathbf{D}^p_{x,y}$ using the multilevel implementation of Recursive Spectral Bisection (RSB) [10]. Mathematically $\mathbf{D}$ can be written as:

$$\mathbf{D} = \bigcup_p \mathbf{D}^p_{x,y} \times (\mathbf{a}, \mathbf{b}). \tag{3.4}$$

This results in a decomposition of $\mathbf{D}$ into columns oriented in the z direction, each of which is assigned to a processor.

During each transport sweep across $\mathbf{D}_{x,y} \times (\mathbf{a}, \mathbf{b})$, each processor may require incident fluxes from other processors, which may or may not have been calculated yet. Let $\oplus$ show the need for incident boundary fluxes and let $\otimes$ show the availability of new outgoing fluxes from a neighboring subdomain. Thus, if $\otimes \equiv \oplus$, then we use the new available information; otherwise, we use the older estimates. Thus, introducing an iteration superscript, the parallel source iteration expression of equation 2.4 can be written, when ξ_m is positive, as :

$$\mu_m \frac{\partial \psi^{g,(l+1)}_{i+\frac{1}{2},m,p}}{\partial x}(x, y) + \nu_m \frac{\partial \psi^{g,(l+1)}_{i+\frac{1}{2},m,p}}{\partial y}(x, y) + (\sigma^g_{i+\frac{1}{2},p}(x, y) + \frac{\xi_m}{\mathbf{c}\Delta z_i})\psi^{g,(l+1)}_{i+\frac{1}{2},m,p}(x, y)$$

$$= \sigma^{s,g\to g}_{i+\frac{1}{2},p}(x, y)\phi^{g,(l)}_{i+\frac{1}{2},p}(x, y) + Q^g_{i+\frac{1}{2},m,p}(x, y) + \frac{\xi_m}{\mathbf{c}\Delta z_i}\psi^g_{m,p}(x, y, z_i), \tag{3.5}$$

$$(3.6)\psi^{g,(l+1)}_{i+\frac{1}{2},m,p}(x,y) = \begin{cases} \psi^{g}_{in,i+\frac{1}{2},m}(x,y) & \text{if } (x,y) \in \Gamma_p, \mu_m n_x(x,y) + \nu_m n_y(x,y) < 0, \\ \psi^{g,(l+1)}_{i+\frac{1}{2},m,p'}(x,y) & \text{if } (x,y) \in \Gamma_{p,p'}, \otimes \equiv \oplus, \\ \psi^{g,(l)}_{i+\frac{1}{2},m,p'}(x,y) & \text{if } (x,y) \in \Gamma_{p,p'}, \otimes \neq \oplus, \end{cases}$$

where $n(x,y)$ is the outer unit normal on the part of the boundary of $\mathbf{D}^p_{x,y}$, $\Gamma_p = \partial \mathbf{D}^p_{x,y}$, that coincides with the outer boundary of $\mathbf{D}_{x,y}$, and $\Gamma_{p,p'}$ is the interface between subdomains $\mathbf{D}^p_{x,y}$ and $\mathbf{D}^{p'}_{x,y}$.

At the beginning of a transport sweep, each processor p, $1 \leq p \leq P$, has estimates for both the incident interface fluxes and the scattering source within the subdomain $\mathbf{D}^p_{x,y} \times (\mathbf{a}, \mathbf{b})$. Processor p executes its task sequentially over the discrete ordinate directions $1 \leq m \leq M$. For each direction it processes each slice z_i, $1 \leq i \leq N_z$, sequentially by updating the inflow flux $\psi^g_{m,p}(x,y,z_{i+1})$ at slice $i+1$ using equation 3.1.

At the end of a transport sweep, new estimates have been computed for exiting fluxes from $\mathbf{D}^p_{x,y} \times (\mathbf{a}, \mathbf{b})$. The updated exiting fluxes are available to neighboring processors p' for use as updated incident fluxes. The processors terminate the task of iteration l by updating the scalar flux for use in iteration $l+1$ by:

$$(3.7) \qquad \phi^{g,(l)}_{i+\frac{1}{2},p}(x,y) = \sum_{m'=1}^{M} \omega_{m'} \psi^{g,(l)}_{i+\frac{1}{2},m',p}(x,y).$$

We first solve equation 3.5 beginning with the highest energy group G of the energy partition (see equations 3.5-3.6). Then the same equation is solved for the other energies in descending order, taking into account scattering from higher energies to low energies (source term $Q^g_{i+\frac{1}{2},m,p}$ - see equation 2.7).

3.1. Implementation. Implementation of the numerical solution of equation 3.5 requires an asynchronous communication pattern. Fluxes must be communicated between processors owning adjacent subdomains during each sweep. Alternatively, only fluxes from a previous iteration could be used (leaving out the $\otimes \equiv \oplus$ boundary condition in equation 3.6); we call this the synchronous algorithm, since fluxes would only have to be communicated between processors once at the end of each iteration. Problems with asynchronous communication are best implemented on shared memory computers [17], because each processor can access a global address space without the participation of other processors. Therefore we have implemented our algorithm using OpenMP, an industry-wide standard for threads-based shared memory parallelization.

The computational kernel of the code, which contains the source iteration, was placed in one OpenMP parallel region and parallelized using the Single Program Multiple Data (SPMD) approach. That is, we did not use the typical approach taken with OpenMP of parallelizing individual loops. Variables in the parallel region were chosen to be private by default, with the notable exception of the flux ψ and various constants, which were set to be shared.

As discussed above, each processor performs transport sweeps over its subdomain sequentially for each discrete ordinate angle. It is desirable to order the transport sweeps in each subdomain so as to maximize the availability of updated incident fluxes from adjacent subdomains. We have shown that this can result in an improvement in the rate of convergence of the asynchronous algorithm [9]. For each subdomain $\mathbf{D}^p_{x,y}$ and for each direction m, we find the first layer that intersects $\mathbf{D}^p_{x,y}$(see equations 3.2,3.3):

$$(3.8) \qquad n_m = \min_i \{i, S^m_i \cap \mathbf{D}^p_{x,y} \neq \emptyset\}.$$

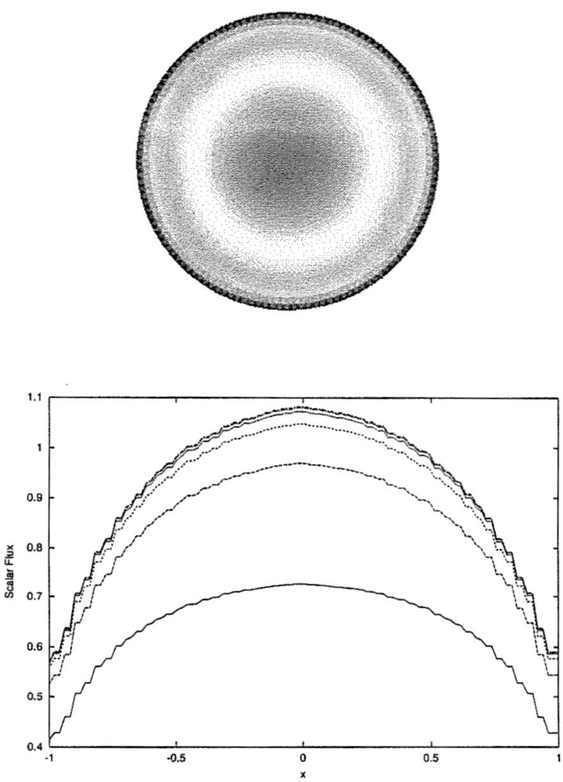

(a)

(b)

FIG. 3.1. *(a) Scalar flux after one iteration of sequential program; (b) scalar flux along horizontal slice through center of (a) for first six iterations (bottom to top)*

We then order the directions for transport sweeps in the subdomain $\mathbf{D}^p_{x,y}$ as $m_1, m_2, ..., m_i, m_{i+1}, ..., m_M$, such that $n_{m_i} \leq n_{m_{i+1}}$. This means that while we sweep in a specified direction in processor p, we sweep in a direction in a neighboring processor p' so that both processors are able to use the new outgoing interface boundary fluxes from their neighbors as soon as possible.

This means, for instance, that sweeping in subdomains on the outer boundary of the domain will be done first for directions that come from outside. When incident fluxes are required from another subdomain they are obtained (updated or not) transparently from global memory.

3.2. Convergence. Since the parallel algorithm breaks the dependency of the transport sweeps, convergence will be slower than the serial algorithm. We illustrate this for the two-dimensional mono-energetic model problem used in previous work [9], which consists of a disk with a vacuum boundary and constant source, total, and scattering cross sections: $Q(x,y) = 1.0$, $\sigma(x,y) = 1.0$, $\sigma^s(x,y) = 0.5$. Convergence of the sequential algorithm is seen in figure 3.1, where the scalar flux already qualitatively has its final shape after two iterations, and converges rapidly within four iterations. The slower convergence of the parallel algorithm is illustrated in figure 3.2, for the case of four subdomains, and for synchronous communication (leaving out $\otimes \equiv \oplus$ in equation 3.6); the subdomain boundaries are clearly seen, and then gradually erased as the iterations proceed.

We showed previously for neutron transport in two dimensions that this problem can be

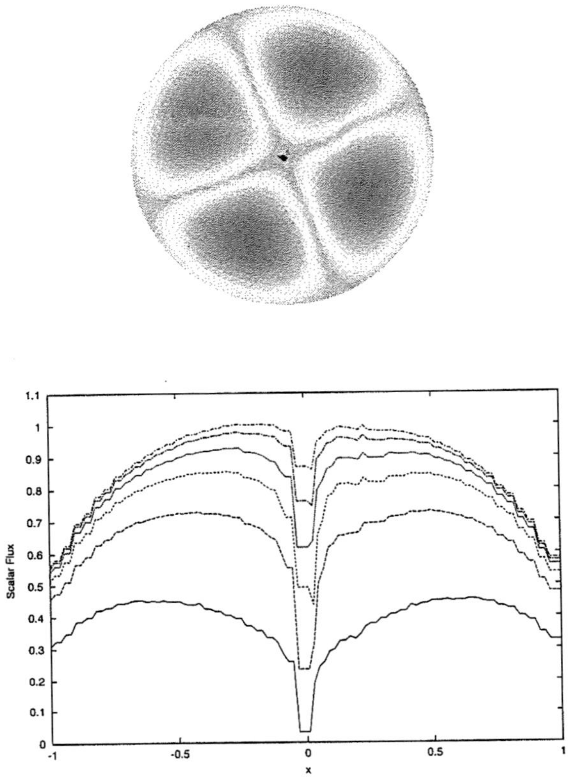

(a)

(b)

FIG. 3.2. *(a)Scalar flux after one iteration of* synchronous *parallel program; (b) scalar flux along horizontal slice through center of (a) for first six iterations (bottom to top)*

mitigated somewhat by the use of our asynchronous algorithm (see equation 3.5), resulting in convergence in a little more than half the number of iterations as the synchronous algorithm. The faster convergence of the asynchronous algorithm is illustrated in figure 3.3. There still remains the fact that in many cases, old boundary subdomain fluxes will still be used ($\otimes \neq \oplus$). This occurs for approximately 40% of triangles that lie on $(x, y) \in \Gamma_{p,p'}$, for the two dimensional problem studied in [9]. As a result, convergence of the asynchronous parallel algorithm is still slower than for the sequential algorithm. Importantly, the number of iterations did not increase rapidly with the number of processors used, reaching a plateau of twice the the number of iterations compared to the serial algorithm.

The convergence of the parallel algorithm is sensitive to the error introduced by using old boundary subdomain fluxes, particularly during the first iteration, when there are no old fluxes available. These old fluxes would normally be set to an initial guess solution, for example to zero, before the first iteration. This situation would be expected to be aggravated in our approach to the three-dimensional problem, since the error resulting from the domain decomposition would propagate in the z direction through the $\psi^{g}_{m,p}(x, y, z_i)$ term in equation 3.5.

However, it is possible to increase the convergence of our multigroup parallel algorithm. Since the problem is solved by using back substitution computation from higher to lower energies, one can use the calculated flux $\psi^{g+1}_{i+\frac{1}{2},m}$ at energy $g+1$ as an initial guess solution $\psi^{g,(0)}_{i+\frac{1}{2},m}$ to compute the flux at energy g:

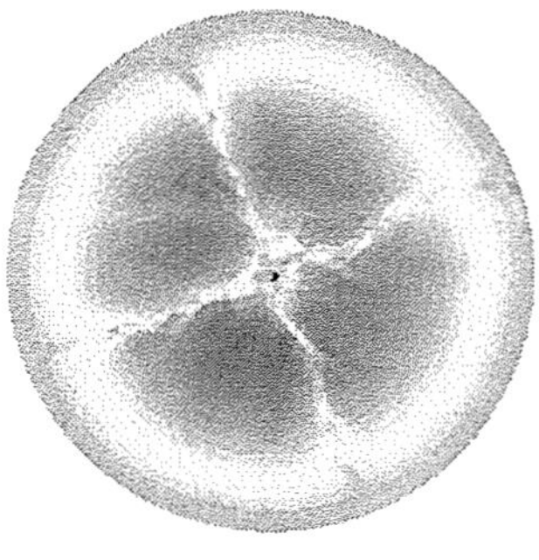

(a)

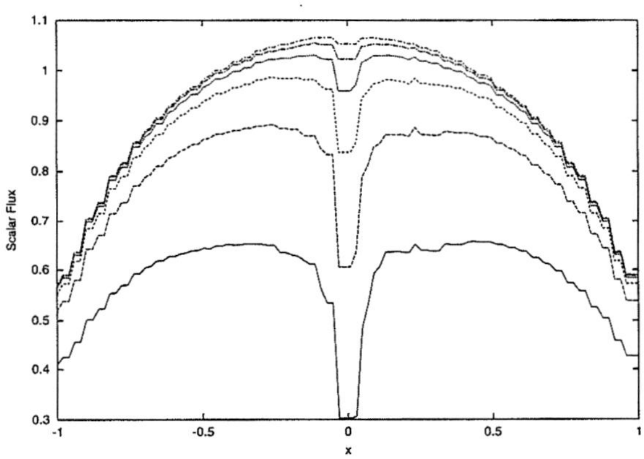

(b)

FIG. 3.3. *(a)Scalar flux after one iteration of* asynchronous *parallel program; (b) scalar flux along horizontal slice through center of (a) for first six iterations (bottom to top)*

$$\psi^{g,(0)}_{i+\frac{1}{2},m}(x,y) = \psi^{g+1}_{i+\frac{1}{2},m}(x,y) \quad if \quad g < G \tag{3.9}$$

For ψ continuous over the energy interval $(\mathbf{E}_0, \mathbf{E}_0/\alpha^G_{max})$, the error introduced by the domain decomposition can be reduced by this procedure.

4. Results. Our algorithm was implemented in Fortran 90, and results were obtained on an SGI Origin 3800 with 64 MIPS R12000 400 MHz processors and 32 GB memory. The Origin 3800 is a distributed shared memory machine, with a "first-touch" data-placement policy. This means that pages are allocated to memory close to the processor that runs the code. Therefore, the shared array containing the flux $\psi^g_{i+\frac{1}{2},m,p}(x,y)$ was initialized in parallel to maximize local memory references. All the processors initiate their work simultaneously after one processor initializes the input data for all. At the end of every iteration a global L_2 relative error norm is calculated for the scalar fluxes:

$$\epsilon = \frac{\|\phi^{(l+1)}_{i+\frac{1}{2}} - \phi^{(l)}_{i+\frac{1}{2}}\|_2}{\|\phi^{(l)}_{i+\frac{1}{2}}\|_2}. \tag{4.1}$$

This is the only serial part of our algorithm, in addition to the initialization described above and any writing of fluxes to disk. If the convergence criterion $\epsilon < 10^{-7}$, then the program proceeds to the next lower energy, after having calculated new source terms.

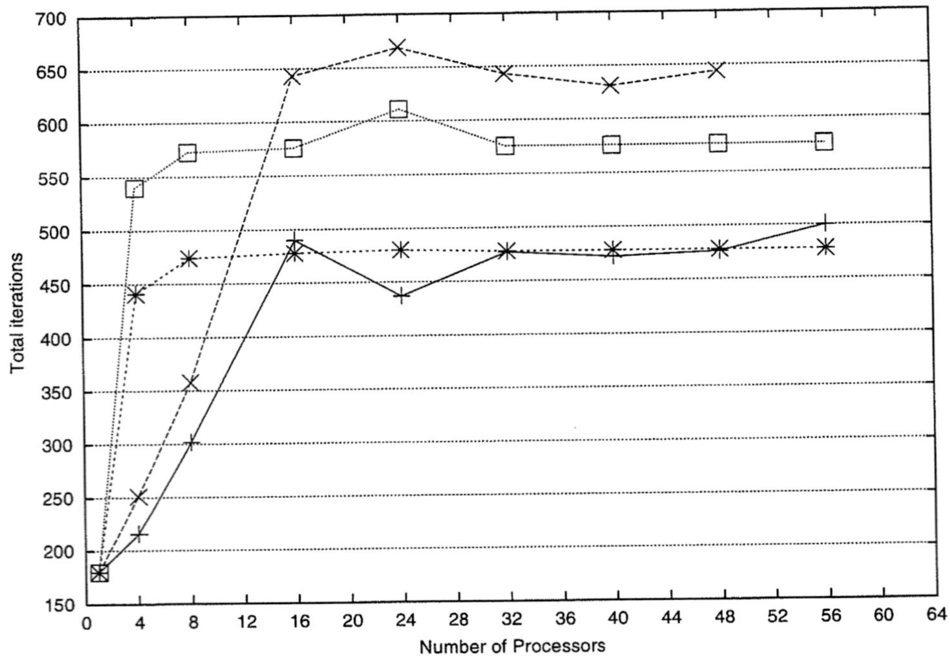

FIG. 4.1. *Total number of iterations (over all energies) for source on the side with flux reuse (+) and without (×) flux reuse between energy groups, and for source on top with flux reuse (∗) and without (□) flux reuse.*

All tests are carry out on the BNCT model. We considered two different neutron sources impinging on a cylinder of 10 cm radius and 20 cm height: (i) incident at a normal to the center of the top of the cylinder with a circular cross-sectional radius of 2 cm; (ii) incident on the center of the side of the cylinder, with a square cross section of 4 cm wide and 2 cm high. Sample plots of the resulting scalar flux are shown in figure 2.2.

We also considered two ways of initializing the flux for energies lower than E_0/α_{max}^G, as discussed in the previous section: using zero as initial guess solution or reusing fluxes from the previous highest energy computation.

4.1. Convergence rate. The sequential source iteration program required 5 iterations per energy group to converge, for a total of 180 iterations over all energies. The number of iterations increased with the number of processors for the parallel source iteration program, but reached a plateau after 8 or 16 processors. The sum of the iterations required to converge over all energy groups is shown in figure 4.1 as a function of the number of processors, for both types of neutron sources, and for both types of flux reuse.

Consider first the effect of reusing fluxes from a higher energy for the initial guess. When fluxes are not reused, the initial guess is set to zero for every energy, and the number of iterations required to converge increases more rapidly and reaches a higher plateau than when they are reused. Consider in detail the case when the source is on the top of the cylinder, and 32 processors are used. If fluxes are not reused, convergence is achieved in 16 iterations for each energy. If they are reused, the convergence occurs in 16 iterations for the highest energy, then in 19 iterations for the second highest, followed by 14 iterations for the third highest and in 13 iterations for the rest. This pattern is typical, and can be explained as follows. Since the external source occurs only at the highest energy (group G), the resulting fluxes are quite different than for the other energies (see figure 2.1), therefore

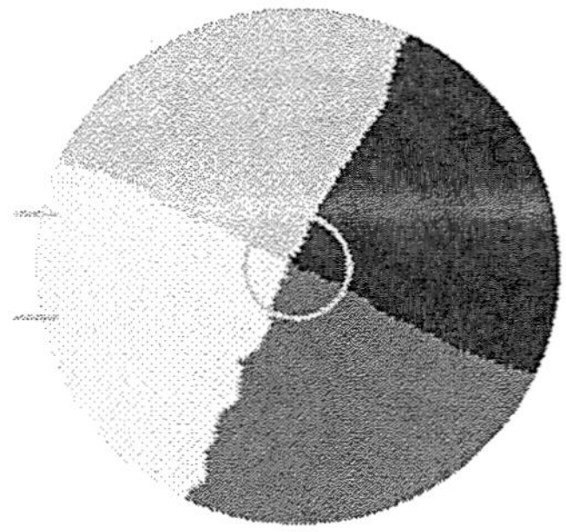

(a)

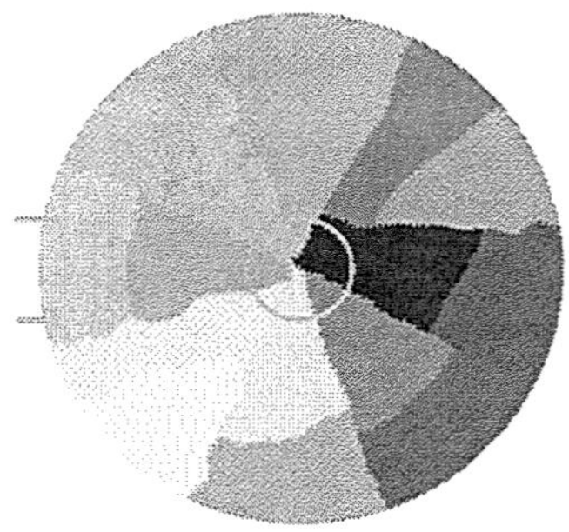

(b)

FIG. 4.2. *Domain decomposition for (a) four and (b) sixteen processors, showing the two locations of the neutron source*

the flux for group G is not a good initial guess for the flux of group $G-1$, and is worse than simply initializing the flux to zero. The fluxes for all energies other than group G are more similar, since there is no external source, therefore reusing them results in a better initial guess when inter-subdomain fluxes are required and consequently leads to a decrease in the number of iterations required to converge. All further discussion will refer to calculations where the fluxes are reused, unless otherwise specified.

Consider next the effect of changing the geometric location of the neutron source. The number of iterations rises much more rapidly for the source on the top than for the source on the side. The reason for this can be seen by looking at how the source intersects with the domain decomposition. Figure 4.2 shows the domain decomposition for 4 and 16 processors, together with the location of the source. For the source on the side, neutrons travel initially in only one subdomain, but for the 16-processor decomposition, they reach other subdomains sooner. Since the flux goes to zero rapidly with distance (see figure 2.1), it stays mostly in one subdomain for the 4-processor decomposition, whereas it is spread over several subdomains for the 16-processor decomposition. Therefore convergence occurs in only 6 iterations in the former case, but in 13 iterations (for most energies) in the latter case. Since the source on the top immediately couples multiple subdomains for all decompositions, the number of iterations rises rapidly starting at 4 processors, with typically 13 iterations required to converge per energy group.

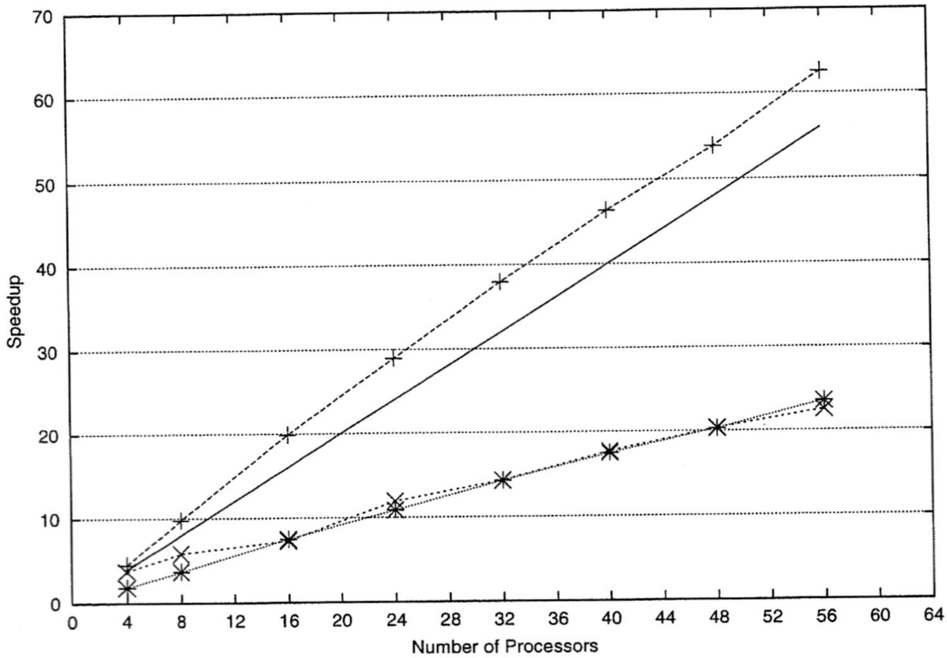

FIG. 4.3. *Parallel speedups per iteration (+) and total speedups for source on side (×) and on top (∗)*

4.2. Parallel speedup. The speedups obtained by our asynchronous parallel algorithm are shown in figure 4.3. Timings were averaged over all iterations and energies. The speedup per iteration was calculated as $S_p = t_s/t_p$, where t_s and t_p are the execution times per iteration of the sequential and parallel (using p processors) programs. Note that this speedup is superlinear, that is its slope is greater than one, for fewer than 16 processors, and slightly superlinear for 16 processors or more. One possible explanation is that the shared array containing the flux requires 1.5 GB storage, which is too large to fit in a single 2-processor node of the Origin 3800 (1 GB). Therefore the serial program must perform a number of memory accesses to a remote node; if the data is layed out in such a way that the memory accesses are localized as much as possible, then the parallel program may have fewer remote memory accesses. However, upon investigation with SGI's Perfex performance monitor, it became clear that the cause lay in the better cache reuse of the parallel programs. This is evident from the L2 cache hit rate (fraction of data accesses satisfied from the L2 cache), which was 0.934 for the serial program, 0.965 for four processors, and 0.976 for greater than four processors. This is an effect common to many memory-bound SPMD parallel programs, where explicit allocation of data with processors leads to better cache reuse.

The overall speedup, given by $(N_{iter,s}/N_{iter,p})(t_s/t_p)$, where $N_{iter,s}$ and $N_{iter,p}$ are the number of iterations required to converge for the serial and parallel calculations respectively, is also shown in figure 4.3, for both neutron sources. The decrease in the convergence rate of the parallel program offsets to some extent the speedups obtained per iteration. However, the overall speedup still increases with the number of processors, and the execution time is reduced to 40 minutes with 48 processors.

5. Conclusions. The formulation of the three-dimensional transport equation as coupled two-dimensional equations allowed us to extend previous work on the parallelization of the transport equation [9]. The proposed asynchronous parallel algorithm is shown to be viable, and we observe no significant degradation in the convergence rates as has been reported [11, 12, 13].

Implementation of our asynchronous parallel algorithm was done using OpenMP. Our results demonstrate that SPMD parallelization together with OpenMP can yield excellent speedup. This was achieved on the SGI Origin 3800, a cc-NUMA machine, by taking advantage of SGI's "first touch" data placement policy and parallel intialization of shared arrays. Our parallel implementation does require more code modification than the loop-level approach, which is usual for OpenMP programs, but it is still far easier than a message-passing implementation.

We achieved superlinear speedups per iteration due to cache effects. Convergence of the parallel program took more iterations than the serial program, but this increase reached a plateau of 2.5 times the number of serial iterations. This is comparable to the relative slowdown in the parallel convergence rate found in our previous results for the two-dimensional mono-energetic Boltzmann equation. The rate of convergence was found to be sensitive to the location of the source of neutrons. Convergence was improved by reusing fluxes between calculations for each energy group, which reduced the error on the first iteration of the parallel programs.

Acknowledgments. Our work made use of the infrastructure and resources of MACI (Multimedia Advanced Computational Infrastructure) funded in part by the CFI (Canada Foundation for Innovation) and the University of Alberta.

REFERENCES

[1] IAEA, *Curent Status of Neutron Capture Therapy*, IAEA-TECDOC-1223 (May 2001).

[2] C. Cercignani, *The Boltzmann equation and its applications*, Springer-Verlag, New York (1988).

[3] M. S. Clowdsley, J. H. Heinbockel, H. Kaneko et.al, *A Comparison of the Multigroup and collocation Methods for Solving the Low Energy Neutron Boltzmann Equation*, Canadian Journal of Physics, 78 (2000) pp. 45-56.

[4] E. E. Lewis and W. F. Miller, *Computational Methods of Neutron Transport*, John Wiley and Sons, New York (1984), reprinted by the American Nuclear Society, La Grange Park (1993).

[5] P. Lesaint, P.A. Raviart, *On a Finite Element Method for Solving the Neutron Transport Equation*, in Mathematical Aspects of Finite Elements in Partial Differential Equations, 89 (1974), Academic Press, New York.

[6] G.R. Richter, *An Optimal-Order Estimate for the Discontinuous Galerkin Method*, Math. Comput., 50 (1988) p. 75.

[7] F.E. Khettabi, C. Lécot, *Characteristic Methods for Discretizing the two-Dimensional Transport Equation on an Unstructured Grid of Triangular Cells*, Proc. Joint International Conference on Mathematical Methods and Supercomputing for Nuclear Applications, 2 (1997), pp. 975-984, American Nuclear Society, La Grange Park.

[8] F. E. Khettabi, *Exponential characteristic Methods for Discretizing the Two-Dimensional Transport Equation on an Unstructured Grid of Triangular Cells*, International Conference on the physics of nuclear science and technology, (1998).

[9] E. E. Aubanel and F. E. Khettabi, *Parallelization of Radiation Transport on Unstructured Triangular Grids with Spatial Decomposition and OpenMP*, Workshop on Parallel and Distributed Scientific and Engineering Computing with Applications, in proc. of the 16th Intl. Parallel and Distributed Processing Symposium (2002).

[10] Stephen T. Barnard and Horst D. Simon, *A Fast Multilevel Implementation of Recursive Spectral Bisection for Partitioning Unstructured Problems*, Concurrency: Practice and Experience, 6 (1994) pp. 101-107.

[11] M. Yavuz and E. Larson,*Iterative Methods for Solving $X - Y$ Geometry S_n Problems on Parallel Architecture Computers*, Nucl. Sci. Eng., 111 (1992), 46.

[12] S.P. Burns and M.A. Christon, *Spatial Domain-Based Parallelism in Large-Scale, Participating Media, Radiative Transport Applications*, Numerical Heat Transfer, Part B, 31 (1997), 401.

[13] J. Goncalves and P.J. Coelho, *Parallelization of the Discrete Ordinates Method*, Numerical Heat Transfer, Part B, **32**, 151 (1997).

[14] P. Nowak and M.K. Nemanic, *Radiation Transport Calculations on Unstructured Grids using a Spatially Decomposed and Threaded Algorithm*, Proc. ANS Conf. on Math. and Computation, Reactor Physics and Environmental Analysis in Nuclear Applications, 379 (1999).

[15] S. PLIMPTON, B. HENDRICKSON, S. BURNS, W. MCLENDON III, *Parallel Algorithms for Radiation Transport on Unstructured Grids*, Proc. SuperComputing 2000, IEEE (2000).

[16] R. HIROMOTO, B.R. WIENKE, R.G. BRICKNER, *The Performance of asynchronous iteration schemes applied to the linearized Boltzmann transport equation*, Parallel Computing, 18 (1992), pp. 241-268.

[17] S.M. PANCAKE, *Is Parallelism for You?*, Computational Science and Engineering Vol. 3, No. 2 (Summer, 1996), p. 18 .

In: Applied Parallel and Distributed Computing
Editors: Yi Pan and Laurence T. Yang , pp. 89-102
ISBN 1-59454-174-4

AN OBJECT-ORIENTED PROGRAMMING FRAMEWORK FOR PARALLEL FINITE ELEMENT ANALYSIS WITH APPLICATION: LIQUID COMPOSITE MOLDING

BRIAN J. HENZ* AND DALE R. SHIRES†

Abstract. The use of object-oriented programming techniques in development of parallel, finite element analysis software enhances software reuse and makes application development more efficient. In this paper, an object-oriented programming framework for developing parallel finite element software is described. All required steps, from data file parsing and equation solving to post processing and graphical user interfaces, are discussed. After development of the framework, a sample parallel finite element code, namely COMPOSE, is extracted from its original functional programming paradigm and implemented in the new object-oriented programming framework. Besides ease of development, the use of generic visualization and interface tools for software utilizing the framework speeds delivery of research codes to end users.

Key words. Object-oriented programming, Parallel processing, Finite element method, Resin transfer molding, Software development

1. Introduction. Scientific computing has provided insights and solutions for numerous classes of scientific and engineering problems. Computational science, the techniques used to arrive at these solutions, requires effective use of computer hardware systems and algorithm development strategies. While these problems can often be computed on a single processor, most often the sheer complexity and size of the problem in question requires the use of parallel computer systems. One of the predominant uses of the many large-scale, parallel computer systems in use today is for the solution of problems in science and engineering. Indeed, the performance of these systems is most often measured by its speed at solving mathematically-oriented benchmark applications.

While great strides have continually been made in hardware and parallel processing speed, software development for these applications remains problematic. The focus on code execution speed combined with early formal language theory to create simple, easy to compile, function-oriented design languages like FORTRAN 77. These early languages had limited features and could generate machine code as efficient as the best hand-coded routines. Since these early days, languages such as C and extensions to FORTRAN, including Fortran 90/95 and High Performance Fortran (HPF), continue to provide more robust functionality. Today, C and Fortran remain the predominant languages of choice for scientific computing codes.

However, these languages suffer common function-oriented design problems. They do not provide for effective code reuse. Most often, this requires copying and modifying code from an existing application to a new application. This inevitably introduces unwanted side effects and buggy code. It also means that the substantial effort already employed to produce viable, efficient code is limited to the current application only. The lack of modularity is also a problem. An operation on data in these codes can often be spread over multiple functions with no clear entry and exit point. This data abstraction, the definition of new data types, and associated functionality is a crucial component that holds the key to resolving many of these problems. It is no surprise that as the Fortran language has continued to evolve, this support has been incorporated into Fortran 90/95 [4].

Object-oriented design and the related object-oriented programming (OOP) is an approach widely offered in place of function-oriented design. It is based on information hiding

* U.S. Army Research Laboratory, Attn: AMSRL-CI-HC, Aberdeen Proving Ground, MD 21005, (bhenz@arl.army.mil).
† U.S. Army Research Laboratory, Attn: AMSRL-CI-HC, Aberdeen Proving Ground, MD 21005, (dshires@arl.army.mil).

and focuses on the software system as a set of interconnected, interfacing objects [20]. Information hiding forces the developments to be modular and allows for built-up systems of components. This promotes software reuse and allows for selective optimization. These concepts, however, have not been widely applied to scientific computing codes. In this paper, we focus on applying these techniques to the finite element method (FEM). The FEM is a technique found in computational engineering that has been used in various serial and parallel codes.

While the use of OOP is not widespread in computational engineering, it has been applied successfully in certain instances [5, 10, 21]. Some parallel OOP formulations for the FEM have also been introduced [11, 15]. These developments focus our current research and extensions to make the approach more generic and robust. The new toolkit described in this chapter is called SPOOCEFEM (Simple Parallel Object-Oriented Computing Environment for the Finite Element Method), pronounced spo͞o'kēfēm. The framework has been designed to allow for extensive software reuse, describes common data file representations to promote interfacing with multidisciplinary codes and scientific visualization packages, and provides functionality on both single and multiprocessor architectures.

2. SPOOCEFEM Goals and Implementation. While there really is no easy way to iterate the goals behind a development effort (usually there are just too many), several in this case are worth noting. The first design goal for SPOOCEFEM was that it be generic. By providing a general OOP FEM framework, new application codes are spared the tedious and laborious effort required to replicate much of the functionality that is common across the various FEM codes. For example, various finite element types are supported with associated routines, such as computation and storage of local coordinates.

The second goal was that it be modular. Base classes with well-defined interfaces are constructed first. More complex objects, such as an FEM object, are composed of these base classes. In a current application using SPOOCEFEM, this practice has allowed for the creation of complex classes using multiple inheritance with no requirements for revisiting the base code. This modularity, even to the level of the input and output data, has allowed it to be easily interfaced with existing scientific visualization codes. The result is a solution built from well-tested components complete with interfaces to complex scientific visualization libraries.

Speed was the final goal in the development of the library. This is an active research area for the SPOOCEFEM developers as the library is still being profiled and studied for performance. Of primary note, however, is that the modularity of the design has allowed for a system where numerical solvers can easily be selected and changed according to the needs of a specific FEM application. As with numerous scientific computing codes, the majority of the times we have seen in codes using SPOOCEFEM require the solution of linear systems of equations. The modularity of the developments foster speed by making these changes virtually effortless, as compared to the colossal effort required to change embedded solvers in functional programming codes. Even if the runtime system required to support operator overloading and polymorphism incurs some overhead compared to historical codes such as those developed with Fortran, we feel the reduced time to solution in the development cycle is worth the slight increase in computer time.

The language of choice for these developments is C++. The authors have had success in porting the newly developed library using this standardized language coupled with the MPI libraries for parallel execution. The current ports include the SGI Origin machines, Linux clusters, and the IBM SP3 and SP4. It should be noted, however, that these benefits do come at a price. The initial ramp-up time to a fully functioning SPOOCEFEM library was significant. However, the authors are already taking advantage of the functionality provided by the library in quickly extending and developing new codes based on the FEM.

3. SPOOCEFEM Structure. An overview of the components from which SPOOCEFEM is constructed is shown in Figure 3.1. Base components are shown at the bottom of the stack with each layer representing new or extended functionalities added to the layers below it. As can be seen in the figure, the SPOOCEFEM environment encompasses and builds upon the functionalities found in numerous languages and libraries. The blocks representing the linear algebra components (PETSc, PSPASES, BLAS, and LAPACK) are all optional. FORTRAN 77 and Fortran 90 are optional and are only required for the use of PETSc and PSPASES, respectively.

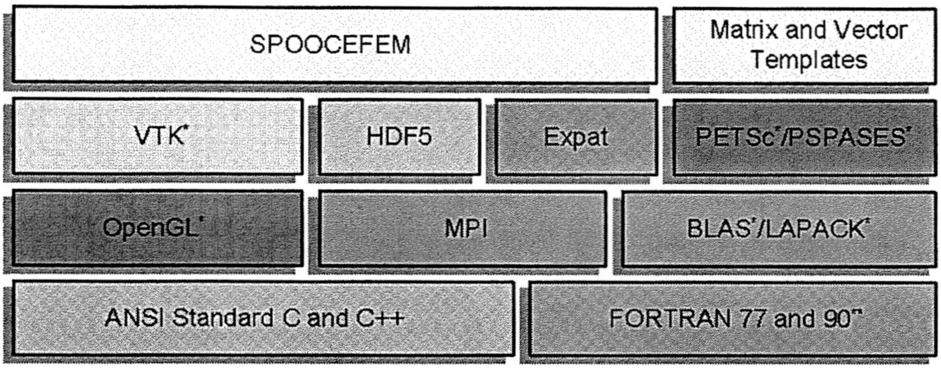

FIG. 3.1. *SPOOCEFEM building block framework.*

The remainder of the paper is devoted to a discussion of the integration of these various components and the functionalities found at the SPOOCEFEM layer. In particular, this section includes discussions of the data format utilized in SPOOCEFEM, some of the classes available, and file converters for NASTRAN and PATRAN neutral files. The work discussed here is applicable to serial or parallel FEM software development and is the framework around which new applications are built. Parallel extensions are described in a later section.

3.1. The FEM data file format. The data format used in SPOOCEFEM is the eXtensible Data Model and Format (XDMF) for communication between interdisciplinary applications in the solution of multi-physics problems [3]. This data format works well for the OOP approach since it is extensible and designed for storing data used/generated by computational software. Although the XDMF format is defined for many types of computational applications, SPOOCEFEM only utilizes a subset for unstructured grid problems as encountered in the FEM.

The data required by computational software is stored in XDMF as either "light" or "heavy" data. "Light" data is typically descriptive in nature and is used to store such information as the number of nodes in a mesh, the number of each type of element, and other small sets of information such as boundary conditions (BC) and material data. Light data is stored in eXtensible Markup Language (XML) files for ease of parsing, writing, and dataset modifications. "Heavy" data is typically large or static datasets required by FEM software such as element connectivity, node locations, and simulation results. Heavy data is stored in Hierarchical Data Format version 5 (HDF5) files for access across architectures. Having heavy data stored in binary files has many advantages including providing for random access to data when only a subset of a large dataset is required.

An advantage of utilizing the XDMF file format is that there are many GUI tools already available for visualizing the data. These include the standard GUI in the Interdisciplinary Computing Environment (ICE) being developed by ARL and its converters to EnSight and OpenDX formats. By wrapping the SPOOCEFEM libraries with The Simplified Wrapper and Interface Generator (SWIG), the Java and Python interfaces developed by these authors is also available for visualization of geometric and simulation results data. Another advantage of using XDMF is that there are a growing number of scientific applications that utilize XDMF for input and output, making the problem solving capabilities of these codes more accessible. This capability is especially important when developing multi-physics software that requires modules from various developers with unique input/output requirements.

The following snippet from a SPOOCEFEM data file is used as an illustrative example of the file format. All of the tags between the SPOOCEFEM tags are recognized and processed by the SPOOCEFEM XML reader. The parameters are defined by the PARAMETER tag and are generic data holders. The number of parameters is defined by the PARAMETERS tag. This methodology is found often in the SPOOCEFEM XML file format as it is a logical description and facilitates the actions of the reader.

```
<?xml version="1.0" ?>
<SPOOCEFEM>
  <PARAMETERS Number="2">
    <PARAMETER Name="TIMESTEP" Type="REAL" Value="0.5" />
    <PARAMETER Name="VISCOSITY" Type="REAL" Value="0.0" />
  </PARAMETERS>
  <NODES Number="3715"
    Location="box_3715.h5:/Geometry/Points/XYZ"
    GlobalIndex="box_3715.h5:/Geometry/Points/GlobalIndex"
  />
  <ELEMENTS Number="7286">
    <E2DTRI3 Number="7286"
       Connectivity="box_3715.h5:/Geometry/Elements/2dTri3/Connectivity"
       GlobalIndex="box_3715.h5:/Geometry/Elements/2dTri3/GlobalIndex"
       Thickness="box_3715.h5:/Geometry/Elements/2dTri3/Thickness"
       Material="box_3715.h5:/Geometry/Elements/2dTri3/Material"
    />
  </ELEMENTS>
  <MATERIALS Number="1">
    <MATERIAL ID="0" NumberProperties="9">
       <PROPERTY Name="KXX" Type="REAL" Value="3.4e-5" />
       <PROPERTY Name="KXY" Type="REAL" Value="0.0" />
       <PROPERTY Name="KYY" Type="REAL" Value="3.4e-5" />
       <PROPERTY Name="IAXIS" Type="INTEGER" Value="3" />
       <PROPERTY Name="ANGLE" Type="REAL" Value="0.0" />
       <PROPERTY Name="VOF" Type="REAL" Value="0.19" />
       <PROPERTY Name="CONDUCTIVITY" Type="REAL" Value="0.0067" />
       <PROPERTY Name="DENSITY" Type="REAL" Value="2.56" />
       <PROPERTY Name="HEATCAPACITY" Type="REAL" Value="0.67" />
    </MATERIAL>
  </MATERIALS>
  <BCS Number="4">
    <BC ID="0" Location="1182" TypeName="BC_FLOWRATE" Value="1.234" />
    <BC ID="1" Location="1183" TypeName="BC_FLOWRATE" Value="1.234" />
    <BC ID="2" Location="1182" TypeName="IC_FILLFRAC" Value="1.0" />
    <BC ID="3" Location="1183" TypeName="IC_FILLFRAC" Value="1.0" />
  </BCS>
</SPOOCEFEM>
```

The NODES tag is parsed and interpreted by the `FEMparser`, whereas the ELEMENTS tag contains some application specific data that is unrecognized by the `FEMparser`. The NODES tag contains the global number of nodes, the location in the HDF5 file of the XYZ values, and the location of the global indices (also stored in an HDF5 file). The ELEMENTS tag contains the global number of elements of all types with the number of the particular type specified in each tag below. For example, this mesh is made entirely of 3-noded triangular elements so the number of E2DTRI3 elements is the same as the total number of ELEMENTS. Each unique type of element contains the location of the elemental connectivities, global indices, and material numbers. The elemental thickness values are later read by an application-specific parser and are stored in application-specific element types.

The MATERIALS tag is parsed by the `FEMparser` and individual properties are stored by name. All properties listed with type REAL are stored as real values and all properties with type INTEGER are stored as integers by the use of a union in C++. This is a powerful method because all materials for any application are already parsed by the `FEMparser` and stored according to their application-specific name.

The boundary conditions and any initial conditions (IC) are listed inside of the BC tag. ICs share many attributes with the BC class. Accordingly, it was decided that for parsing and data storage it was simpler to consider ICs as BCs and have each application define unique methods of application and other functionality. For illustration, consider the fill fraction IC that requires a node location and real value for data storage. This is exactly the same data required for the flow rate BC and therefore, except for the method of application, the IC and BC are be stored in the same way.

3.2. NASTRAN and PATRAN neutral format parsers/converters. Parsers for reading geometric data from NASTRAN and PATRAN neutral files are included in the `FEM` class. Currently, the converters support reading of geometric information and material numbers for many element types including triangles, quadrilaterals, and tetrahedrons. For access to more information that may be contained in NASTRAN and PATRAN neutral files, such as BCs, it is simply a matter of creating a converter inside of the `FEM` class. Having converters available for standard data formats and implemented inside of the `FEM` class provides for quick development of robust preprocessing routines that are sometimes neglected in favor of other application specific routines in research applications.

3.3. The finite element class. The hierarchy of the `FEM` class utilized is shown in Figure 3.2. This class contains all of the generic finite element functionality required for developing a complete application. Some of the data includes BCs, material data, geometric information, and data file parsing utilities. The `FEM` class itself is a container class and is used to hold all of the FEM data and to perform utility functions for the stored data.

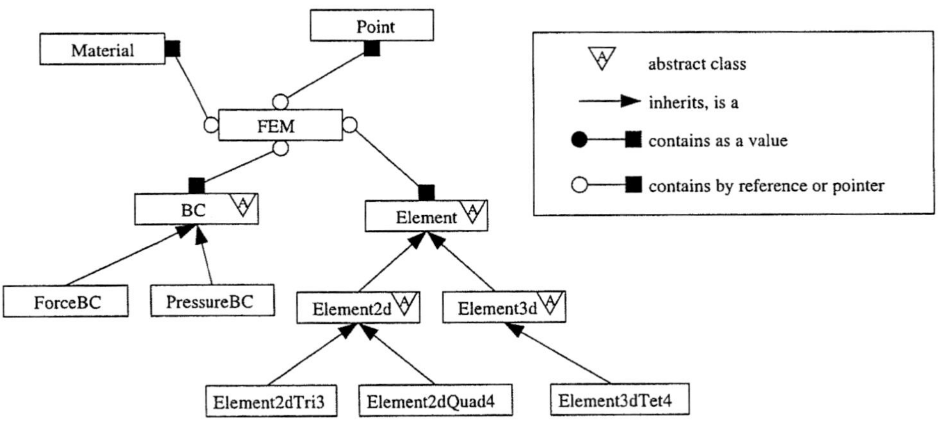

FIG. 3.2. *Hierarchy of the* `FEM` *object used by all applications.*

There are many types of finite elements available in SPOOCEFEM and all inherit from the base `Element` class. This class contains the lowest common data structures and functionality required of all elements. The data stored in this class includes a pointer to the specified material and an `Array` with the connectivity list. Inheriting from the `Element` class are the `Element2d` and `Element3d` classes. These are for 2- and 3-dimensional elements, respectively. At the moment these classes do not contain any data of their own but are useful for differentiation between element types. Inheriting from the `Element2d` class are the `Element2dTri3` and the `Element2dQuad4` classes for 3-noded triangles and 4-noded quadrilaterals, respectively. These classes contain more specific information such as the number of nodes in each element and the function for computation of the local coordinates. At this time the only 3-dimensional element type is the `Element3dTet4` class for 4-noded tetrahedrons. These elements do not require local coordinate computations and therefore are only currently used for data storage.

Boundary and initial conditions both inherit from the `BC` class and are stored in an `FEM` object as a linked list. This method of storage allows for easy addition and removal of any IC or BC and is useful for preprocessing in a GUI. The `BC` class itself only stores an integer that indicates the location of a BC or IC and all functionality thereafter is defined by the specific type of BC or IC. In the `PressureBC` class, the pressure value is stored as a real and is interpreted as pressure on a node for COMPOSE but could just as easily be pressure on an element edge or face for 2- and 3-dimensional stress analysis respectively. The actual application of the BC is left to the application designer at this time, as it would be difficult to assume how a BC is used in each case.

3.4. The helper classes. There are many common data structures and algorithms that are useful in the FEM. Some of these are included as separate classes and templates that are accessible to all objects. These helper classes include an adjacency list, a list template, an array template, a binary tree, and an XML writer. The adjacency list is especially useful because it is used to compute the connectivity of the finite element mesh and then the sparsity pattern of the stiffness matrices. The adjacency list is also useful for computing external nodes, or those nodes that are on the outside of a geometry, which will be used in several planned mesh optimization passes. The XML writer provides functionality for creating indented, correct, and easy to read XML files. Arrays are useful containers that enable run time bounds checking for developmental and code testing revisions. Binary trees are used in several cases to provide $O(log\ n)$ fast searches and for priority queue construction.

4. SPOOCEFEM Parallel Extensions. In this section the software developments that pertain only to parallel finite element analysis are discussed. The goal for SPOOCEFEM is to remove many of the hurdles and concerns for a developer of parallel finite element software. To this end, the following classes and templates were created to alleviate the burden on the application developer.

4.1. The finite element class. Parallelism in SPOOCEFEM is achieved by partitioning the problem domain. That is, the finite element mesh is domain decomposed where roughly equal-sized problems are assigned to various parallel processors. The `FEM` class contains the functionality for partitioning an unstructured finite element mesh by nodes or elements by utilizing the Metis [8] graph partitioning tool. The partitioning is accomplished at run-time so that any number of processors can be utilized with a simple command line option. One advantage of this method over storing partition information in the data file is that a simulation can be executed in parallel without having to worry about whether or not the proper partition information is available.

Once the partition numbers are known by the `FEM` object, the shared or ghost nodes are computed. All of this is facilitated by the `FEM` object and therefore the application developer is relieved of this cumbersome task. Generation of partitioning datasets and maintenance of the bookkeeping required for parallel computation are rather tedious and time-consuming operations. This integration of parallel bookkeeping into the `FEM` class allows for other optimizations, such as the minimization of communication between distant processors [18], to be applicable to all applications developed with SPOOCEFEM. Optimization of the communication routines and the bookkeeping operations independent of any application code is possible since they have been encapsulated in the class.

4.2. The vector and matrix classes. Typically, much of the time spent in FEM software is in the solution of the system of equations. This is the case in the Composite Manufacturing Process Simulation Environment (COMPOSE) application that is built on SPOOCEFEM technology. In this code, 80% to 90% of the runtime is spent in the solution of the associated linear equations. For this reason, great care has been taken to improve efficiency of the vector and matrix routines. One of the novel approaches in SPOOCEFEM is the inclusion of multiple equation solver packages. The `Matrix` and `Vector` template class interfaces provided by SPOOCEFEM ensure a consistent and transparent interface to all solvers. These interfaces are implemented to provide maximum flexibility to the developer in choosing an optimal solution method.

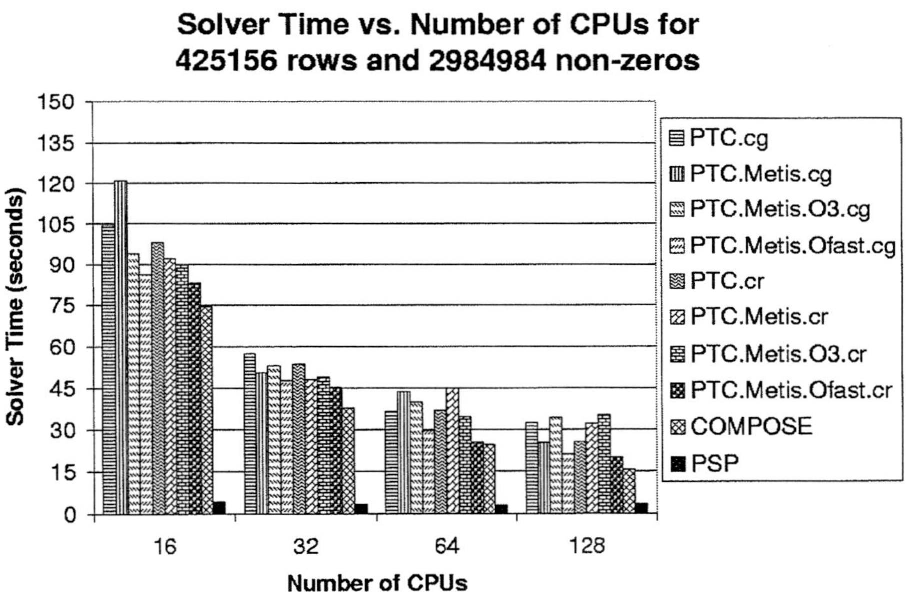

FIG. 4.1. *Comparison of solution times for linear system of equations from COMPOSE.*

It has been shown in COMPOSE that for typical problem sizes ($< 1 \cdot 10^6$ nodes) a direct solver is often the preferred solution method (see Figure 4.1). The linear system solved for the bar chart in Figure 4.1 is taken from the COMPOSE software simulation of a part when the resin has infused 95% of the mold. At this point the problem is much more difficult to solve because as the simulation progresses the stiffness matrix contains more nonzero terms throughout. In Figure 4.1, PTC refers to solvers from PETSc [2], PSP is the PSPASES [7] direct solver, COMPOSE [9] is the current application solver, METIS refers to matrix partitioning performed by Metis, `O3` and `Ofast` are compiler optimization levels defined by the SGI MIPS compiler, and cg or cr refers to conjugate gradient (CG) and conjugate residual solvers, respectively. For example, the PTC.Metis.O3.cg bar refers to the system solution computed by PETSc, partitioned by Metis, compiled with `O3` optimizations, and utilizing the CG solver.

For various problem sizes it would be optimal to take advantage of the best solver for the situation, whether in a parallel or serial environment. Therefore, the `Matrix` and `Vector` classes can store data in multiple formats including those used by PETSc, PSPASES, SPOOLES [1], the Vectorized Sparse Solver (VSS) from the NASA Langley Research Center, and the solver currently used in COMPOSE. The interface to all matrix objects is consistent, and the user is only required to decide during object instantiation which solver type(s) should to be accessible to the matrix and vector object. For example, in the non-isothermal COMPOSE software where symmetric and non-symmetric systems of equations are to be solved, the stiffness matrix associated with the flow simulation may require PSPASES for the solution of the symmetric system of equations, whereas the thermal problem is non-symmetric and therefore may have a stiffness matrix stored in the PETSc format for access to the Generalized Minimum Residual (GMRES) solver. Once created, all of the interfaces to the matrices are consistent and the storage details are hidden from the application. There is some overhead associated with accessing the matrix data, but since so much time is required by the solution routines this overhead is viewed as minimal [16].

The matrix data for COMPOSE is stored in the Yale or Compressed Sparse Row (CSR) format. The stiffness matrix is partitioned by rows so that each process has a contiguous set of data. This is the only information the user is required to be aware of for the generation of parallel FEM software in the SPOOCEFEM framework. Once the problem is read and partitions generated with Metis, the elemental stiffness matrices are generated and assembled into the global stiffness matrix stored according to the partition information. The problem is then solved in parallel using the requested solver. This description is for partitioning based on nodal domain decompositions.

5. Application Development with the SPOOCEFEM Framework. In this section, we describe the re-implementation of the FEM software COMPOSE in the SPOOCEFEM framework to improve software reuse and maintenance and to allow for the use of direct solvers. COMPOSE was originally developed using a top-down functional design decomposition coded in Fortran 90. Of primary concern is the ultimate performance of the SPOOCEFEM version of COMPOSE compared with that of the original version. The problem is first described mathematically and shown in discretized form. Next, the application-specific code required for COMPOSE is discussed, and finally, performance of the parallel COMPOSE versions are compared.

5.1. Problem description. The liquid composite molding process, namely the resin transfer molding (RTM) process, is utilized in many U.S. DoD applications for the manufacture of composite components. Originally developed by Mohan et al. [14, 12], the implicit pure finite element mold filling formulation tracks the transient flow front of the resin in the fibrous preform for the manufacture of composite components. A brief discussion of the governing equations follows. Starting from the continuity equation and using the methods described by Mohan, the following representation is derived:

$$\int_{\Omega} \frac{\partial \Psi}{\partial t}\, d\Omega + \int_{\Omega} \Psi \nabla \cdot \mathbf{u}\, d\Omega = 0. \tag{5.1}$$

where Ψ is the fill fraction and $\mathbf{u}$ is the resin velocity. Using Darcy's law, given as

$$\mathbf{u} = -\frac{\bar{\mathbf{K}}}{\mu} \cdot \nabla P; \tag{5.2}$$

to substitute for **u** in equation 5.1 the following is obtained

$$\int_\Omega \frac{\partial \Psi}{\partial t}\, d\Omega = \int_\Omega \Psi \nabla \cdot \left(\frac{\bar{\mathbf{K}}}{\mu} \cdot \nabla P \right) d\Omega, \tag{5.3}$$

where $\bar{\mathbf{K}}$ is the permeability tensor of the fibrous preform, μ is the resin viscosity, and P is pressure. After applying the FEM the semi-discretized equation is given as

$$\mathbf{C}\dot{\mathbf{\Psi}} + \mathbf{KP} = \mathbf{q}, \tag{5.4}$$

where

$$\begin{aligned}
\mathbf{C} &= \int_\Omega \mathbf{N}^{\mathbf{T}}\mathbf{N}\, d\Omega \\
\mathbf{K} &= \int_\Omega \mathbf{B}^{\mathbf{T}} \frac{\bar{\mathbf{K}}}{\mu} \mathbf{B}\, d\Omega \\
\mathbf{q} &= \int_\Gamma \mathbf{N}^{\mathbf{T}} \left(\frac{\bar{\mathbf{K}}}{\mu} \cdot \nabla P \cdot \mathbf{n} \right) d\Gamma \\
\dot{\mathbf{\Psi}} &= \frac{\mathbf{\Psi}_{\mathbf{n+1}} - \mathbf{\Psi}_{\mathbf{n}}}{\Delta t}.
\end{aligned} \tag{5.5}$$

In equation 5.5, **N** is the elemental shape function and $\mathbf{B} = \nabla\mathbf{N}$. Equation 5.4 is solved in the structured FEM software COMPOSE utilizing element-based domain decomposition. The same equation is solved with SPOOCEFEM with node-based domain decomposition, otherwise everything else including element types (3-noded triangle, 4-noded quadrilateral, and 4-noded tetrahedral), the stiffness matrix storage format (CSR), and iterative CG based solvers remain the same.

5.2. Application specific FEM code. Some application specific code for COMPOSE is required in order to use the SPOOCEFEM framework. The bulk of the application specific code is included in the various element types used in COMPOSE. For the 2.5-dimensional simulation code there are two types of elements, namely 3-noded triangles and 4-noded quadrilaterals. The 3-noded triangular elements will be described in detail with the assumption that all developments are equally applicable to the 4-noded quadrilateral element type. The COMPOSE 3-noded triangular element class is called `ComposeElement2dTri3` and inherits from the `Element2dTri3` class, Figure 5.1. From this inheritance the `ComposeElement2dTri3` class has access to storage of material data, connectivity, calculation of local coordinates, and reading and writing to XML and HDF5 files. The `ComposeElement2dTri3` class expands this functionality with calculation of the elemental stiffness matrix for resin flow in the RTM process. Some other application functionality was discovered to be the same for all 2-dimensional element types in COMPOSE and so a `ComposeElement2d` class was created to handle calculation of the local permeabilities, the lumped mass matrix, and storage of the elemental thickness. The storage and retrieval of viscosity information is required of 2- and 3-dimensional element types in COMPOSE and so one more class was created for this purpose; `ComposeElement`. The inheritance diagram for the `ComposeElement2dTri3` class is shown in Figure 5.1 and shows visually the multiple inheritance required for this level of abstraction.

The BCs required for an isothermal COMPOSE simulation are either pressure at a node (Dirichlet) or flow rate at a node (Neumann). These two BC types have already been included in the SPOOCEFEM framework and therefore no extensions are required.

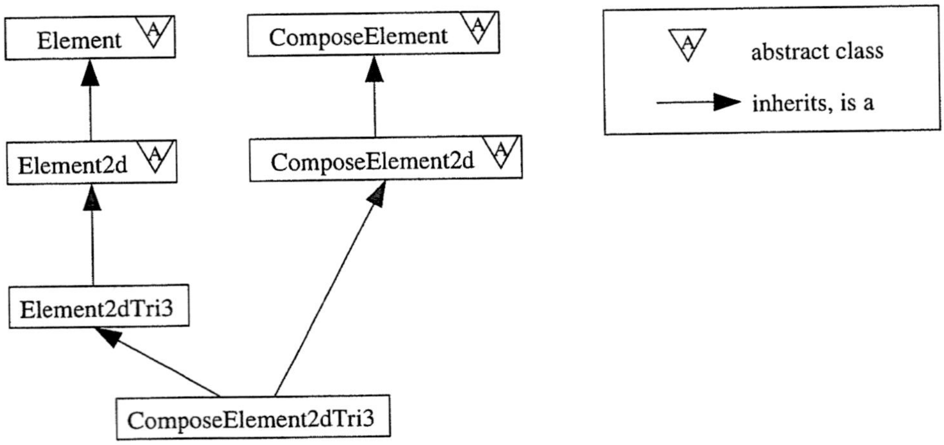

FIG. 5.1. *Hierarchy of the* `ComposeElement2dTri3` *class showing multiple inheritance.*

The application of Dirichlet BCs is handled by the `MatrixCSR` class for serial and parallel matrices. The Neumann BC is set by the application by modification of the right hand side vector value, in COMPOSE the vector is the right hand side of Equation 5.4, namely q. Data files in COMPOSE are parsed by the generic SPOOCEFEM parser with a new attribute for the thickness of 2-dimensional element types. By utilizing the FEM parser, functions for standard finite element data such as elemental connectivity, nodal XYZ data, BCs, and material properties, few new parsing routines are required in COMPOSE.

The final class created for COMPOSE is the `ComposeFEM` class that contains all of the routines required to execute a COMPOSE simulation. These routines include the time-stepping and mass convergence routines. Two advantages of putting all of this functionality into the `ComposeFEM` class is that the algorithm used for 2- and 3-dimensional analysis and serial and parallel simulations is the same, only the data storage is different. The addition of new element types and performance enhancements are mostly external to this part of the application and so upgrades are simple and accomplished by replacing the old shared libraries with new ones or recompiling and linking with static ones. The addition of other enhancements, such as the "One Shot" [22] fill time computation routine and sensitivity analysis [6], are accomplished for all isothermal COMPOSE simulations with one version of the algorithm. In the past the "One Shot" algorithm required modification of the serial and parallel versions of the COMPOSE code base, but with the object-oriented code-base the new routines work for all types of analysis possible within COMPOSE.

5.3. Performance comparison: structured and OOP-based COMPOSE software. Extensive performance testing and code enhancements have been performed on the structured COMPOSE code [13, 19, 17]. It is against this software that the current OOP developments are compared. Simulation results are presented here for the SPOOCEFEM-based COMPOSE software with the direct PSPASES solver and the iterative CG solver from PETSc. The simulation time is the time required for COMPOSE to simulate complete mold filling in a complex geometry with a large number of nodes. The speedup results are scaled to assume perfect speedup with 8 processors. Empirical evidence, based on numerous simulation runs, seems to indicate that at this number of processors the problem decomposition is of a size that maps better to cache and local memory. The times for the 425,156 node simulation are also presented for 8 processors, but the problem is somewhat larger and superlinear speedup is observed between 8 and 16 processors.

In a complete filling simulation it is observed in Table 5.1 that for 8 processors the PSPASES-based software out performs the original COMPOSE software by a factor of

TABLE 5.1
Simulation time in seconds for 105,722 node RTM simulation.

No. CPUs	PSPASES	PETSc	COMPOSE
8	7070	97973	14945
16	5362	38261	8944
32	4439	19143	5742
64	4891	11841	5856

TABLE 5.2
Speedup results for 105,722 node RTM simulation, assuming perfect speedup at 8 processors.

No. CPUs	PSPASES	PETSc	COMPOSE
8	8.000	8.000	8.000
16	10.548	20.485	13.368
32	12.743	40.944	20.822
64	11.565	66.192	20.417

about 2. This increase in performance is encouraging and performance enhancements in SPOOCEFEM will continue to increase this lead. The PETSc-based code is about 6 times slower than the original COMPOSE software but this can be partially explained by the overhead incurred in the various routines within COMPOSE, besides the linear solver. During a time step of mold filling the stiffness matrix is modified many times, and this modification has a large amount of overhead associated with it in PETSc. This point is being worked on diligently and will hopefully be alleviated in future versions of SPOOCEFEM. One point to make here is that the solutions obtained from the PSPASES- and PETSc-based parallel simulations match the serial solution with VSS to machine accuracy, but the original solver in COMPOSE has a noticeable error associated with it. This would mean that the results obtained from the SPOOCEFEM version of COMPOSE are much more reliable and therefore a small loss in performance is not an issue if results are more accurate.

Some quick notes about implementation are required at this point. First and foremost it must be noted that the structured version of COMPOSE utilizes element-based domain decomposition, whereas SPOOCEFEM currently only supports node-based domain decomposition. This is important because in the formation of the stiffness matrices within SPOOCEFEM COMPOSE for the individual processes, some redundant computation is required for elements contained in multiple partitions. Second, the preconditioned conjugate gradient (PCG) solver used by the structured code computes the residual slightly differently than the OOP-based code so that the number of iterations changes as the number of domains changes in the structured code but stays approximately constant in the OOP-based code.

Tables 5.5 and 5.6 show simulation timing results for the same geometries as those in Tables 5.1 and 5.3, respectively. The difference from the previous results is that the full range of material properties, specifically the fiber permeability tensors, is used in Tables 5.5 and 5.6. In order to obtain accurate results from the iterative solvers, it was decided that for timings in Tables 5.1 and 5.3, a simplified set of fiber permeability tensors would be used to ensure a well-formed problem. In real world situations though, the permeability varies widely across a composite component and these numbers affect the condition of the problem solved in the FEM software. Tables 5.5 and 5.6 show that the PSPASES direct solver is unaffected by the condition of the problem, whereas the structured COMPOSE solver requires more time to obtain accurate results from the less well-conditioned problem. In Figures 5.2(a) and 5.2(b), the increase in simulation time for the PSPASES-based software

TABLE 5.3
Simulation time in seconds for 425,156 node RTM simulation.

No. CPUs	PSPASES	PETSc	COMPOSE
8	25405	N/A	123113
16	22578	N/A	59865
32	17300	141043	26426
64	11554	63582	16049

TABLE 5.4
Speedup results for 425,156 node RTM simulation, assuming perfect speedup at 8 processors.

No. CPUs	PSPASES	PETSc	COMPOSE
8	8.000	N/A	8.000
16	9.002	N/A	16.452
32	11.748	N/A	37.270
64	17.591	N/A	61.369

is due to the fact that more mass convergence iterations are required for each time step. The increase in time for the original version of COMPOSE is due to more mass convergence iterations and more iterations in the linear equation solver, thus making the percentage of time increase greater than that for the PSPASES-based software. This is an important point to highlight since choosing a direct or iterative solver in SPOOCEFEM is as easy as changing one variable in the call to the solve routine in the `Vector` class, whereas adding a new solver to the structured COMPOSE software would require rewriting many routines and changes to a large portion of the application code.

6. Conclusions. The SPOOCEFEM framework discussed in this paper has demonstrated its usefulness in the development of parallel FEM software. The ease of development, software reuse, and the GUI tools are all advantages of utilizing SPOOCEFEM. As with other OOP designs, the SPOOCEFEM framework required a higher investment in time and thought vs. functional programming approaches. After SPOOCEFEM was developed though, implementation of the application COMPOSE was swift and required little additional code. Much of the functionality available in C++ is utilized to make developing FEM applications simpler, but making the base FEM development complex. An example of the extensive OOP work is the use of multiple inheritance by COMPOSE in the development of the element classes. Another example is the use of polymorphism in the element and BC classes, making extensions by individual applications efficient. The greatest complexity comes from the `Vector` and `Matrix` classes, where various combinations of data and parallel algorithms are located, but accessed through a consistent interface. This complexity is warranted though, as now the applications developer is relieved of the task of changing solver calls and data storage to accommodate various new packages or solvers.

7. Future Development. The original impetus to develop SPOOCEFEM was the current work of extending COMPOSE to model the non-isothermal resin flow and cure kinetics in RTM with parallel computers. Since much work would have gone into parallelizing the current serial code with little usable source code for future projects it was decided to create a reusable framework for FEM software development. Now that the isothermal version of COMPOSE is implemented in the SPOOCEFEM framework, the job of creating the parallel non-isothermal COMPOSE software is much easier and will be available for other projects yet to come. Other sparse matrix formats besides CSR will be added to SPOOCEFEM in the future along with the associated equation solvers. Element-based

TABLE 5.5

Simulation time in seconds for 105,722 node RTM simulation with full range of material properties.

No. CPUs	PSPASES	COMPOSE
8	7165	36299
16	5433	20873
32	4520	13967
64	4891	11652

TABLE 5.6

Simulation time in seconds for 425,156 node RTM simulation with full range of material properties.

No. CPUs	PSPASES	COMPOSE
8	31574	327502
16	27137	157100
32	24034	72669
64	13878	45303

domain decomposition requires refinement in SPOOCEFEM so that applications can take advantage of it.

8. Acknowledgments. This research was made possible by a grant of computer time and resources by the Department of Defense High Performance Computing Modernization Program (HPCMP). Parallel versions of COMPOSE were developed through support from the Common HPC Software Support Initiative (CHSSI) project.

REFERENCES

[1] C. C. ASHCROFT, R. G. GRIMES, D. J. PIERCE, AND D. K. WAH, *Solving Linear Systems using SPOOLES 2.2*, Boeing Phantom Works, 2002.

[2] S. BALAY, W. GROPP, L. C. MCINNES, AND B. SMITH, *PETSc Users Manual*, Argonne National Laboratory, 2001.

[3] J. A. CLARKE AND R. R. NAMBURU, *A Distributed Comuting Environment for Interdisciplinary Applciations*, Concurrency and Computation: Practice and Experience, 14 (2002), pp. 1–14.

[4] T. M. ELLIS, I. R. PHILIPS, AND T. M. LAHEY, *Fortran 90 Programming*, Addison-Wesley, Reading, MA, 1994.

[5] B. R. FORD, R. O. FOSCHI, AND S. F. STIEMER, *Object-Oriented Finite Element Analysis*, Computers and Structures, 34 (1990), pp. 355–374.

[6] B. J. HENZ, K. K. TAMMA, R. KANAPADY, N. D. NGO, AND P. W. CHUNG, *Process modeling of composites by resin transfer molding: Sensitivity analysis for isothermal considerations*, in AIAA-2002-0790, 40 th Aerospace Sciences Meeting, Reno, NV, Jan. 2002.

[7] M. JOSHI, G. KARYPIS, AND V. KUMAR, *PSPASES: Scalable Parallel Direct Solver Library for Sparse Symmetric Positive Definite Linear Systems*, Department of Computer Science, University of Minnesota, 1999.

[8] G. KARYPIS AND V. KUMAR, *METIS: A Software Package for Partitioning Unstructured Graphs, Partitioning Meshes, and Computing Fill-Reducing Orderings of Sparse Matrices*, University of Minnesota and the Army HPC Research Center, 1997.

[9] K. H. LAW, *A Parallel Finite Element Solution Method*, Computers & Structures, 23 (1985), pp. 845 - 858.

[10] R. I. MACKIE, *Object-Oriented Programming of the Finite Element Method*, International Journal on Numerical Methods in Engineering, 35 (1992), pp. 425–436.

[11] S. MODAK AND E. D. SOTELINO, *An Object-Oriented Programming Framework for the Parallel Dynamic Analysis of Structures*, Computers and Structures, 80 (2002), pp. 77–84.

[12] R. V. MOHAN, N. D. NGO, AND K. K. TAMMA, *On a Pure Finite Element Methodology for Resin Transfer Mold Filling Simulations*, Polymer Engineering and Science, 39 (1999), pp. 26–43.

[13] R. V. MOHAN, D. R. SHIRES, A. MARK, AND K. K. TAMMA, *Advanced Manufacturing of Large Scale Composite Structures : Process Modeling, Manufacturing Simulations and Massively Parallel Computing Platforms*, Journal of Advances in Engineering Software, 29 (1998), pp. 249–264.

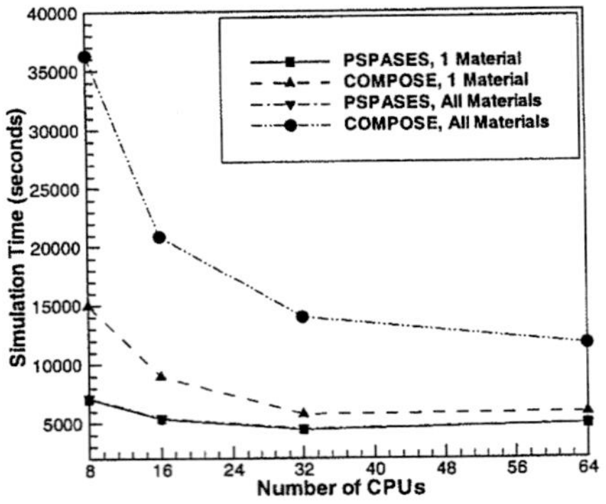

(a) Plot of solution times for PSPASES and COMPOSE solvers with 105,722 nodes for single and multiple material models.

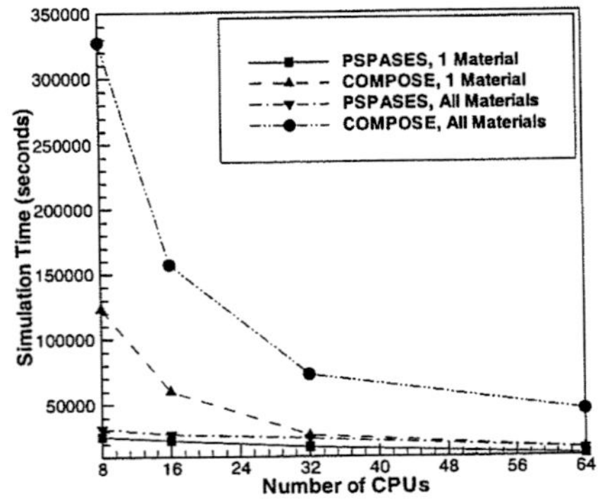

(b) Plot of solution times for PSPASES and COMPOSE solvers with 425,156 nodes for single and multiple material models.

FIG. 5.2. *Results of PSPASES vs. COMPOSE comparison.*

[14] N. D. NGO, R. V. MOHAN, P. W. CHUNG, AND K. K. TAMMA, *Recent Developments Encompassing Non-Isothermal/Isothermal Liquid Composite Molding Process Modeling/Analysis: Physically Accurate, Computationally Effective and Affordable Simulations and Validations*, Journal of Thermoplastic Composite Materials, 11 (1998), pp. 493–532.

[15] R. NIEKAMP AND E. STEIN, *An Object-Oriented Approach for Two- and Three-Dimensional Adaptive Finite Element Computations*, Computers and Structures, 80 (2002), pp. 317–328.

[16] B. NORRIS, S. BALAY, S. BENSON, L. FREITAG, P. HOVLAND, L. MCINNES, AND B. SMITH, *Parallel components for PDEs and optimization: some issues and experiences*, Parallel Computing, 28 (2002), pp. 1811–1831.

[17] D. SHIRES, R. MOHAN, AND A. MARK, *An Evaluation of HPF and MPI Approaches and Peformance in Unstructured Finite Element Simulations*, International Conference on Parallel and Distributed Processing Techniques and Applications, 2001.

[18] D. R. SHIRES, B. J. HENZ, AND R. V. MOHAN, *Architecture-Based Communication Improvements for Domain Decompositions*, in International Conference on Parallel and Distributed Processing Techniques and Applications, Las Vegas, NV, June 2002.

[19] D. R. SHIRES, R. V. MOHAN, AND A. MARK, *Optimization and Performance of a Fortran 90 MPI-Based Unstructured Code on Large Scale Parallel Systems*, in International Conference on Parallel and Distributed Processing Techniques and Applications, Las Vegas, NV, June 2001.

[20] I. SOMMERVILLE, *Software Engineering*, Addison-Wesley Publishing Company, New York, NY, 1989.

[21] S. SUN AND T. R. MARRERO, *An Object-Oriented Programming Approach for Heat and Mass Transfer Related Finite Element Analyses*, Computers in Chemical Engineering, 22 (1998), pp. 1381–1385.

[22] V. R. VOLLER AND Y. F. CHEN, *Prediction of Filling Times of Porous Cavities*, international Journal for Numerical Methods in Fluids, 23 (1996), pp. 661–672.

In: Applied Parallel and Distributed Computing
Editors: Yi Pan and Laurence T. Yang , pp. 103-116

ISBN 1-59454-174-4

PARALLEL COMPUTING AIDED DESIGN OF EARTHING SYSTEMS FOR ELECTRICAL SUBSTATIONS IN NON HOMOGENEOUS SOIL MODELS

IGNASI COLOMINAS*, JAVIER GÓMEZ*, FERMÍN NAVARRINA*, MANUEL CASTELEIRO* AND JOSÉ M. CELA†

Abstract. An accurate design of grounding systems is essential to assure the safety of the persons, to protect the equipment and to avoid interruptions in the power supply. In order to attain these targets, it is necessary to compute the equivalent electrical resistance of the system and the potential distribution on the earth surface in fault conditions. In this paper, a numerical approach for grounding analysis embedded in stratified soils and its implementation in a high-performance parallel computer are presented. The feasibility of this system is shown with its application to the grounding analysis in layered soils by using the geometry of real grounding grids.

Key words. Parallel computing, Grounding, Boundary elements, Numerical computations

1. Introduction. The interest for the prediction and the numerical simulation of problems related to the security have increased in last years with the construction of grounding systems of large electrical installations. The "grounding" or "earthing" systems comprises all interconnected grounding facilities of an specific area, being the "grounding grid" the main element of these systems. A grounding grid in most of real electrical substations consists of a mesh of interconnected cylindrical conductors, horizontally buried and supplemented by ground rods vertically thrusted in specific places of the installation site.

The main objective of a grounding system is to provide means to carry and dissipate electrical currents into the ground, in order to guarantee the continuity of the power supply and the integrity of the equipment and to ensure that a person in the vicinity of the grounded installation is not exposed to a critical electrical shock. Thus, the apparent electrical resistance of the grounding system must be low enough to guarantee that fault currents dissipate mainly through the earthing electrode into the ground, while the values of electrical potentials between close points on earth surface that can be connected by a person must be kept under certain maximum safe limits (step, touch and mesh voltages)[1, 2].

Taking into account these previous aspects, it is obvious that the design of safe grounding systems in electrical installations is essential to assure the security of the persons, to protect the equipment and to avoid interruptions in the power service. Since the sixties, several methods and procedures for the analysis and design of grounding systems of electrical substations have been proposed, most of them based on practice, on semi-empirical works or on intuitive ideas. Although these techniques represented an important improvement in the grounding analysis area, some problems were reported such as large computational requirements, unrealistic results when segmentation of conductors was increased, and uncertainty in the error bounds[1, 3].

Since the early days of the industrial use of the electricity the problem of obtaining the potential sdistribution produced when a fault current is derived into the ground through an earthing grid has been a challenging one. Although the physical phenomena of fault currents dissipation into the earth is a well-known problem that can be modelled by means of Maxwell's Electromagnetic Theory, its application and resolution for the computing of grounding grids of large installations in practical cases present some difficulties. First, it is obvious that no analytical solutions can be obtained in a real case. Moreover, the

*Applied Mathematics Dpt., Civil Engineering School, Universidad de A Coruña, Campus de Elviña, 15192 A Coruña, SPAIN (colominas@iccp.udc.es)

†Architecture of Computers Dpt., Universitat Politècnica Catalunya, Campus Nord-UPC mòdul D-6, Jordi Girona 1-3, 08034 Barcelona, SPAIN (cela@ac.upc.es)

specific geometry of the grounding systems (a mesh of interconnected bare conductors in which ratio diameter/length is relatively small) precludes the use of standard numerical techniques (such as the Finite Element Method or Finite Differences) since discretization of the domain (the whole ground) is required, and obtaining sufficiently accurate results should imply unacceptable computing efforts in memory storage and CPU time. For these reasons, during the last years the authors have developed a general numerical formulation based on the Boundary Element Method for the analysis of earthing systems embedded in uniform soil models, which has been successfully applied to real grounding grids[4, 5, 6]. At present, for real problems, single-layer models ("uniform models") run in real-time in personal computers[7], while multiple-layer models break off the design process since the computing time is out of range.

Next, we present a generalization of the BEM formulation for the analysis of grounding systems embedded in stratified soils and the study of the parallelization of that code for its implementation in a high-performance parallel computer. Furthermore, we apply this approach to the analysis of a real grounding system in a layered soil model.

2. Mathematical Model of the Problem. Fault current dissipation into the ground through a grounding grid can be described by means of Maxwell's Electromagnetic Theory. Thus, if one restricts the analysis to the electrokinetic steady-state response and neglects the inner resistivity of the earthing conductors (then, potential can be assumed constant in every point of the grounding electrode surface), the 3D problem can be written as

$$\begin{gathered}\operatorname{div}(\boldsymbol{\sigma})=0, \quad \boldsymbol{\sigma}=-\boldsymbol{\gamma}\,\mathbf{grad}(V) \text{ in } E\ ;\\ \boldsymbol{\sigma}^t\boldsymbol{n}_E=0 \text{ in } \Gamma_E\ ; \quad V=V_\Gamma \text{ in } \Gamma\ ;\\ V\rightarrow 0, \text{ if } |\boldsymbol{x}|\rightarrow\infty;\end{gathered} \tag{2.1}$$

where E is the earth, $\boldsymbol{\gamma}$ is its conductivity tensor, Γ_E is the earth surface, $\boldsymbol{n}_E$ is its normal exterior unit field and Γ is the electrode surface [5, 6]. Therefore, when the earthing electrode is energized to a voltage V_Γ (Ground Potential Rise, or GPR) relative to a remote earth, the solution to problem (2.1) gives potential V and current density $\boldsymbol{\sigma}$ at an arbitrary point $\boldsymbol{x}$.

The current density vector field $\boldsymbol{\sigma}$ describes the stream of electric charges in the vicinity of each point. Thus, the scalar product $\boldsymbol{\sigma}^t(\boldsymbol{x})\boldsymbol{n}$ gives the electric charge flux, i.e. the amount of charge flowing per unit of surface and unit of time, in the direction of the vector $\boldsymbol{n}$ at the point $\boldsymbol{x}$. In the steady state, by definition, the amount of charge does not vary at any point. Therefore, the equilibrium equation $\operatorname{div}(\boldsymbol{\sigma})=0$ in E is just a standard conservation law that expresses the indestructibility of charge. Obviously, this law can easily be derived from Maxwell's equations [8, 9].

The constitutive equation $\boldsymbol{\sigma}=-\boldsymbol{\gamma}\ \mathbf{grad}(V)$ is a generalized version of Ohm's law. In essence, Maxwell's equations predict an ir-rotational electric field intensity $\boldsymbol{\mathcal{E}}$ for the steady state. Therefore, a so-called electric scalar potential V must exist, such that $\boldsymbol{\mathcal{E}}=-\,\mathbf{grad}(V)$ [8, 9]. Thus, the above constitutive equation establishes a linear relation between the current density $\boldsymbol{\sigma}$ and the electric field intensity $\boldsymbol{\mathcal{E}}$ at each point, in terms of the so-called conductivity tensor $\boldsymbol{\gamma}$. If the medium being dealt with is homogeneous, the conductivity tensor is constant. If the medium is isotropic, the conductivity tensor can be substituted by a scalar conductivity γ. Hence, in the case of a one-dimensional homogeneous and isotropic medium, the constitutive equation simply says that the current intensity per unit of surface is proportional to the loss of electric potential per unit of length, that is a known form of Ohm's law.

Since the scalar product $\boldsymbol{\sigma}^t\boldsymbol{n}_E$ gives the electric charge flux in the direction of the normal to the earth surface, it must be clear now that the natural boundary condition $\boldsymbol{\sigma}^t\boldsymbol{n}_E=0$ in Γ_E is equivalent to consider the air as a perfect insulator. On the other hand, the essential boundary condition $V = V_\Gamma$ in Γ comes from neglecting the resistivity of the earthing electrode.

On the other hand, the essential boundary condition $V \to 0$ if $|\boldsymbol{x}| \to \infty$ assigns a null (arbitrary but convenient) value to the reference potential at remote earth [9]. Additionally, the potential V must satisfy some theoretical regularity requirements at infinity, the so-called "normal conditions" [9, 10, 11].

Now, for known values of V on Γ_E and $\boldsymbol{\sigma}$ on Γ, it is straightforward to obtain the design and safety parameters of the grounding system[1, 2]. Thus, the leakage current density $\sigma(\bar{\xi})$ at an arbitrary point $\bar{\xi}$ on the earthing electrode surface, the ground current I_Γ (total surge current being leaked into the earth) and the equivalent resistance of the earthing system R_{eq}, can be written as

$$\sigma(\boldsymbol{\xi}) = \boldsymbol{\sigma}^t(\boldsymbol{\xi})\boldsymbol{n}, \quad I_\Gamma = \int_{\boldsymbol{\xi}\in\Gamma} \sigma(\boldsymbol{\xi})d\Gamma, \quad R_{eq} = \frac{V_\Gamma}{I_\Gamma}, \tag{2.2}$$

being $\boldsymbol{n}$ the normal exterior unit field to Γ. Since V and $\bar{\sigma}$ are proportional to the GPR, the assumption $V_\Gamma = 1$ is not restrictive at all and it will be used from now on.

Most of the methods proposed for grounding analysis are based on the hypothesis that soil can be considered homogeneous and isotropic, and thus $\boldsymbol{\gamma}$ is substituted by an apparent scalar conductivity γ that must be experimentally obtained[1]. It is obvious that this assumption does not introduce significant errors if the soil is essentially uniform (both in horizontal and vertical directions) in the surroundings of the grounding grid[1], and this model can be used with loss of accuracy if the soil resistivity changes slightly with depth. However, since parameters involved in the grounding design can significantly vary if soil electrical properties change through the substation site (e.g., changes of the material nature, changes of humidity), it seems advisable to develop advanced models that could take into account variations of soil conductivity in the surroundings of the installation.

It is clear that to take into account the real variation of the soil conductivity in the vicinity of a grounding site would never be affordable, neither from the economical nor from the technical point of view. Hence, a more practical proposed soil model (and still quite realistic when conductivity is not markedly uniform with depth) consists of considering the soil stratified in a number of horizontal layers, defined by an appropriate thickness and an apparent scalar conductivity that must be experimentally obtained. In fact, it is widely accepted that two-layer (or even three-layer) soil models should be sufficient to obtain good and safe designs of grounding systems in most practical cases[1]. This chapter is devoted to studying the application of high performance computing techniques to two-layer soil models by means of parallelization, and its final implementation.

Consequently, if the soil is formed by C horizontal layers with different conductivities and the grounding electrode is buried in the layer b, the mathematical problem (2.1) can be written in terms of the following Neumann exterior problem[12, 13, 14]

$$\begin{gathered} \operatorname{div}(\boldsymbol{\sigma}_c) = 0,\ \boldsymbol{\sigma}_c = -\gamma_c\,\mathbf{grad}(V_c) \text{ in } E_c,\ 1 \le c \le C; \\ \boldsymbol{\sigma}_1^t \boldsymbol{n}_E = 0 \text{ in } \Gamma_E,\ V_b = 1 \text{ in } \Gamma; \\ V_c \to 0 \text{ if } |\boldsymbol{x}| \to \infty,\ \boldsymbol{\sigma}_c^t \boldsymbol{n}_c = \boldsymbol{\sigma}_{c+1}^t \boldsymbol{n}_c \text{ in } \Gamma_c, \\ 1 \le c \le C-1; \end{gathered} \tag{2.3}$$

being E_c each one of the soil layers, γ_c the scalar conductivity of layer E_c, V_c the potential at an arbitrary point of layer E_c and $\boldsymbol{\sigma}_c$ the corresponding current density, Γ_c the interface between layers E_c and E_{c+1} and $\boldsymbol{n}_c$ the normal field to Γ_c[12, 14].

3. Variational Form of the Boundary Value Problem. As we have exposed, the real geometry of grounding systems in most of real electrical substations consists of a grid of interconnected bare cylindrical conductors, horizontally buried and supplemented by rods, so ratio diameter/length uses to be relatively small ($\sim 10^{-3}$).

Although this geometry is straightforward to describe, it implies serious difficulties to the modellization of the problem: it is obvious that no analytical solutions can be obtained in a real case, and the use of standard numerical techniques (FEM or FD) should involve a completely out of range computing effort since discretization of the domain (the 3D domains E_c) is required. Consequently, and taking into account that potential values are only required on the earth surface and the equivalent resistance can be easily obtained in terms of the leakage current density σ on Γ ($\sigma = \boldsymbol{\sigma}^t \boldsymbol{n}$, where $\boldsymbol{n}$ is the normal exterior unit field to Γ), we turn our attention to a Boundary Element approach which would only require the discretization of the grounding surface Γ[5, 6]. For this, it is first necessary to derive an expression to relate the potential V and the leakage current density σ.

Since the surroundings of the substation site are levelled and regularized during the construction of the electrical installation, earth surface Γ_E and interfaces Γ_c between layers can be assumed horizontal. Thus, with this assumption the application of the "method of images" and Green's Identity to problem (2.3) yields the following integral expression[12, 14] for potential $V_c(\boldsymbol{x}_c)$ at an arbitrary point $\boldsymbol{x}_c \in E_c$, in terms of the unknown leakage current density $\sigma(\boldsymbol{\xi})$ at any point $\boldsymbol{\xi}$ of the electrode surface $\Gamma \subset E_b$:

$$V_c(\boldsymbol{x}_c) = \frac{1}{4\pi\gamma_b} \int\!\!\int_{\boldsymbol{\xi}\in\Gamma} k_{bc}(\boldsymbol{x}_c, \boldsymbol{\xi})\, \sigma(\boldsymbol{\xi}) d\Gamma, \ \forall \boldsymbol{x}_c \in E_c, \tag{3.1}$$

where integral kernels $k_{bc}(\boldsymbol{x}_c, \boldsymbol{\xi})$ are formed by infinite series of terms corresponding to the resultant images obtained when Neumann exterior problem (2.3) is transformed into a Dirichlet one[12, 14, 16]. In the case of uniform soil, the series are reduced to only two summands, since there is only one image of the original grid[4, 5, 6].

Weakly singular kernel $k_{bc}(\boldsymbol{x}_c, \boldsymbol{\xi})$ depends on the conductivity of the layers, and on the inverse of the distances from the point $\boldsymbol{x}_c$ to the point $\boldsymbol{\xi}$ and to all the images of $\boldsymbol{\xi}$ with respect to the earth surface Γ_E and to the interfaces Γ_c between layers[12, 14]. A general form to express these integral kernels is given by:

$$k_{bc}(\boldsymbol{x}_c, \boldsymbol{\xi}) = \sum_{l=0}^{\infty} k_{bc}^l(\boldsymbol{x}_c, \boldsymbol{\xi}), \quad k_{bc}^l(\boldsymbol{x}_c, \boldsymbol{\xi}) = \frac{\psi^l(\kappa)}{r(\boldsymbol{x}_c, \boldsymbol{\xi}^l(\boldsymbol{\xi}))}, \tag{3.2}$$

being ψ^l a weighting coefficient that only depends on a certain ratio κ defined in terms of the layer conductivities and $r(\boldsymbol{x}_c, \boldsymbol{\xi}^l(\boldsymbol{\xi}))$ the Euclidean distance between the points $\boldsymbol{x}_c$ and $\boldsymbol{\xi}^l$, being $\boldsymbol{\xi}^o$ the point $\boldsymbol{\xi}$ on the electrode surface ($\boldsymbol{\xi}^o(\boldsymbol{\xi}) = \boldsymbol{\xi}$), where $\boldsymbol{\xi}^l$ ($l \neq 0$) are the images of $\boldsymbol{\xi}$ with respect to the earth surface and to the interfaces between layers[12, 14]. For example, in the particular case of a two-layer soil model ratio κ is given by $(\gamma_1 - \gamma_2)/(\gamma_1 + \gamma_2)$ and four cases must be considered depending on the layer where the points $\boldsymbol{x}_c$ and $\boldsymbol{\xi}^l$ are located. In each case, several series with different locations of their images and different weighting coefficients are added. Explicit expressions of these kernels can be found in [12, 14, 16].

Now, since the expression for the potential (3.1) also holds on electrode surface Γ (where potential is known by the boundary condition $V_b(\boldsymbol{\chi}) = 1, \forall \boldsymbol{\chi} \in \Gamma$), the leakage current density σ must satisfy the following Fredholm integral equation of the first kind on Γ:

$$\int\!\!\int_{\boldsymbol{\chi}\in\Gamma} w(\boldsymbol{\chi}) \left(\frac{1}{4\pi\gamma_b} \int\!\!\int_{\boldsymbol{\xi}\in\Gamma} k_{bb}(\boldsymbol{\chi}, \boldsymbol{\xi}) \sigma(\boldsymbol{\xi})\, d\Gamma - 1 \right) d\Gamma = 0, \tag{3.3}$$

for all members $w(\boldsymbol{\chi})$ of a suitable class of test functions defined on Γ[4, 5, 6]. It is obvious that a numerical approach based on the Boundary Element Method seems to be the best choice to solve equation (3.3).

4. BEM Numerical Formulation.

4.1. General 2D approach. The numerical resolution of the variational form (3.3) requires the discretization of the domain (the surface of the cylindrical conductors) and the leakage current density that flows from the grounded electrode. Thus, for given sets of $\mathcal{N}$ trial functions $\{N_i(\boldsymbol{\xi})\}$ defined on Γ, and $\mathcal{M}$ two dimensional boundary elements $\{\Gamma^\alpha\}$, the leakage current density σ and the electrode surface Γ can be discretized as follows:

$$\sigma(\boldsymbol{\xi}) = \sum_{i=1}^{\mathcal{N}} \sigma_i N_i(\boldsymbol{\xi}), \qquad \Gamma = \bigcup_{\alpha=1}^{\mathcal{M}} \Gamma^\alpha, \tag{4.1}$$

Now, if we take into account that kernels (3.2) are given by series, integral expression (3.1) for potential $V_c(\boldsymbol{x}_c)$ can also be discretized as

$$V_c(\boldsymbol{x}_c) = \sum_{i=1}^{\mathcal{N}} \sigma_i V_{c,i}(\boldsymbol{x}_c); \;\; V_{c,i}(\boldsymbol{x}_c) = \sum_{\alpha=1}^{\mathcal{M}} \sum_{l=0}^{l_V} V_{c,i}^{\alpha l}(\boldsymbol{x}_c); \tag{4.2}$$

$$V_{c,i}^{\alpha l}(\boldsymbol{x}_c) = \frac{1}{4\pi\gamma_b} \iint_{\boldsymbol{\xi}\in\Gamma^\alpha} k_{bc}^l(\boldsymbol{x}_c, \boldsymbol{\xi})\, N_i(\boldsymbol{\xi})\, d\Gamma^\alpha; \tag{4.3}$$

where l_V represents the number of terms that is necessary to consider until convergence is achieved.

On the other hand, for a given set of $\mathcal{N}$ test functions $\{w_j(\boldsymbol{\chi})\}$ defined on Γ, variational form (3.3) is reduced to the following linear system:

$$\begin{aligned} &\sum_{i=1}^{\mathcal{N}} R_{ji}\sigma_i = \nu_j \qquad (j = 1, \ldots, \mathcal{N}) \\ &R_{ji} = \sum_{\beta=1}^{\mathcal{M}} \sum_{\alpha=1}^{\mathcal{M}} \sum_{l=0}^{l_R} R_{ji}^{\beta\alpha l}, \qquad \nu_j = \sum_{\beta=1}^{\mathcal{M}} \nu_j^\beta, \end{aligned} \tag{4.4}$$

being coefficients $R_{ji}^{\beta\alpha l}$ and ν_j^β:

$$R_{ji}^{\beta\alpha l} = \frac{1}{4\pi\gamma_b} \iint_{\boldsymbol{\chi}\in\Gamma^\beta} w_j(\boldsymbol{\chi}) \iint_{\boldsymbol{\xi}\in\Gamma^\alpha} k_{bb}^l(\boldsymbol{\chi}, \boldsymbol{\xi}) N_i(\boldsymbol{\xi}) d\Gamma^\alpha d\Gamma^\beta, \tag{4.5}$$

$$\nu_j^\beta = \iint_{\boldsymbol{\chi}\in\Gamma^\beta} w_j(\boldsymbol{\chi}) d\Gamma^\beta, \tag{4.6}$$

where l_R represents the number of terms that is necessary to consider until convergence is achieved.

It is important to emphasize that the solution of linear equations (4.4) provides the values of the intensities σ_i $(i = 1, \ldots, \mathcal{N})$ leaking from the nodes of the grid. With these values, it is possible to compute the potential at any point on the earth surface or even at any inner point —by means of (4.2) and (4.3)— , the leakage current density σ —by means of (4.1)—, and all the design and safety parameters of the grounding system[1, 5, 6].

Nevertheless, the statement of the above linear system requires the discretization of a 2D domain: the whole surface Γ of the grounding electrodes, which implies a large number of degrees of freedom in practical cases. Besides, its matrix is full and the computation of its coefficients requires to perform double integration on 2D domains. For all these reasons, it is necessary to introduce some additional hypotheses in order to decrease the computational cost.

4.2. Approximated 1D boundary element approach. An approximated boundary element numerical approach to the previous one presented can be derived if the real geometry of the grounding systems in practice is considered. Thus, since the ratio between the diameter and the length of the grounded conductors is very small ($\sim 10^{-3}$), the hypothesis of circumferential uniformity (i.e., the leakage current density σ is constant around the cross section of the cylindrical conductors of the grounding grid) can be assumed producing a notable fall of the computational cost[1, 5, 6]. In this way, discretizations (4.1) and (4.4) become much simpler, since the classes of test and trial functions are restricted to those with circumferential uniformity, while only the axial lines of the grounding electrodes have to be discretized[5, 6].

Now, for a given level of mesh refinement, the number of element contributions $R_{ji}^{\beta\alpha}$ and ν_j^{β} that we need to compute in order to state linear system (4.4), as much as the number of unknowns σ_i are significantly smaller than in the previous 2D approach, since it is required the discretization of a simpler domain: the axial lines of the grounding electrodes. Despite of this important reduction in the computation effort, extensive computing is still necessary mainly because of the circumferential integration on the perimeter of the electrodes that are involved in the integral kernels[5, 6]. However, these circumferential integrals can be performed in an approximated way if suitable simplifications in the general approach are introduced[12, 14].

The selection of different sets of trial and test functions in the numerical scheme allows to derive different formulations. Further discussion in this paper is restricted to the case of a Galerkin type approach, since the matrix of coefficients is symmetric and positive definite[5, 6]. As the 1D approximated expressions for terms $V_{c,i}^{\alpha l}$ and $R_{ji}^{\beta\alpha l}$ in (4.3) and (4.5) are formally equivalent to those obtained in the case of uniform soil models[12, 14], these terms can be computed by using the highly efficient analytical integration techniques derived by the authors to compute these coefficients for the uniform soil case[5, 6, 9, 12, 14].

The example presented in the next section corresponds to the analysis of a grounding system embedded in a two-layer soil model. Obviously, this boundary element formulation can be applied to any other case with a higher number of layers. However, CPU time may increase up to un-admissible levels, mainly due to the poor rate of convergence of the underlying series expansions, and the need to evaluate double series (in three-layer models), triple series (in four-layer models), and so on.

4.3. Total efficiency of the numerical approach. An important aspect of the numerical formulation proposed is its total computational cost. Thus, for specific discretization ($\mathcal{M}$ elements of p nodes each, and a total number of $\mathcal{N}$ degrees of freedom), a linear system (4.4) of order $\mathcal{N}$ must be generated and solved.

Matrix generation process requires $O(\mathcal{M}^2 p^2/2)$ operations, since p^2 series of contributions of type (4.5) have to be computed for every pair of elements, and approximately half of them are discarded because of symmetry. In uniform soil models these series are formed by only two terms, while in two-layer models the series have an infinite number of them, that will be numerically added up until a tolerance is fulfilled or an upper limit of summands is achieved. Consequently, matrix generation will be much more expensive in two-layer models. In connection with the linear system solving process, it requires $O(\mathcal{N}^3/3)$ operations (since the matrix is symmetric but not sparse) if the resolution is carried out with a direct method.

Hence, most computing effort is devoted to matrix generation in small/medium problems, while linear system resolution prevails in medium/large ones. In these cases, the use of direct methods for the linear system resolution is out of range. Therefore iterative or semiiterative techniques will be preferable. The best results have been obtained by a diagonal preconditioned conjugate gradient algorithm with assembly of the global matrix[5].

This technique has turned out to be extremely efficient for solving large scale problems, with a very low computational cost in comparison with matrix generation. So the cost of the system resolution should never prevail.

On the other hand, once the leakage current has been obtained, the cost of computing the equivalent resistance is negligible. The additional cost of computing potential at any given point (normally at the earth surface) by means of (4.2) only requires $O(\mathcal{M}p)$ operations, since p series of contributions of type (4.3) have to be computed for every element. However, if it is necessary to compute potentials at a large number of points (i.e. to draw contours), computing time may be important.

5. Application Examples to Grounding Analysis. This boundary element approach has been integrated in a Computer Aided Design system for grounding analysis. The computer program has been developed for running in sequential mode (in conventional computers) or in parallel mode (in parallel computers). In this section two examples of earthing analysis are presented by using the geometry of grounding grids of real electrical substations. Further on, we will discuss the implementation of the numerical code and its parallelization, that is, the distribution of different tasks of the program among several processors.

5.1. Example 1: the Barberá grounding system. The first example we present is the grounding grid of the Barberá substation. This earthing grid is formed by a grid of 408 segments of cylindrical conductor of the same diameter (12.85 mm) buried to a depth of 80 cm. The grounding system has a right-angled triangle shape of 143×89 m and protects a total area of 6,600 m^2 (Figura 5.1). The grid has been discretized in 408 linear leakage current elements which implies 238 degrees of freedom. The Ground Potential Rise (GPR) considered in this study has been 10 kV.

In order to illustrate the capacity of the numerical approach, this grounding system has been calculated by using a uniform soil model ($\gamma = 0.016\,(\Omega m)^{-1}$), and a more interesting two-layer soil model (the conductivities of the upper and the lower layer are $\gamma_1 = 0.005(\Omega m)^{-1}$ and $\gamma_2 = 0.016(\Omega m)^{-1}$ respectively, and the thickness of the upper layer is 1.0 m).

Figure 5.2 shows the potential distribution on the earth surface obtained for the uniform soil case and for the two-layer soil model. The equivalent resistance and the total surge current of the earthing system computed in each case has been 0.3128 Ω and I=31.97 kA (for the uniform soil model), and 0.3704 Ω and I=26.99 kA (for the two-layer soil model).

5.2. Example 2: the Balaidos grounding system. Next we present the analysis of a substation grounding considering 3 different soil models by using the presented BEM approach. The earthing grid is formed by a mesh of 107 cylindrical conductors (diameter: 11.28 mm) buried to a depth of 80 cm, supplemented with 67 vertical rods (each one has a length of 1.5 m and a diameter of 14.0 mm) (Figure 5.3). The Ground Potential Rise considered has been 10 kV, and the numerical model used in the analysis has been a Galerkin formulation with a discretization in 241 elements.

The different soil models considered are the following: Model A is a uniform soil model with a conductivity of 0.020 $(\Omega m)^{-1}$; Model B is a 2-layered soil model formed by an upper layer of 0.0025 $(\Omega m)^{-1}$ and a thickness of 70 cm and a lower layer with a conductivity of 0.020 $(\Omega m)^{-1}$ (consequently, all electrodes of the grounding grid are buried in the lower layer); and Model C is also a 2-layered soil model formed by an upper layer of 0.0025 $(\Omega m)^{-1}$ and a thickness of 1 m and a lower layer with a conductivity of 0.020 $(\Omega m)^{-1}$ (consequently, most electrodes of the grounding grid are buried in the upper layer while part of the vertical rods are in the lower layer).

Figure 5.4 shows the potential distribution ($\times 10kV$) on the earth surface obtained by using the soil models A, B and C. Table 5.1 shows the Equivalent Resistance of the grounding

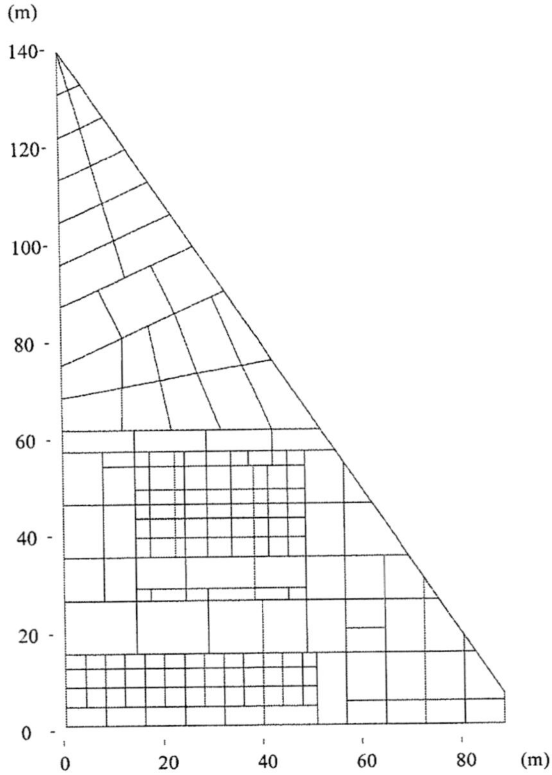

FIG. 5.1. *Barberá grounding system: Plan of the grounding grid.*

TABLE 5.1
Balaidos Grounding System: Equivalent Resistance of the grounding grid and Total Current leaked to the ground for the different soil models

Soil Model	Equivalent Resistance (Ω)	Total Current (kA)
A	0.3366	29.71
B	0.3522	28.39
C	0.4860	20.58

system and the Total Current that flows to the ground for each case. As it is shown, results noticeably vary when different soil models are used, and in consequence, the grounding design parameters (Equivalent Resistance, Touch-Voltage, Step-Voltage and Mesh-Voltage) significantly change.

As we can see in these examples, results obtained by using a multiple-layer soil model can be noticeably different from those obtained by using a single layer (or uniform) soil model. Therefore, it could be advisable to use multi-layer soil formulations to analyze grounding systems as a general rule, in spite of the increase of the computational effort. In fact, the use of this kind of advanced models should be mandatory in cases where the conductivity of the soil changes markedly with depth.

However, while single-layer models run in real time in conventional computers for the analysis of medium/big size grounding grids, multiple-layer models require in general an out of order computing time. In the next section, the main aspects of the parallelization of the multi-layer boundary element numerical approach for grounding analysis are discussed.

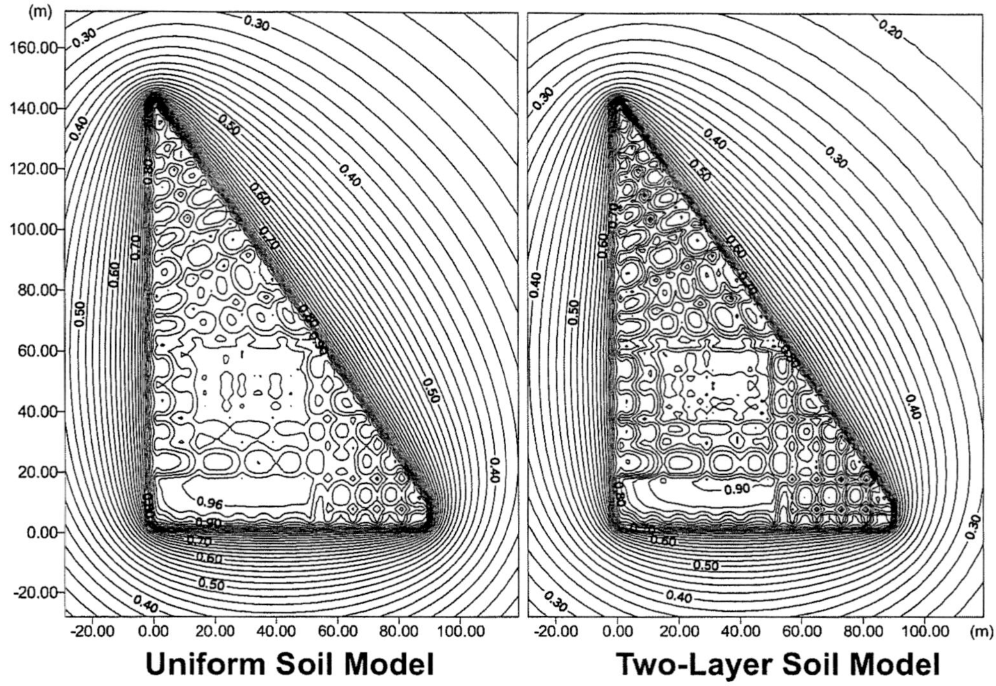

FIG. 5.2. *Barberá grounding system: Potential distribution on earth surface (×10 kV) obtained by using uniform and two-layer soil models.*

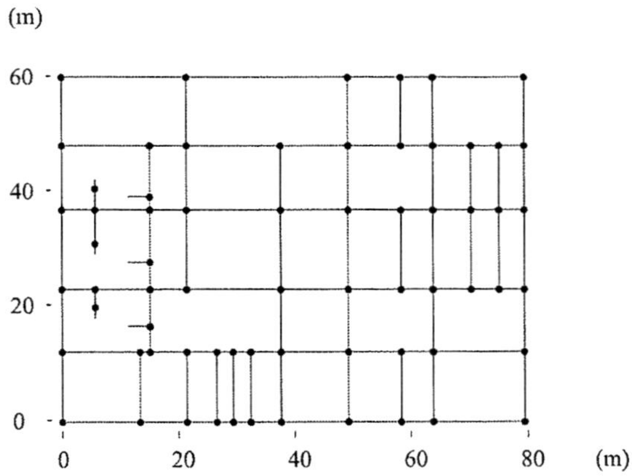

FIG. 5.3. *Balaidos Grounding System: Plan of the grounding grid (vertical rods are marked with black points).*

6. Parallelization of the Proposed BEM Approach.

6.1. Parallel computer and parallelization mode. The numerical approach has been implemented on a CAD system, which has been compiled and run onto an *Origin 2000 Silicon Graphics* computer at the *European Center for Parallelism of Barcelona* (CEPBA). The compilation process of the code has been made in sequential and parallel modes, and the executions have been run for the uniform and the two-layer models [15].

As we have exposed in previous sections, the most critical time-consuming process of this numerical formulation based on the Boundary Element Method is matrix generation,

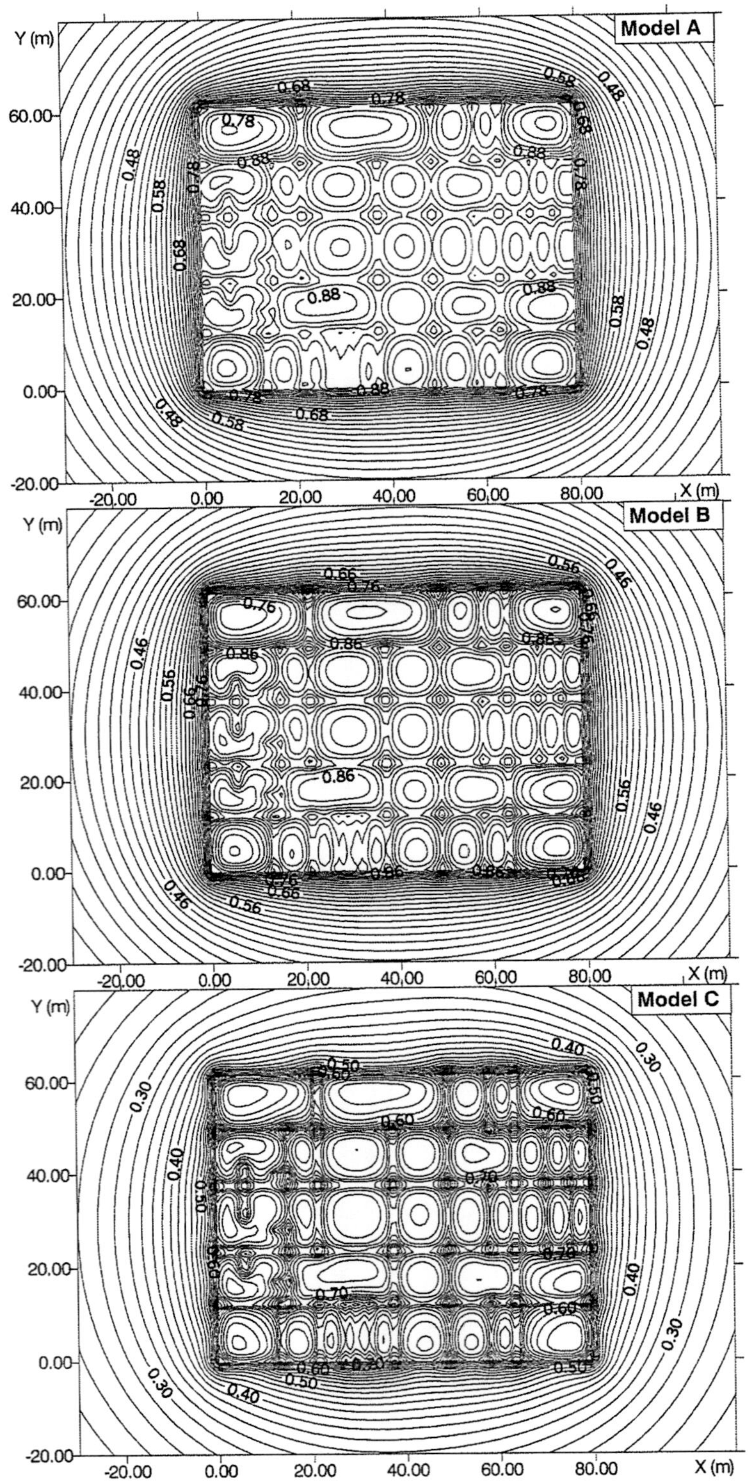

FIG. 5.4. *Balaidos Grounding System: Potential distribution (×10kV) on the earth surface for different soil models.*

TABLE 6.1
Barberá Grounding System: CPU time in sequential execution for each process of the program in the two-layer grounding analysis obtained with the O2000 computer

Process	CPU time(s)
Data Input	0.737
Data Preprocessing	0.045
Matrix Generation	1723.207
Linear System Solving	0.211
Resuts Storage	0.015

followed by computation of potential at a large number of points once the leakage current density has been obtained. Since both processes accept massive parallelization, computing time could be reduced under acceptable levels, even for cases of extremely large models, if the number of available processors is high enough, in spite of the efficiency loses due to the data transfer overhead and the system administration workload. Table 6.1 summarizes the CPU time required in each process of the implementation of the numerical approach for the Barberá grounding system in the two-layer soil model case. It is evident that the matrix construction is the most expensive part of it.

The O2000 used in our work is a high-performance computer with 64 MIPS R10000 processors at 250 MHz. It has a peak performance of 32 GFlops. Internally, the O2000 is organized in clusters of 2 processors sharing a main memory of 256 Mbyte. Each processor has 4 Mbyte of cache memory. The clusters are connected by an hypercube network. Each processor can access all the distributed main memory through the network. Then, the O2000 can be programmed as an 8 Gbyte shared memory machine. The input/output devices have a capability of 1.2 Gbytes/s.

The parallelization mode selected for this problem has been the use of compiler directives, following the present OpenMP standard. This selection is justified because: *a)* a shared memory computer is available for running the program (necessary condition for using compiler parallelization directives), *b)* the use of compiler directives grants clearness to a parallel code that may be handled in the future, *c)* the OpenMP syntax assures the portability of the parallel code to any shared memory computer, and *d)* as we will see below, the loop to be run in parallel is transformable into an adequate form so that directives are efficient. A parallelization scheme that mixes threads and message passing in boundary element applications can be found in reference [17].

6.2. Parallelization of the code. In the sequential program, the matrix generation process is performed by means of a double loop that couples every element with all the other $\mathcal{M}(\mathcal{M}+1)/2$ cycles. Into each cycle, the elemental matrix corresponding to a pair of elements is calculated and immediately assembled into the system matrix. If we try to parallelize this double loop, we find that the assembly of the elemental matrices causes a dependency between the actions of the threads or processes. This drawback can be avoided by taking the assembly process out of that loop, which implies first the computation and the storage of all the elemental matrices and, after this step, the assembly in a sequential mode. This scheme requires approximately twice the memory space than the original one, but in any case this memory space is not very large. If $\mathcal{N} = O(10^3)$ then the matrix size is $O(10^6)$ bytes.

Then, the target code is the nested DO loops that compute the elemental matrices, and we can parallelize the outer loop or the inner one. This is the first choice studied. Figure 6.1 shows the evolution of the speed-up factor obtained with different number of processors for both types of parallelization in the analysis of the Barberá grounding system with a two-layer soil model (the speed-up factor has been referenced to the sequential CPU time).

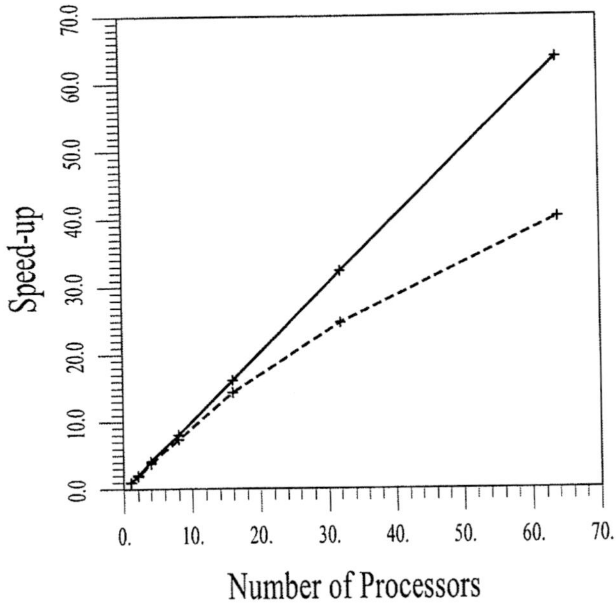

FIG. 6.1. *Barberá grounding system: Comparison between the speed-up obtained with the parallelization of the outer loop (in continuous line) and the inner loop (in discontinuous line).*

These results have been obtained with the schedule option "Dynamic,1" (we will discuss the schedule options below), and they correspond to the minimum of 4 CPU time measures made for the same option (the variance of the four ones is very small, anyway), in order to approximate better the strict value. In some cases, we have obtained speed-ups bigger than the number of processors due to small errors in the measurement of CPU time by the processors, and to the additional optimization of the code that the parallel compiler introduces.

Results are better when the outer loop is parallelized because the granularity is bigger in that way, and so the cost of managing the parallel execution is minor: since the numerical approach leads to a symmetric formulation, the coupling of every element of the grid with each one of the others can be represented by a triangle of $\mathcal{M}$ columns, of which the first one has $\mathcal{M}$ rows and the last one has 1 row. Hence, if the outer loop is parallelized, the columns of the triangle, that is, the cycles of the outer loop, are distributed among the processors. Whereas, if the inner loop is parallelized, the rows of one column are distributed among the processors. In this case, when computations on that column are finished the program moves sequentially to the next one, where another distribution of its rows among the processors is performed. This effect of granularity is, of course, more sensible when the number of processors grows, as figure 6.1 shows.

As the parallelization of the outer loop is preferable, and the cycles that it is necessary to distribute among the processors have very different sizes, the way to do this distribution becomes a decisive question. Table 6.2 summarizes the speed-up factors (referenced to the sequential CPU time) obtained for the outer-loop parallelization with different number of processors by using different "schedule" OpenMP options. Since the size of the cycles is linearly decreasing, "static" schedules with a high "chunk" (i.e., the number of cycles in a task) are the less profitable ones. When no chunk value is specified, all the columns are uniformly distributed in the beginning. "Dynamic" schedules improve this behavior because as each processor finishes a task, it dynamically takes the next one. Best results are obtained for a dynamic schedule with a chunk parameter of 1 column. This is the most lively

TABLE 6.2
Barberá Grounding System: Speed-up factors for different schedules and number of processors in the outer loop parallelization for the two-layer soil model

Schedule ()	Number of Processors			
	1	2	4	8
Static	1.01	1.32	2.32	4.38
Static,64	1.02	1.76	1.86	3.55
Static,16	1.02	1.94	3.59	6.23
Static, 4	1.01	2.01	3.96	7.36
Static, 1	1.02	2.03	4.03	7.99
Dynamic,64	1.02	2.02	3.56	3.55
Dynamic,16	1.02	2.02	4.08	7.87
Dynamic, 4	1.01	2.04	3.99	7.90
Dynamic, 1	1.02	2.03	4.09	8.05
Guided,64	1.02	1.97	3.56	3.56
Guided,16	1.02	1.99	3.96	8.03
Guided, 4	1.02	2.01	4.11	7.93
Guided, 1	1.02	2.07	3.95	8.38

TABLE 6.3
Balaidos Grounding System: CPU Time (in s) by using 1,2,4 and 8 processors for different soil models (in brackets, the speed-up factors).

Soil Model	Number of Processors			
	1	2	4	8
A	2.44 (1)	—	—	—
B	81.26 (1)	40.85 (1.98)	20.41 (3.98)	10.09 (8.05)
C	443.28 (1)	218.10 (2.03)	111.38 (3.98)	53.53 (8.28)

scheme, since there are never waiting processors, although it requires the biggest amount of parallelization management. "Guided" schedules distribute initially all the columns among all the processors into pieces with size exponentially varying. In this case, results are very similar to those obtained with the "dynamic" ones. In general, for any schedule, we obtained worse results when the chunk parameter and the number of processors are high because then some processors do not get any work.

Therefore, as we can see, speed-up factors obtained for the outer parallelization are very close to the number of processors for good schedules, that is, "dynamic" or "guided" with low chunk parameters. This fact reveals that the parallelization of this loop is very profitable: in the example, the Barberá grounding analysis in a two layer soil model, 99.9% of the work of the whole processing program is dealt with only 408 tasks.

The conclusions of this analysis with the Barberá grounding system have been applied to the second example. Table 6.3 shows the CPU times and speed-up factors obtained in the matrix generation process of the grounding analysis for the three soil models considered by using different number of processors. As we can see, the results agree with those obtained for the Barberá case. Now, as in the previous example, in some cases speed-up factors bigger than the number of processors are obtained due to small errors in the measurement of CPU time by the processors and to the additional optimization of the code that the parallel compiler introduces. Finally, it is important to remark that the increase in the CPU time in the model C is due to the type of soil model considered. In this case, a part of the vertical rods are in the upper layer and other part in the lower, and consequently integral kernels combining electrodes in different layers have to be used [12]. These integral kernels are different from those used in the model B (all the electrodes are in the same layer) and they involve series with a lower rate of convergence.

7. Conclusions. Accurate analysis of grounding systems of electrical installations requires the use of multilayer soil models when the soil is not essentially uniform in the surroundings of the earthing grid. At present, while uniform soil models run in real-time in conventional computers, the use of models with a small number of soil layers breaks off the design process due to the important computing time required in practical cases.

In last years, the authors have developed a BEM numerical approach for the analysis of grounding systems embedded in stratified soils that has been implemented in a high performance parallel computer. This numerical approach accepts massive parallelization since most of the computing time is required in the computation of the elemental matrices corresponding to the contribution of each electrode of the grounding grid. Results obtained with different parallelization options prove that the proposed multi-layer Boundary Element formulation can be a real-time design tool, as high-performance parallel computing becomes a widespread available resource in engineering.

Acknowledgements. This work has been partially supported by the *Ministerio de Ciencia y Tecnología* of the Spanish Government (grants # DPI2001-0556 and # 1FD97-0108), cofinanced with European Union FEDER funds, by the power company *Unión Fenosa Ingeniería, UFISA*, and by research fellowships of the *European Center for Parallelism of Barcelona, CEPBA* and the *Universidad de A Coruña*.

REFERENCES

[1] IEEE Std.80, *IEEE Guide for safety in AC substation grounding*, New York, 2000.
[2] Sverak J.G., *Progress in Step and Touch Voltage Equations of ANSI/IEEE Std.80*, IEEE Trans. Power Delivery,**13**, 762–767, 1999.
[3] Garret D.L., Pruitt J.G., *Problems Encountered with the APM of Analyzing Grounding Systems*, IEEE Trans. P.A.S.,**104**, 4006–4023, 1985.
[4] Navarrina F., Colominas I., Casteleiro M., *Analytical Integration Techniques for Earthing Grid Computation by BEM*, Num. Met. in Eng. and Appl. Sci., 1197–1206, CIMNE, Barcelona, 1992.
[5] Colominas I., Navarrina F., Casteleiro M., *A boundary element numerical approach for grounding grid computation*, Comput. Methods Appl. Mech. Engrg., **174**, 73-90, 1999.
[6] Navarrina F., Colominas I., Casteleiro M., *Why Do Computer Methods For Grounding Analysis Produce Anomalous Results?*, IEEE Trans. on Power Delivery, In press, 2002.
[7] Casteleiro M., Hernández L.A., Colominas I. and Navarrina F., *Memory and User guide of system TOTBEM for CAD of grounding grids in electrical installations*, Civil Engrg. Sch., Universidad de La Coruña, 1994.
[8] Silvester P.P. and Ferrari R.L., *Finite Elements for Electrical Engineers*, Cambridge University Press, Cambridge, U.K., 1996.
[9] Colominas I., *A CAD System for Grounding Grids in Electrical Installations: A Numerical Approach Based on the Boundary Element Integral Method*, Ph.D. Thesis, Universidad de A Coruña, Spain, 1995.
[10] Durand E., *Électrostatique*, Masson, Paris, France, 1966.
[11] Kellog O.D., *Foundations of Potential Theory*, Springer-Verlag, Berlin, Germany, 1967.
[12] Colominas I., Navarrina F., Casteleiro M., *A Numerical Formulation for Grounding Analysis in Stratified Soils*, IEEE Trans. on Power Delivery, **17**, 587–595, 2002.
[13] Colominas I., Navarrina F., Casteleiro M., *A Boundary Element Formulation for the Substation Grounding Design*, Advances in Engineering Software, **30**, 693–700, 1999.
[14] Colominas I., Gómez J., Navarrina F., Casteleiro M., *Computer Analysis of Earthing Systems in Horizontally or Vertically Layered Soils*, Electric Power Systems Research, **59**, 149–156, 2001.
[15] Colominas I., Navarrina F., Mosqueira G., Eiroa J.M., Casteleiro M., *Numerical modelling for grounding grids in high-performance parallel computers*, Intern. Series on Adv. in Boundary Elements: Boundary Elements XXII, Comp. Mech. Pub., Southampton, UK, 2000.
[16] Tagg G.F., *Earth Resistances*, Pitman Pub. Co., New York, 1964.
[17] Cela J.M., Julia A., *High performance computing on boundary element simulations*, Intern. Series on Adv. in Boundary Elements: Boundary Elements XXII, Comp. Mech. Pub., Southampton, UK, 2000.

In: Applied Parallel and Distributed Computing ISBN 1-59454-174-4
Editors: Yi Pan and Laurence T. Yang , pp. 117-131

AN IMPLICITLY PARALLEL OBJECT-ORIENTED MATRIX LIBRARY AND ITS APPLICATION TO MEDICAL PHYSICS

JONAS LÄTT AND BASTIEN CHOPARD*

Abstract. We introduce VLADYMIR, a matrix library that permits the development of array-based code in C++. It is especially useful for numerical simulation tasks and parallelizes automatically, without any need for parallelization-specific instructions. Thanks to the underlying data-parallel model, it shows up an excellent scalability, even on large parallel machines. VLADYMIR has been successfully tested so far on simulations of physical systems by cellular automata and lattice Boltzmann models. In this paper, an application to emboli detection in medical physics is presented. Occurrence of emboli in the brain presents a risk for cardio-vascular accidents, which one tries to avoid by ultrasonography methods. Simulations using lattice Boltzmann methods help to analyze the interaction of an embolus with ultrasounds and lead towards a better understanding of the structure of the signal in ultrasonography measurements.

Key words. Data-parallelism, Array-based computation, Lattice Boltzmann models, Emboli detection, Transcranial Doppler ultra-sonography

1. VLADYMIR — A C++ Matrix Library for Data-Parallel Applications.

1.1. Array-based computations and data-parallelism.

1.1.1. Introduction. A very natural and widely used approach in computational sciences is to express the computations in terms of matrix datatypes and to treat the whole matrices as one abstract entity. This approach applies very well to computations on a grid, and in particular to cellular automata and lattice Boltzmann simulations which now gain in popularity among the scientists and engineers [2, 15]. In an array-based programming-paradigm, the fundamental scalar datatypes, e.g. integer or float, are replaced by a vector, a matrix or a similar higher dimensional construct. Those new datatypes enclose a set of scalar data permitting to address them by one collective operation.

Some of the most popular programming languages that were designed for scientific and engineering purposes support this programming style. As for an example, Fortran 90 and Matlab offer d-dimensional arrays as a basic data structure that is very straightforward to use.

In addition to its conceptual elegance, array-based code offers a very important advantage in terms of performance: it can be parallelized without difficulty using a data-parallel model. The key to the simplicity of data-parallelism is that it makes a clear distinction between a single instruction flow and large, abstract and parallelized data structures. It is close to the level of abstraction we are used to in mathematics and results in more readable programs with less errors [12, 6].

Although, as we said, quite a big amount of developing tools exist that implement array-based programming concepts, it is difficult to find one that takes full advantage of the possibilities of data-parallelism. For example, HPF (High Performance Fortran) has been an attempt to offer data-parallelism on modern parallel computers. However, it never showed up the expected performance, due probably to the impossibility to combine the flexibility of the language with an efficient parallelization.

In this area we therefore think that there is still room for some work to be done, in order to develop a tool that fits the needs of scientific applications. For this purpose we introduce a matrix library that may be useful for developing numerical applications in the language C++. In this way, it combines the power of the high-level language C++, the simplicity of array-based programming and the performance of a data-parallel execution.

*University of Geneva, Computer Science Department, CH-1211 Geneva 4, Switzerland ({Jonas.Latt, Bastien.Chopard}@cui.unige.ch)

1.1.2. The use of an array-based paradigm. When a scientific problem is to be formulated in a programming language, the matrix is often the datatype of choice. Let us for example look at a simple application, the computation of the Mandelbrot set. This set is determined by successive iterations of the complex function $f(z) = z^2 + \mu$, where the complex parameter μ is taken to represent the geometrical coordinates of a two-dimensional set. There are two possible outcomes for such an iteration: for a given subset of the parameter space μ all values of the iterations are confined inside a circle of radius 1. Those parameters represent the Mandelbrot set. For all other parameters the iteration will quit this circle after a finite number of iterations *nstep* and then start to diverge. In that case, one utilizes this number *nstep* to characterise the corresponding parameter μ. In a classical programming language, the core of a program for the computation of the Mandelbrot set would look somewhat like this:

```
complex z(MAX_Y, MAX_X)          // two-dimensional array z
complex mu(MAX_Y, MAX_X)         // two-dimensional array z
complex nStep(MAX_Y, MAX_X)      // two-dimensional array z
...                              // some code to initialize mu
for x =1 to MAX_X                // loops over space dimensions
  for y = 1 to MAX_Y
    nStep(y,x) = 0
    z(y,x) = 0
    for iterStep = 1 to MAX_STEP          // time loop
      if (abs(z(y,x)) <= 2)
        nStep(y,x) = nStep(y,x) + 1
        z(y,x) = sqr(z)y,x)) + mu(y,x)  // computations
      end if
    end for
  end for
end for
```

In a array-based approach, the loops over space dimensions are not needed any more:

```
complex z(MAX_Y, MAX_X)          // two-dimensional array z
complex mu(MAX_Y, MAX_X)         // two-dimensional array z
complex nStep(MAX_Y, MAX_X)      // two-dimensional array z
nStep = 0                        // matrix initialization
z = 0
...                              // some code to initialize mu
for iterStep = 1 to MAX_STEP     // one loop over iterations
  where(abs(z) <= 2)
    nStep = nStep+1
    z = sqr(z)+mu                // computations in easy
                                 // array notation
  end where
end for
```

Thus, the array-based code looks more intuitive and readable than its scalar counterpart. Furthermore, it offers a serious advantage in terms of performance: it can be parallelized without difficulty. Indeed, the array-based formulation of the code encourages the use of a data-parallel model in which the computationally intensive data, being stored in a regular matrix, are distributed over the parallel machine.

Data-parallelism uses a sequential flow of instructions (i.e. each line of the above program is executed one after the other) but each instruction applies on a full data structure and parallelism can be exploited to process coherently all the element of the data structure.

This clear distinction between a single instruction flow and large, abstract, parallelized data structures is the key to the simplicity of this programming model. It is close to the level of abstraction we are used to in mathematics and results in more readable programs with less errors [6].

1.1.3. VLADYMIR, an overview. The library VLADYMIR(Visualised LAttice DYnamics Matrix InteRface) was specifically designed to support numerical simulations that are based on nearest-neighbour dynamics. Although it can very well be used in different domains, it should be expected to show especially good performance in applications akin to lattice Boltzmann simulations as mentioned in the previous subsection. The best way to get a feeling for the library is probably to look directly at a programming example. We show in the following a typical code that implements the dynamics of a lattice Boltzmann model. As one can see, the syntax is quite close to the one used by Fortran 90:

```
for (int t=0; t<tmax; t++) {
  f1.column(0)=A*sin(omega*t);
  f3.column(l-1)=0;

  psi=f1+f2+f3+f4;

  where(obstacle);
    f1_ = -f3;
    f2_ = -f4;
    f3_ = -f1;
    f4_ = -f2;
  elsewhere();
    f1_ = 1./2.*psi-f3;
    f2_ = 1./2.*psi-f4;
    f3_ = 1./2.*psi-f1;
    f4_ = 1./2.*psi-f2;
  endwhere();

  f1 = f1_.rrotate();
  f2 = f2_.urotate();
  f3 = f3_.lrotate();
  f4 = f4_.drotate();
}
```

The precise meaning of the code will become more clear from the discussion of the model in section 2.1. It is based on four floating point matrices $f_1 \cdots f_4$ that can be represented as a particle density distribution in phase space. The first part of the code contains a series of arithmetic operations corresponding to a collision between the particle flows. The second part implements a propagation step with pure nearest-neighbor interaction.

That VLADYMIR is not simply an "implementation of Fortran 90 in C++" becomes clear when one discusses the parallelization of the code. A compiler option suffices to turn the serial code into a parallel one, based on the parallel library PVM. In that case, an additional configuration file specifies the setup of the virtual machine and optionally defines the data layout on the processors. This functionality is somehow similar to the corresponding compiler directive used in HPF.

1.2. Features of VLADYMIR. The purpose of the library presented here is to offer an intuitive interface for the scientific programmer. It does in no way implement a generic matric datatype in the tradition of the Standard Template Library of C++. On the contrary, it implements a specific set of functions that are defined and optimized for the integer and floating point datatypes.

A series of overloaded operations make the matrix behave as an integrated datatype of the language:

Arithmetic and trigonometric functions. Basic arithmetic operators as well as the functions of the library *math.h* are defined as collective operations on a matrix.

Logical operators. They make it easy to formulate domain specifications of the dynamics. This technique is discussed later in this section.

Matrix manipulation routines. Those global manipulation routines enable for example to extract submatrices from a matrix.

Reduction operations.

Input/output routines. Thanks to the interface to Matlab, a sophisticated graphical output of the data is no problem.

A special feature is the ability to specify complex domains and boundaries for the dynamics. In that case, the effect of collective matrix operations is restricted to a subdomain. Consider for example a numerical simulation on a lattice that is divided in two domains (boundaries and bulk), each of them subject to some particular dynamics. As in Fortran 90, the instruction `where` enables to express this separation:

```
where(special_dynamics);
 ...    ! implement the special dynamics
elsewhere();
 ...    ! implement the usual dynamics
endwhere();
```

The command `where` can be seen as a multi-dimensional generalization of the scalar `if` command. It takes as its argument a matrix with boolean values that specifies the subdomain for the special dynamics. All collective operations enclosed between a `where()` - `endwhere()` block are subject to this domain restriction.

1.3. The virtual matrix: getting rid of the object-oriented overhead. Hiding the implementation of a parallelized data structure behind an object-oriented interface is not without problems. On the one hand, one suffers from a loss of performance as compared to an array-based compiler, because the access to the data structure is handled at run time. On the other hand, one looses part of the flexibility for the design of an algorithm that evaluates the matrix expressions. Indeed, the object-oriented semantics of C++ determines in a rigid way the scheme in which overloaded algebraic expressions are evaluated. Both those problems can be partially solved with the help of a special data structure which we call a virtual matrix. The present section is devoted to the presentation and discussion of this data structure.

1.3.1. The problem: returning a matrix per value. A typical object in C++ makes an intense use of the concept of a copy-constructor. The copy-constructor permits to create a clone of a given object by duplication of its complete dataspace. It is implicitly called every time an object is passed by value as a parameter to a function. Applying this procedure to an object with a small dataspace may be a reasonable thing to do, but calling the copy-constructor of a 1000×1000 matrix without a good reason can be a big waste of time. Thus any person with basic programming skills will be very attentive to pass big matrices by reference rather than by value to a function.

On the other hand, it is sometimes impossible to avoid the use of a copy constructor. This is the case for the returned value of an arithmetic operator, as will be made clear by the following example. Suppose we have defined a datatype `matrix` which we use to implement a matrix addition, e.g.

```
A=B+C;    // A,B and C are matrices
```

The C++ compiler will interpret this line as one single instruction similar to the following:

```
A.operator=(B.operator+(C));
```

The two operators used in this code may be implemented like this:

```
matrix matrix::operator+(matrix& rhs)
{
  matrix temp;
  ...   // add rhs to current matrix and
        // store result in temp
  return temp;  // returning a matrix
}               // by value !!!


matrix& matrix::operator=(matrix& rhs)
{
  ...   // copy rhs to current matrix
  return *this;
}
```

Here, operator+ is instructed to return the matrix temp by value[1]. It is impossible to return it by reference, because a reference to the local matrix temp would get out of scope as soon as the frame of the function is left. It is not possible either to return a pointer to a dynamically created temporary matrix: the language C++ does not define a garbage collector, and one can therefore not ensure a correct deletion of temp. A more detailed discussion of this topic is given in [11](Item 23). Incidentally, note that additionally to the copy procedure inside the constructor, the whole matrix data is copied once more during the execution of the operator=.

In whatever way we turn the problem, it is not possible to avoid the resulting matrix to be returned by value. The question remains then, how to avoid that the whole content of the matrix be copied during this process. One solution would be to implement a copy constructor that simply copies the pointer to the data, without touching to the data themselves. This in its turn asks for advanced techniques like reference counting, in order to avoid an unwanted behavior of the copy constructor.

1.3.2. The solution: defining a matrix with empty dataspace. In this text, we suggest a slightly different approach. The idea is to replace the matrix which is to be returned by value by a virtual matrix (note that the term "virtual" in the designation of a virtual matrix has nothing in common with the notion of a virtual function in C++ and should not be mixed up with it). The virtual matrix is implemented by a dataspace that is of constant size against the "real" dimensions of the matrix and is therefore cheap to copy. The key to this technique is the abstraction of data in the object oriented environment. Indeed, the implementation of the matrix data, which might be a simple array, is hidden in the private data space of a matrix object. The only way to access them is through a member function as, in our case, the function call operator operator(). For this reason, a matrix class can choose not to implement any data at all until the very last moment when the data is requested through a corresponding member function. This is precisely the concept of the virtual matrix: it offers the same interface as a conventional matrix, but implements the data in a more abstract manner.

In our example on the return value of the operator+, the VLADYMIR library constructs a virtual matrix that simply keeps a pointer to the matrix operands of the addition operation. The corresponding code looks somewhat like this:

```
v_matrix matrix::operator+(matrix& rhs)
```

[1]To be fully honest towards the C++ standard, let us remark that modern compilers might skip in some cases the creation of a temporary through the use of the so-called return-value optimization.

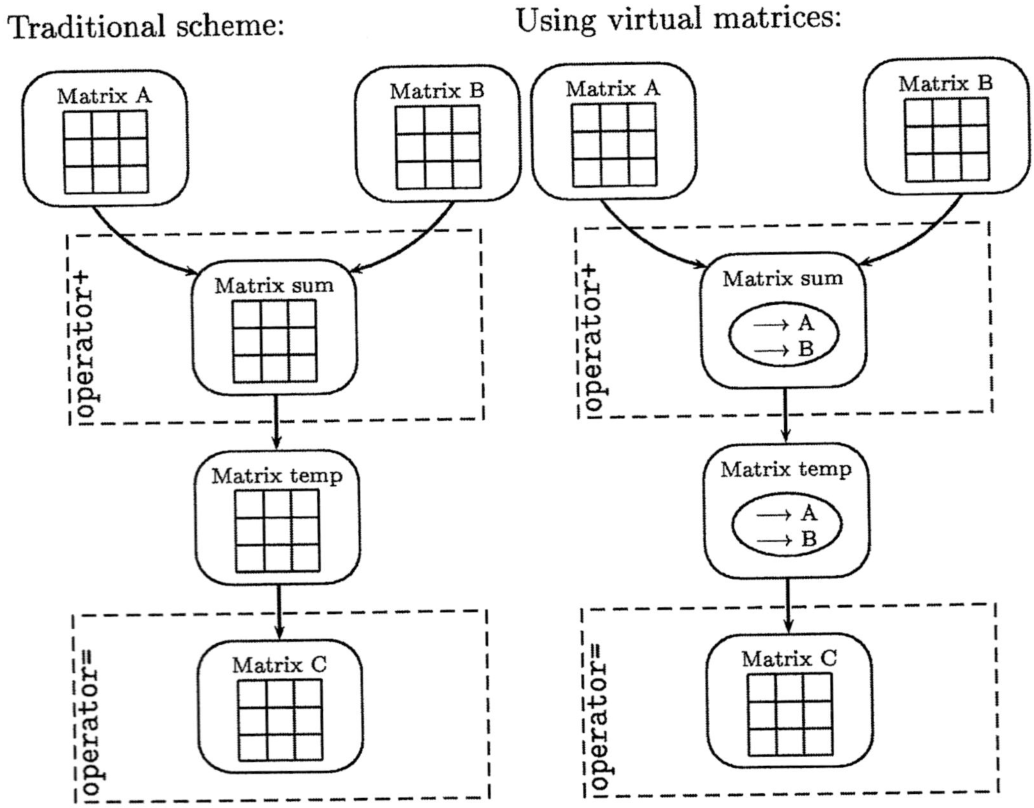

FIG. 1.1. *Creation of temporaries during an arithmetic matrix operation*

```
{
    // build a virtual matrix to be
    // passed as return value
  v_matrix temp(*this, rhs, addition);
    // the parameter addition is of
    // type enum{add, substr, etc.}
  return temp;
}
```

The data space of the matrix `temp` consists of merely two pointers on the operands and one identifier for the kind of operation to perform. It is cheap to duplicate by copy construction but sufficient for constructing the data when the need should arise. And this need arises at the point where the data is copied to another matrix, namely at the use of the `matrix::operator=`:

```
matrix& matrix::operator=(matrix& rhs)
{
  ...  // ask rhs to explicit its dataspace and to deliver
       // a pointer to it
  ...  // replace old data with the data from rhs
  return *this;
}
```

This way of doing permits to avoid the construction and copying of two value arrays.

The technique is illustrated on figure 1.1.

We finally remark that the parameters to the `operator+` may very well be virtual matrices themselves, thus allowing for composed operations like the following one:

```
A=B+C*D-E
```

During the execution of this code, a sequence of virtual matrices is built up that refer to each other in the form of a graph. During the execution of the `operator=`, all arithmetic operations are performed through a recursive evaluation of this graph. The specifications of VLADYMIR state that a virtual matrix never points to matrices that do not exist any more. To ensure this, virtual matrices will only be used *locally* as return values of an operator and never quit the scope of the objects they refer to. The user of the matrix library may not refer explicitly to virtual matrices and will most probably not even know about their existence.

1.3.3. Other advantages of the virtual matrix. Making fully abstraction of the implementation of a matrix offers several additional advantages. For example, the increased freedom in deciding when to effectively execute a matrix operation permits to coordinate more efficiently the time invested for communication between processors on one side and the computations on the other side.

Another useful feature is to exploit virtual matrices as *proxy classes* ([11], Item 30), for example in order to distinguish between their right-hand side and left-hand side use.

1.4. Parallelization.

1.4.1. General concepts. When a program is to be run on a parallel machine, it must be decomposed into a set of sub-problems, each of which are executed on a different processor. In general this decomposition of an algorithm is a delicate task, and there does not exist a generic procedure that applies on any chosen problem and ensure satisfying performance.

In our case, however, there is no need to address the problem in its full generality because VLADYMIR is intended to perform well only on applications that make use of an array-based paradigm. In this case there is a single stream of arithmetic operations that are performed on every element of the matrix. This encourages the use of a data-parallel programming model in which the distribution of the computation tasks to the nodes of a parallel machine is realized through a regular subdivision of the arrays. This kind of parallelization is very straightforward and the parallel semantics is already inherent to the array-based formulation of the program.

We take advantage of this ease of implementation to offer a completely implicit parallelization of VLADYMIR programs: a code that was designed for a sequential environment can also be run in a parallel one without any single change. This is possible thanks to the fact that the parallel structure is hidden behind the matrix interface and implemented at run time. In this way, there is no need to add any syntactical extension to the language C++ nor to treat the code by a preprocessor.

Load balancing issues, i.e. differences of work that may typically result from a `where` statement (as exemplified by the calculation of the Mandelbrot set) are not yet addressed in the current implementation. Again we focus on well conditioned problems and assume that computational irregularities are sufficiently few or uniformly distributed on the domain.

1.4.2. The parallelization techniques. The parallel VLADYMIR code implements a Single Program Multiple Data (SPMD) execution model in which every node of the parallel machine executes exactly the same code, without synchronization, except when communication is needed.

The idea behind this is that every processor treats the program just as if it had been written for a serial machine. Every line of C++ code that does not make use of the array-based library is then executed on all nodes, thus running at the speed of a single processor.

Things get more interesting when a collective operation on a matrix is executed. In that case, the nodes restrict their calculations to a submatrix whose coordinates are determined at run time, thus reducing the calculation time in the best case by a factor equal to the number of nodes.

In the actual version of VLADYMIR, the matrices are divided in regular rectangles of static and user-defined size. The information on the configuration of the parallel machine and the repartition of the data need to be defined by the programmer in a configuration file that is read at run time.

We finally note that VLADYMIR is implemented based on PVM, which permits to run the code even on a heterogeneous parallel machine. Because of the underlying SPMD model, it can be ported to MPI without difficulty.

The VLADYMIR functions that produce inter-processor communications are the global data motion methods such as `f.xrotate()` or the reduction operations like `sum`.

1.5. Comparison to existing libraries. There exists a huge amount of compilers, programming tools and libraries that allow for programming with a matrix data-type. All of them have their own features, advantages and disadvantages, and it might be useful to situate VLADYMIR in this crowd. One important issue shall be pointed out before we start this discussion. It can be noticed that most people, when thinking of matrices, think of linear algebra. Indeed, matrix libraries often also offer a variety of numerical algorithms for the resolution of linear algebra problems. This is not the case of VLADYMIR: it is intended to offer no more than an interface for the simulation of (physical) dynamics on a lattice structure. In this context a couple of widely used compilers and libraries will be introduced now and discussed through the application of two simple benchmarks. These comparisons are performed in a non-parallel environment: performance issues of VLADYMIR on a parallel machine will be discussed in section 2.3.

1.5.1. State of the art. Many programming tools for array-based computing can be classified by one of the following three groups:

Compilers. Fortran 90, for example, supports d-dimensional arrays as a basic data structure and contrasts with C or C++ in which the handling of matrices is quite awkward. We will also discuss the widely used program Matlab which implements a matrix structure in a very natural way.

Dynamic object-oriented interfaces. In C++, new datatypes can easily be added to the basic language through the overloading of operators. This technique has been used by numerous libraries such as Lapack++ [4]. VLADYMIR also fits into this category. Although very elegant, this way of doing is often quite un-effective due to the overhead of object-oriented function calls.

Expression templates. They offer a compromise between the two previous groups. Through the use of templates in C++, expressions involving matrix types are evaluated during the compilation and produce code comparable to one by a compiled language (cf. [13]). We will discuss the popular library Blitz++ [14].

A lot of scientific programmers develop their applications with the well established Fortran 90 compiler. This language lacks however object-oriented features or some other higher-level constructs. This explains probably the increasing popularity of numeric libraries for modern languages such as C++ or Java.

The choice between a library with a static respectively dynamic evaluation of expressions is not easy at all. The library Blitz++ has clearly shown that expression templates are unbeatable in terms of pure performance. Our point of view however is that a dynamic library offers more flexibility for the implementation of algorithms, especially in the context of a parallel execution. The following benchmark show that thanks to the technique explained in the previous sections, the object-oriented interface of VLADYMIR can compete

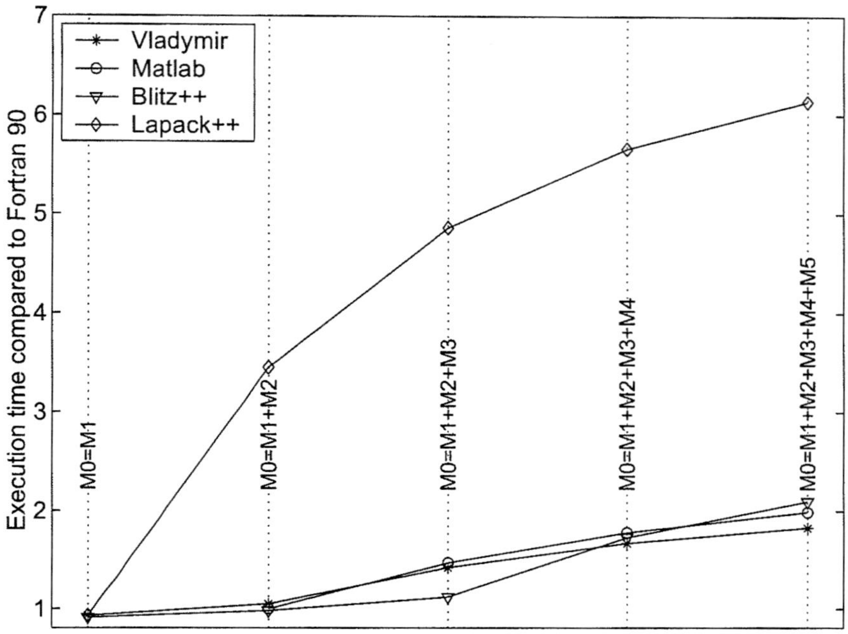

FIG. 1.2. *Relative performance of matrix additions*

with the other approaches.

1.5.2. Benchmarks. Through a simple call to consecutive matrix additions one can see in what way the performance of an arithmetic computation is influenced by the overhead of function calls. Figure 1.2 shows the relative performance of up to 5 matrix additions as compared to Fortran 90. Blitz++, Matlab and VLADYMIR range all three equally well but lose up to a factor of two against Fortran.

To discuss a more interesting example we test now the code for a Lattice Boltzmann simulation that was presented in section 1.1.3. Again, the four libraries are compared to Fortran 90 (figure 1.3). This time, both Blitz++ and VLADYMIR show up good performance.

There is an obvious difference between Lapack++ and the other tested libraries. This can be taken as an indication that the technique implemented by VLADYMIR is indeed very successful. One should remark however that Lapack++ is first of all an interface to linear algebra routines. For that reason, its bad performance in the present context is not really surprising.

2. Application to Numerical Simulations.

2.1. Introduction to a lattice Boltzmann model. In the first part of this paper, we introduced a code for the numerical simulation of wave propagation. The aim of the present section is to give it some theoretical background in the more general context of inhomogeneous wave propagation. Detailed information on this model can be found in the reference [8].

Let us start with the wave equation in an inhomogeneous space:

$$\partial_t^2 \Psi - c^2 \nabla^2 \Psi = 0 \tag{2.1}$$

where the speed of sound is isotropic but space and time dependent: $c = c(\vec{r}, t)$. We propose a lattice Boltzmann scheme to treat this equation numerically. The idea is to split up the

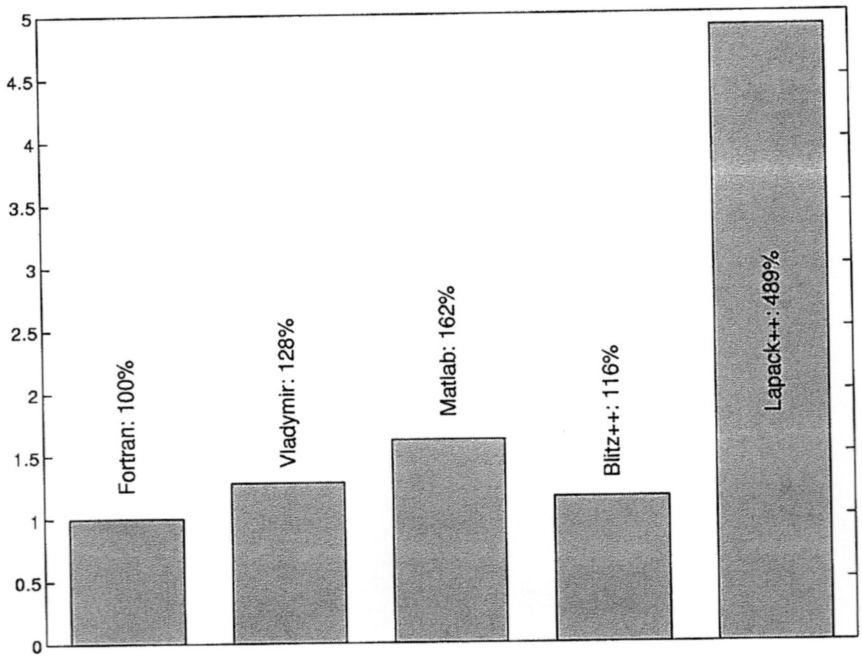

FIG. 1.3. *Benchmark of a lattice Boltzmann simulaion*

scalar quantity Ψ into four components, corresponding to density fluxes in the position-velocity space:

$$\Psi(\vec{r}, t) = \sum_{i=1}^{4} f_i(\vec{r}, t) \tag{2.2}$$

This equation can be interpreted on a regularly spaced grid, the four directions heading from a grid node towards its nearest neighbors being characterized by the velocity constants $v_i, i = 1 \cdots 4$. The value of f_i are then understood as a generalized particle density in the direction of $\vec{v}_i$. In the same way, one introduces a generalized momentum:

$$\vec{J}(\vec{r}, t) = \frac{1}{\rho(\vec{r}, t)} \sum_{i=1}^{4} f_i(\vec{r}, t)\vec{v}_i \tag{2.3}$$

The dynamics is formulated in the BGK (from its inventors Bhatnagar, Gross and Krook) approximation, in terms of a relaxation towards an equilibrium distribution $f_i^{(eq)}$:

$$\begin{aligned} f_i(\vec{x} + \vec{v}_i \Delta t, t + \Delta t) - f_i(\vec{x}, t) = \\ -\frac{1}{\tau}\left(f_i(\vec{x}, t) - f_i^{(eq)}(\vec{x}, t)\right). \end{aligned} \tag{2.4}$$

The equilibrium distribution is a function of Ψ and $\vec{J}$ alone and determines the properties of the flow. In order to represent the wave equation, one chooses a linear expression:

$$f_i^{(eq)} = a_i \Psi + b_i \vec{u} \cdot \vec{J}_i \tag{2.5}$$

where a_i and b_i are some well chosen constants.

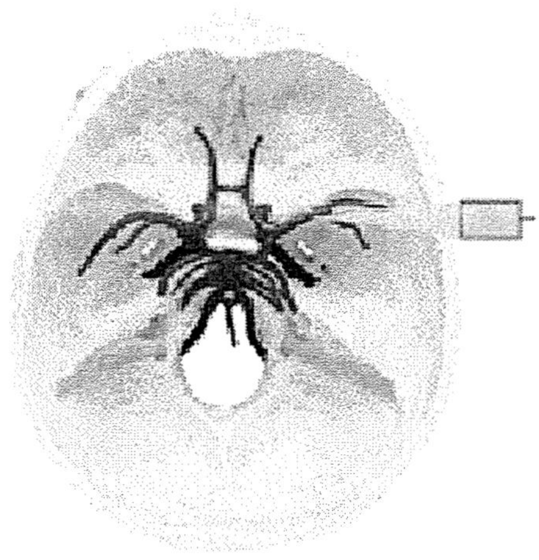

FIG. 2.1. *Setup of a TCD measurement*

We remark that equation 2.4 expresses a nearest-neighbor dynamics and can be especially well formulated in an array-based programming paradigm. Indeed, in the case when the speed of sound c is independent of space and time, the complete dynamics is implemented by the piece of code which was discussed in section 1.1.3. This fact has determined our choice of a lattice Boltzmann model and the library VLADYMIR to perform the simulation presented in the next section.

2.2. Numerical simulation of transcranial Doppler ultrasonography by a lattice Boltzmann method.

2.2.1. Emboli detection through invasive ultrasonography. In medicine, the surveillance of vascular pathologies gains in importance due to the increasing amount of injuries caused by stroke. Stroke is caused by a local interruption in the cerebral blood flow, with the result that one part of the brain is not being supplied with oxygen. Very often, stroke is caused by embolic processes. These are due to the occurrence of *emboli* (sg. embolus), small particles of undisolved matter that are carried by the blood stream and tend to occlude the tiny intracranial vessels. As a consequence of such a stroke, a part of the brain may cease to function, provoking various symptoms, such as lack of sensitivity or motricity in some part of the body, or even leading to death.

There exist efficient methods for detecting the occurrence of emboli in the brain. One of them, the transcranial Doppler ultrasonography (TCD), is a non invasive ultrasound technique that is primarily used to evaluate the blood flow velocity in the major basal intracranial arteries [7]. Figure 2.1 explains the setup of this method. It consists of a device emitting a beam of pulsed ultrasounds that is directed towards the artery under investigation. The beam is reflected inside the blood vessel and propagates back, carrying information on the blood flow velocity as well as on the specific contents of the vessel. There remains then to catch up the returning signal and analyze it with some imaging modality.

Although this method has proven to be very successful for the detection of emboli, there still remain serious problems as when to specify their precise nature. It is especially useful to be able to distinguish between gaseous emboli, i.e. small air particles, and solid emboli. Indeed, solid and gaseous emboli have very different immediate consequences for the patient; solid emboli carry a high risk for stroke, while gaseous embolisation is known to be more benign in the short term. Identifying the type of circulating emboli therefore allows the physician to navigate efficiently in the medical decision tree, and is mandatory

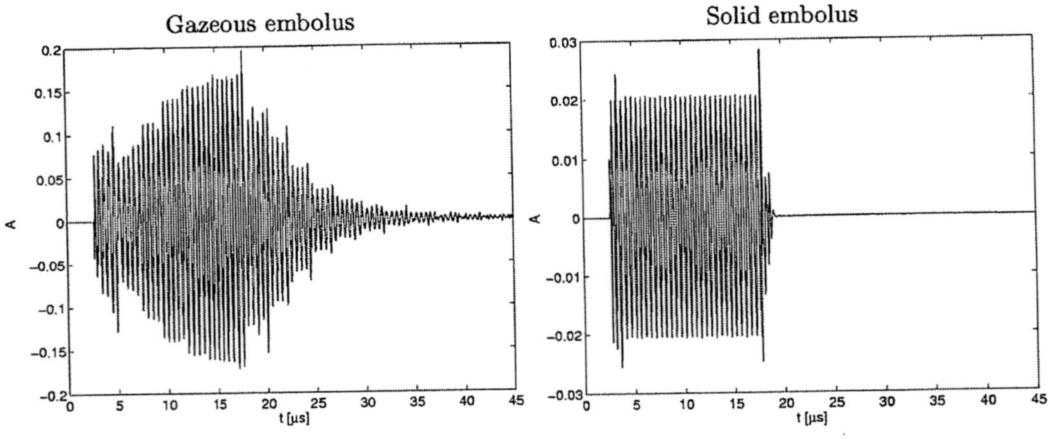

FIG. 2.2. *Comparison of the signal obtained from the simulation on a gaseous respectively solid embolus*

before administering potentially dangerous drugs such as anticoagulants or neuroprotectors.

A series of *in vitro* experiments have been performed with the aim to come up with better distinction criteria between gaseous and solid emboli. During those experiments, a large data-base of TCD signals has been collected and analyzed by pattern-recognition algorithms. As a result, one has been able to come up with decision-trees that offer distinguishing criteria based on a well chosen set of properties of the signal.

In a similar spirit we present a series of numerical simulation of a TCD signal. Rather than just collecting more raw data, we propose with these simulation to obtain a better understanding of the physical processes involved. This should help to give a conceptual background to the results of the *in vitro* experiments. The *in vitro* and the numerical experiments should therefore be understood as two complementary approaches.

2.2.2. The numerical setup. On its trajectory through the human brain, the Doppler ultrasound signal is influenced by the inhomogeneities of its surrounding medium. This influence is very complex and differs from patient to patient. We therefore considered it as a noise and concentrated merely on the physics of the interaction between the signal and the embolus.

The numerical model simulates the ultrasound signal by solving the wave equation in an inhomogeneous, time dependent space. The properties of different emboli are characterized by the distribution of their wave absorption coefficient and the speed of sound. For example, inside a gaseous embolus the speed of sound as well as the absorption coefficient are lower than in a solid one. The emboli are modelled by sizes that range between $50 - 400\,\mu m$. The signal is generated at frequencies close to 2 MHz with a pulse repetition frequency of around 6 kHz and a pulse size of 30 wave periods.

2.2.3. Results of the simulation. Figure 2.2 shows two typical signals, measured on a simulation on a gaseous and on a solid embolus. As a striking property one observes that the gaseous signal is much richer than its solid counterpart. With numerical experiments in which the internal properties of the emboli are varied, it can be shown that this difference arises from internal reflections on the inner surface of the embolus. Indeed, giving a closer look at the signal from a gaseous embolus (figure 2.3), one sees that its striking patterns simply reflect the global structure of the embolus under investigation.

Encouraged by the discovery that internal reflection plays an important role in the measurement of gaseous emboli, we now try to find frequencies at which there is a resonance between the signal and the embolus. For this purpose we generate a signal that contains a

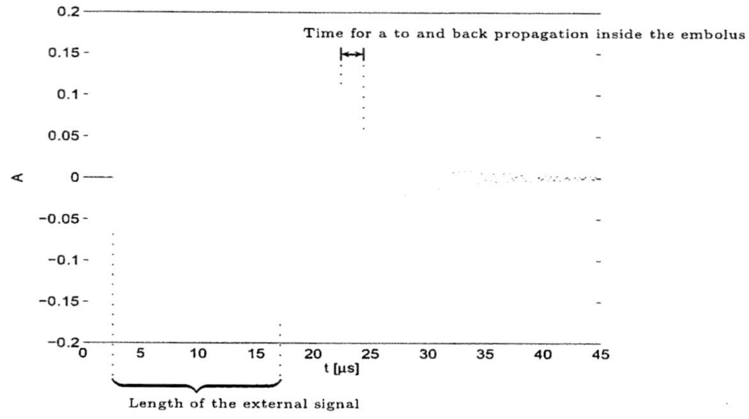

FIG. 2.3. *Analysis of the gaseous signal*

sweep over some range of frequencies.

As one might have expected, the signal shows up resonance in regular intervals that express a proportionality between the size of the embolus and an integer multiple of the wavelength:

$$2d = n\lambda + k \tag{2.6}$$

where d is the diameter of the embolus, λ the wavelength in the gaseous medium and k a numerically determined parameter.

Figure 2.4 shows the detailed spectrum of the measured signal. We remark that the distance between two peaks in the signal permits to determine the size of the embolus.

Discussions with the physicists who perform *in vitro* experiments have shown that there is a reasonable agreement between those experiments and the numerical predictions. Furthermore, the simulations have permitted to characterize more clearly some basic properties of the TCD signal.

2.3. Discussion of performance issues. The numerical experiments discussed in the previous subsections were all performed with the library VLADYMIR in a parallel environment. The parallel machine consisted of a cluster of PCs with 50 nodes. Figure 2.5 shows that even on this large number of nodes, a parallelizing performance of more than 75% could be obtained. Different elements permitted a particularly efficient execution of the code. Among others, we state that

1. The problem is well formulated through a lattice Boltzmann scheme with nearest-neighbor dynamics.
2. The computations are done on a large domain. For this reason, the communication overhead of the parallel execution is diminished.
3. The domain is quite regular and makes load-balancing issues easier.

2.4. Conclusion. We have introduced a parallel matrix library that is suited for the development of array-based C++ application. Through the use of a special technique it avoids important performance problems attached to implementing large matrices in an object-oriented environment. Some comparisons with other numerical libraries showed that our method is indeed promising.

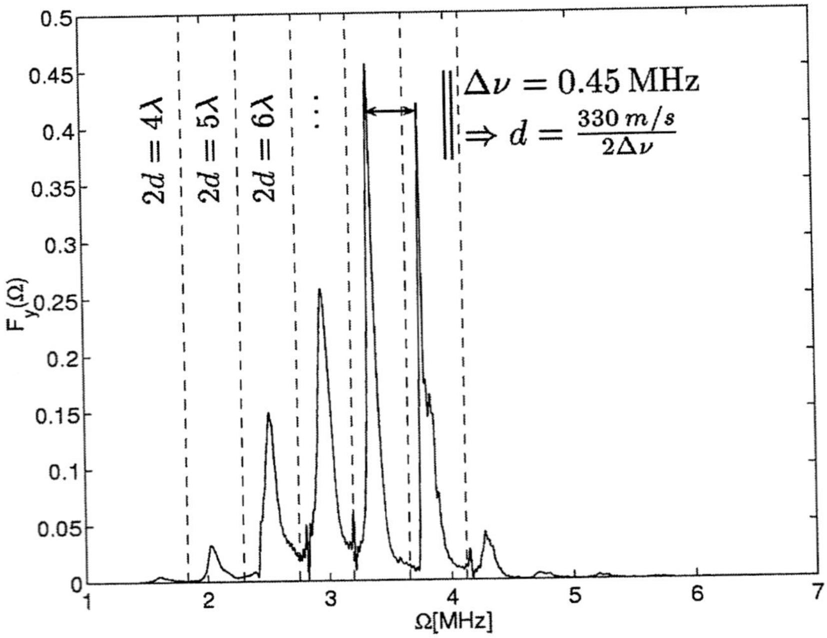

FIG. 2.4. *Spectrum of a gaseous signal*

Furthermore, a research project in medical physics has been discussed which made a successful use of our library. We conclude that, at least in the domain of lattice Boltzmann simulations and similar array-based problems, the library offers a useful alternative to other numerical tools.

To conclude this section, we remark that VLADYMIR has been conceived as an open source project and is still in its beginnings. More information, as well as details on the benchmarks can be found at the internet address `http://cui.unige.ch/~latt`.

REFERENCES

[1] Guy E. Blelloch. *Vector models for Data-parallel Computing.* The MIT Press, 1990.
[2] Bastien Chopard and Michel Droz. *Cellular Automata Modeling of Physical Systems.* Cambridge University Press, Cambridge, 1998.
[3] Julian C. Cummings and William F. Humphrey. Parallel particle simulations using the pooma framework. In *Proceedings of the 8th SIAM Conference on Parallel Processing for Scientific Computing*, 1997.
[4] Jack J. Dongarra, Roldan Pozo, and David W. Walker. A design overview of object-oriented extensions for high performance linear algebra. In *IEEE Proceedings of Supercomputing*, pages 162–171, 1993.
[5] Alexandre Dupuis and Bastien Chopard. An object oriented approach to lattice gas modeling. *Future Generation Computer Systems*, 16(5):523–532, March 2000. Best selected papers from HPCN'99.
[6] Ian Foster. *Designing and Builiding Parallel Programs.* Addison Wesley, 1995.
[7] Jorgen A. Jensen. *Estimation of Blood Velocities Using Ultrasound: A Signal Processing Approach.* Cambridge University Press, Cambridge, 1996.
[8] Pascal O. Lüthi. *Lattice Wave Automata; From Radio Waves to Fractures Propagation.* PhD thesis, Université de Genève, Geneva, 1998.
[9] Claudio Lucchesi. Biomedical data, algorithms & software: The case of brain emboli identification through transcranial doppler ultrasonography. Master's thesis, Université de Lausanne, 2001.
[10] Jean-Marc Girault. *Apport des Techiques du Traitement du Signal à l'Analyse et Détection de Signaux Emboliques.* PhD thesis, Université de Tours, 1999.
[11] Scott Meyers. *More Effective C++; 35 New Ways to Improve Your Programs and Designs.* Addison-Wesley Professional Computing Series. Addison-Wesley, 2001.

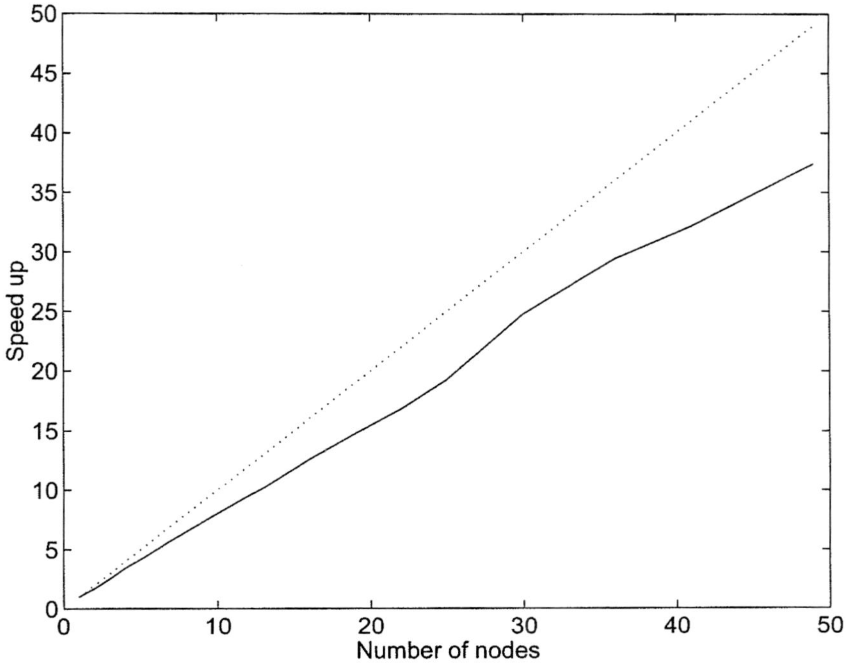

FIG. 2.5. *Parallelization of a lattice Boltzmann simulation using VLADYMIR.*

[12] Dan. I. Moldovan. *Parallel Processing: From application to Systems.* Morgan Kauffmann, San Mateo, California, 1993.

[13] Todd L. Veldhuizen. Expression templates. *C++ Report*, 7(5):26–31, June 1995. Reprinted in C++ Gems, ed. Stanley Lippman.

[14] Todd L. Veldhuizen. Arrays in blitz++. In *Proceedings of the 2nd International Scientific Computing in Object-Oriented Parallel Environments (ISCOPE'98)*, Lecture Notes in Computer Science. Springer-Verlag, 1998.

[15] Dieter A. Wolf-Gladrow. *Lattice-Gas Cellular Automata and Lattice Boltzmann Models.* Number 1725 in Lecture Notes in Mathematics. Springer, Berlin Heidelberg, 2000.

In: Applied Parallel and Distributed Computing
Editors: Yi Pan and Laurence T. Yang , pp. 133-142
ISBN 1-59454-174-4

THE FEELFEM SYSTEM: A REPOSITORY SYSTEM FOR THE FINITE ELEMENT METHOD

HIDEHIRO FUJIO*

Abstract. We have developed a finite element method (FEM) software repository tool named feelfem that serves as a code generator. One important feature of feelfem is that it is designed to generate various program models of FEM analysis, including users' own newly developed numerical schemes. Another feature is that interfaces to newly developed parallel programming paradigms and parallel solvers can easily be added to it. Software reuse is an important target of the feelfem system. To achieve flexibility and expandability for the system, we adopt an object-oriented technique and implementation-oriented pseudo-code representation of numerical algorithms. In its latest released version, feelfem has strong interaction with the personal pre/post processor GiD. By using a combination of feelfem and GiD, users can generate prototype parallel FEM applications with newly developed solvers very easily and quickly.

Key words. Finite element method, Code generator, Object-oriented approach

1. Introduction. Code generators and software tools for solving partial differential equations (PDEs) are not new ideas. Since the historic Ellpack system [1] by John Rice in the early 80's, many similar systems have been developed. We also developed an FEM code generator system FEEL in 1994 [2]. But rather few of these systems are still being used now. One reason is that the target of these code generators or tools was to generate up-to-date programs at that time, but the lifetime of programs in the scientific computing field is not so long, especially in the HPC area.

While developing the old FEEL system, we learned that developing a code generator itself is a huge task (the total code size of the FEEL system is more than 100,000 lines of C code). Furthermore, to enable code generation of up-to-date parallel algorithms requires an easy expendability mechanism in the code generator system itself. Another crucial issue is to develop code generators that are easy to maintain.

We solved these problems by developing a new system that uses object-oriented technology and pseudo-code representation of numerical algorithms. The development of the new system, named 'feelfem', started in late 1999 and the first public version was released in April 2002. Like the former FEEL system, it makes use of a code generator, because using a code generator is the easiest way to establish interfaces to newly developed parallel programs.

One of the usual approaches to apply object-oriented technology for scientific software is to make an object- oriented programming framework. Diffpack [3] and Deal II [4] are examples of successful frameworks. But compared with a code generator, newly developed parallel algorithms must be implemented in their own manner, while feelfem can easily add such new algorithms and libraries because it is designed as a repository of the FEM programs. We will explain this issue in detail later.

2. Objectives and System Overview.

2.1. Objectives of feelfem. One of the main objectives of feelfem is to provide users with a high-level programming interface for FEM analysis. A user may desire to apply a state-of -the art numerical scheme, or try newly developed parallel solvers for their own problems. With this system, users may generate program codes merely by specifying their problems in feelfem scripts. Another objective is to provide an FEM program repository. To achieve this, solvers, schemes and data structures are represented in feelfem script or inside of the feelfem system, then stored and reused by code generation.

*NEC Corporation Internet System Research Laboratories, Miyazaki 4-1-1 Miyamae Kawasaki, Japan, 216-8555 (fujio@ccm.cl.nec.co.jp).

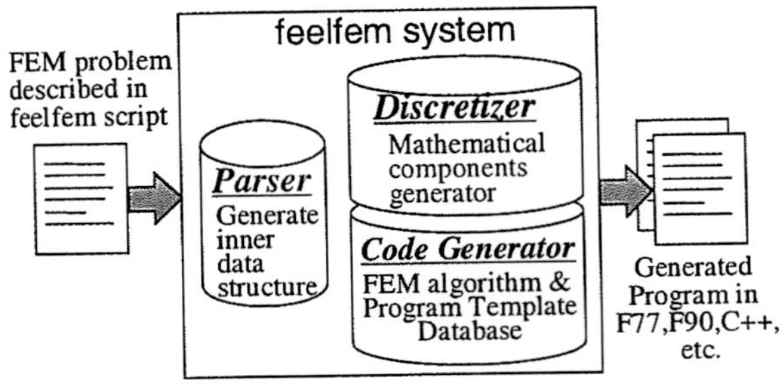

FIG. 2.1. *The feelfem system overview*

2.2. System overview. Fig.2.1 shows the overview of the feelfem system. A user specifies the PDE boundary value problem in the feelfem script language, and the feelfem system reads it and generates a complete FEM program. Roughly speaking, the feelfem system consists of three major components. They are,

- FEM data objects and their representations (*Parser* and script grammar)
- Mathematical discretization (*Discretizer*)
- FEM data /program structure (*Code Generator*)

An example script is shown in Fig.2.2. Since users can express most FEM objects by abstract symbols, PDE problems can be expressed in mathematical style. The *Discretizer* and *Code Generator* treat the parsed data of the script, and finally a complete FEM code is generated.

3. Script Description - ***Parser*** **and** ***Grammar*****.** A feelfem script is composed of a number of functional blocks. This section introduces an outline of the feelfem script language. The feelfem system generates an FEM program by applying the stored FEM theory mechanically. And quadratures, interpolation functions, and variational formulations can be specified if they are expressed in an analytical form.

3.1. Geometry block. For 3-dimensional problems, feelfem adopts GiD [5] as a default pre/post processor. Users can label geometry objects such as '`point`', '`edge`', '`surface`' and '`region`', and the labelled names can be handled in the GiD graphical interface. Fig.3.1 shows how the labelled names appear in the GiD pre-processor. With GiD, users can specify boundary surfaces; in the figure, surfaces labelled 'fix' are specified. The interaction with GiD will be explained in more detail in section 7.

3.2. Element block. In the feelfem system, frequently used elements, such as linear and quadratic triangle elements (`P1`, `P2`), bilinear and 8-node serendipity rectangle elements (`Q1`, `Q2`), and tetrahedral linear element and quadratic elements (`T1`, `T2`) are pre-defined in built-in data. On the other hand, users can also define a new element by using the element statement if it has an explicit analytical expression. In Fig.2.2, `T2` element definition is shown as an example of how to define an element.

3.3. Quadrature block. Some frequently used quadratures are incorporated in the system already. Users can also define a new quadrature by adding a new `quadrature` block; an example is shown in Fig.2.2. In this example, a tetrahedral cubic order quadrature rule named `tet3` is defined. Quadratures are defined by the pairs of coordinates in the reference coordinate with their corresponding weight values.

```
geom {          /* interface for GiD mesh generator */
  mesher gid;
  problem stress3d;
  dimension 3;
  surface (fix,u_fix,v_fix,w_fix);
  surface (press);
  region  (mat);
}
```

Region name definitions GiD interface

```
/* definition of quadrature */
quadrature tet3[tetra] {  /* Cubic order */
  double p2,p4,p6;
  double w,wm;
  p2 =  1.0 / 2.0;
  p4 =  1.0 / 4.0;
  p6 =  1.0 / 6.0;
  w  = 9.0 / 20.0 / 6.0;
  wm = -4.0 /  5.0 / 6.0;
  (p4,p4,p4) : wm;
  (p2,p6,p6) : w;
  (p6,p2,p6) : w;
  (p6,p6,p2) : w;
  (p6,p6,p6) : w;
}
```

Numerical Integration Definition

```
element T2[tetra] {
  (0,0,0): (1.0-r-t-s)*(2.0*(1.0-r-t-s) - 1.0);
  (1,0,0): r *(2.0*r - 1.0);
  (0,1,0): s *(2.0*s - 1.0);
  (0,0,1): t *(2.0*t - 1.0);
  (0.5,0,0) : 4.0*r*(1.0-r-t-s);
  (0.5,0.5,0) : 4.0 * r * s ;
  (0,0.5,0)  : 4.0 * s * (1.0-r-t-s);
  (0,0,0.5)  : 4.0 * t * (1.0-r-t-s);
  (0.5,0,0.5): 4.0 * r * t;
  (0,0.5,0.5): 4.0 * s * t;
}
```

Interpolation (element) definition

```
var {
  fem u[T2],v[T2],w[T2];
  fem fx[T2],fy[T2],fz[T2];
  double c11,c12,c13;
  double c21,c22,c23;
  double c31,c32,c33;
  double          c44,c55,c66;
  ewise e[tet3],nyu[tet3];
  double p;     /* pressure */
  double c;

  ewise ex[tet3],ey[tet3],ez[tet3];
  ewise exy[tet3],eyz[tet3],ezx[tet3];
  ewise sx[tet3],sy[tet3],sz[tet3];
  ewise sxy[tet3],syz[tet3],szx[tet3];
  ewise k1[tet3],k2[tet3],k3[tet3];
  ewise ps[tet3];
  function pstres(a,b,c);
}
```

Variables Definition

```
scheme {
 ProgramModel feelfem90mpi;
```

ProgrmModel (f90-MPI model in this case)

```
fx = 0.0; fy = 0.0; fz = 0.0;
e  = 200000.0;
p  = 2000.0;
nyu = 0.3;
c  = e*(1.0-nyu)/(1.0+nyu)/(1.0-2.0*nyu);
c11 = c * 1.0; c12 = c * nyu / (1.0-nyu);
c13 = c * nyu / (1.0-nyu);
c21 = c12); c22 = c * 1.0;
c23 = c * nyu / (1.0-nyu);
c31 = c * nyu / (1.0-nyu);
c32 = c23; c33 = c * 1.0;
c44 = c * (1.0 - 2.0*nyu)/2.0 / (1.0 - nyu);
c55 = c * (1.0 - 2.0*nyu)/2.0 / (1.0 - nyu);
c66 = c * (1.0 - 2.0*nyu)/2.0 / (1.0 - nyu);
```

Stress-Strain relationship in 3D

```
solve[u,v,w; tu,tv,tw] {
  quadrature tet3;
  solver MUMPS;
```

Quadrature, solver definition

Variational expression of PDE

```
  weq: integral( (c11*dx(u)+c12*dy(v)+c13*dz(w))*dx(tu)) +
       integral(  c44*(dy(u)+dx(v))          *dy(tu)) +
       integral(  c66*(dz(u)+dx(w))          *dz(tu)) =
       integral( fx * tu) + bintegral( Sx * tu);

  weq: integral( (c21*dx(u)+c22*dy(v)+c23*dz(w))*dy(tv)) +
       integral(  c44*(dy(u)+dx(v))          *dx(tv)) +
       integral(  c55*(dz(v)+dy(w))          *dz(tv)) =
       integral( fy * tv) + bintegral( Sy * tv);

  weq: integral( (c31*dx(u)+c32*dy(v)+c33*dz(w))*dz(tw)) +
       integral(  c55*(dz(v)+dy(w))          *dy(tw)) +
       integral(  c66*(dz(u)+dx(w))          *dx(tw)) =
       integral( fz * tw) + bintegral( Sz * tw);

  dbc: u = 0, on fix,u_fix,uv_fix,wu_fix;
  dbc: v = 0, on fix,v_fix,vw_fix,uv_fix;
  dbc: w = 0, on fix,w_fix,wu_fix,vw_fix;
```

Dirichlet, Neumann conditions

```
  nbc: Sx = nx*p,Sy = ny*p, Sz = nz* p, on press;
 }
 ex = dx(u);      ey = dy(v);      ez = dz(w);
 exy = dy(u)+dx(v); eyz = dz(v)+dy(w); ezx = dx(w)+dz(u);
 sx  = c11*ex + c12 * ey + c13 * ez;
 sy  = c21*ex + c22 * ey + c23 * ez;
 sz  = c31*ex + c32 * ey + c33 * ez;
 sxy = c44*exy; syz = c55*eyz;szx = c66*ezx;

 /* principal stress */
 k1  = sx+sy+sz;
 k2  = sx*sy+sy*sz+sz*sx - sxy*sxy - syz*syz-szx*szx;
 k3  = sx*sy*sz+2*sxy*syz*szx-sx*syz*syz-sy*szx*szx-sz*sxy*sxy;
```

Calculation of principal stress

```
 ps  = pstres(k1,k2,k3);
 output[ps](label="primary stress");
 output[u,v,w](label="displacement");
}
```

Interface to postprocessor (GiD)

FIG. 2.2. *The feelfem script sample(3D linear structural analysis)*

3.4. Variable block. In addition to Fortran compatible integer and double variables, a user can define fem, ewise and material variables. For example, a definition "`fem u[P1]`" indicates that the variable u is an `fem` variable, and is based on the `P1` basis function. Once a user defines a new element, one can use that new element merely by specifying its name. The fem variables are assumed to have some continuity between elements and are used to approximate unknown functions, while ewise variables are defined within an individual element. There are three types of ewise variables. The first one is a normal one that has one value at each element, and is specified as "`ewise rho;`". The second one is specified with an interpolation function such as "`ewise e[P1];`". This type of ewise variable is interpolated by a specified basis function, but no continuity between elements is assumed.

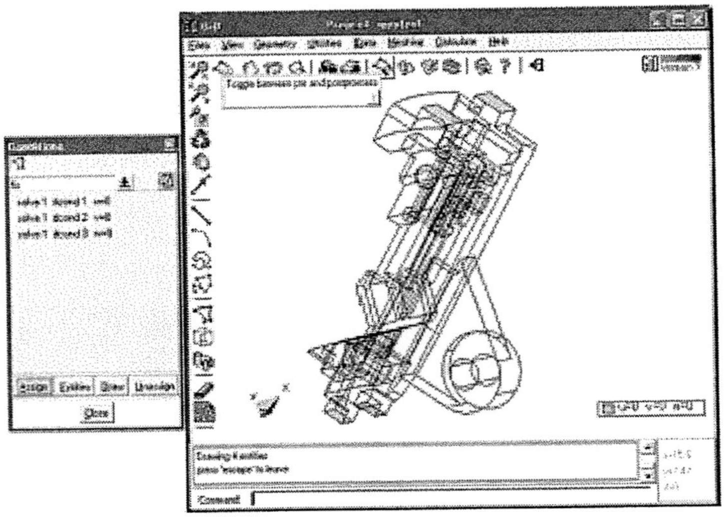

FIG. 3.1. *GiD geometry interface to specify boundary surfaces for specific conditions. In this example, surface labelled 'fix' are specified.*

The third ewise variable is defined at each quadrature point, and specified as, e.g., "`ewise ux[tet3];`". Ewise variables of this type are used as differential values of fem variables. In Fig.3.1, `ex`, `ey`, `ez`, `exy`, `eyz`, and `ezx` are used to calculate differential values and principal stress at each quadrature point named by `tet3`.

3.5. Scheme block. For numerical scheme description, several statements are prepared such as `goto`, *label*, and `if`. In a scheme block, a numerical scheme is realized by using one or more solve statements that solve each variational problem. Integration calculation operators are also supported so that users can calculate various norms and error estimators. Output statements are used to connect post-processors, and there is a tight coupling functionality with the GiD post processor. One important statement is `ProgramModel` statement with solver specification in a solve block to select which computer language, which FEM data model, what kind of data structure of parallel matrix array, and which parallel solver to use are specified. This will be discussed in the next section.

3.6. Solve block. A solve block is a sub block where users specify a PDE problem in a variational formulation. In the block, an '`integral`' operator for regional integration and a '`bintegral`' operator for boundary integration can be used. (In the feelfem system, each operator can have its own quadrature method.) For specifying Dirichlet and Neumann boundary conditions, please refer to Fig.2.2. Solvers, quadratures and transformation function can be specified by `solver`, `quadrature`, and `parametric` statements respectively. A transformation function is used for coordinate transformation between reference and real elements. In simultaneous systems, a user can use different element types for every unknown function, so mixed methods can also be handled.

4. Generator of Mathematical Components - Discretizer. The Discretizer generates mathematical program components, such as a calculation program of numerical integration. In the FEM, integration plays the most important role. The greater part of the Discretizer is occupied by the processing of the code generation for regional and boundary integration.

In the feelfem system, we use the GiNaC GNU C++ library [6] for formula manipulation. GiNaC enables differentiation and interpretation of formulas within C++. Since GiNaC is quite flexible, we can easily use it to convert the input integrand formula to the formulas necessary for its numerical integration. Readers who are interested in applying formula manipulation to the FEM should refer to [7].

5. Pseudo-code Representation of FEM Algorithm - Code Generator. The most significant improvement in the current feelfem system over the former version is that it adopts object-oriented techniques for code generation. The main idea is using implementation-oriented pseudo-codes to represent the numerical algorithms. These pseudo-codes are classified into 4 layers, and the use of layered pseudo-code representation makes it possible to add new algorithms, new parallel programming paradigms, and new parallel solvers very easily.

5.1. Pseudo-code representations of algorithms. Generally speaking, a numerical algorithm does not depend on any individual implementation. For example, the assembling element matrices to the global matrix in the FEM can be written as,

Begin *Subroutine*;
  Allocate *Global Matrix;*
  Repeat *for i* = 1, *number of elements;*
    Calculate *element stiffness matrix and element load;*
    Assemble *the global matrix;*
  End *repeat;*
  Apply *Neumann conditions;*
  Apply *Dirichlet conditions;*
  Solve *the linear equation;*
End *Subroutine*;

This succession of processes does not vary for any FEM procedures when the problem is a linear boundary value problem. Thus, this is a basis of the code generator for storing algorithms; however, we divide these abstract pseudo-codes into smaller sections according to their implementation factors.

5.2. Implementation oriented layered pseudo-code. The implementation of the FEM involves a hierarchical layer structure. (Fig.5.1)

Every implementation of a specific level depends on the lower layers. And when the lower layers are the same, the upper layers can be varied easily and the lower layers may be implemented identically. For example, if two linear solvers use the same matrix structure, the implementation of the lower 3 layers should be the same for both solvers. We use this characteristic structure of the FEM implementation hierarchy to classify the implementation-oriented pseudo-codes.

Fig.5.2 is an example of implementation-oriented pseudo code representation of the matrix assembly FEM algorithm mentioned in section 5.1. This is an actual feelfem code written in C++. In feelfem, all implementation-oriented pseudo-codes are realized as virtual (code generator) functions, and every FEM algorithm unit is represented by a succession of such virtual functions. The instances of these virtual functions are implemented in each layer class (Fig.5.3).

5.3. Class of code generator virtual functions. In the feelfem system, as mentioned above, implementation-oriented pseudo-codes are realized as virtual functions in C++, and the instances of these virtual functions are implemented in an individual class. These classes have a tree-structure inheritance structure (Fig.6.1). For example, the gray

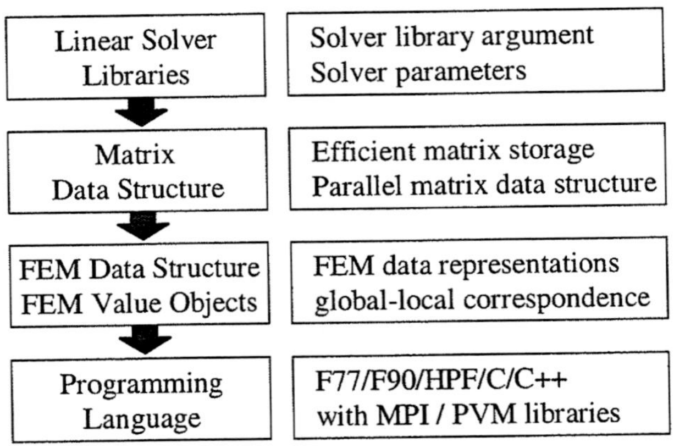

FIG. 5.1. *Hierarchical structure of the FEM implementation*

colored pseudo-codes in Fig.5.3 are related to the matrix level, so these inheritances are implemented in one matrix-level class.

6. Discussion.

6.1. Advantages of the object oriented code generator. There are two advantages to the features described in section 5. The first is that it is very easy to add new numerical algorithms to the feelfem system. If this is done and a similar algorithm has already been implemented as is usually the case, the existing virtual code generator functions can be reused or newly made by copying existing generator programs with only small modifications. Fig.6.2 demonstrates this advantage. The code generator in the figure is an FEM assemble matrix algorithm for *nonlinear* problems. Compared with the *linear* assembling shown in Fig.5.2, only the three pseudo-codes enclosed within solid lines need to be added for expanding the code generator to deal with nonlinear assembling.

The second advantage is the easy expansion of the code generator for newly developed program paradigms, parallel matrix data structures, and parallel solvers. For example, in Fig.6.1, if the newly developed parallel linear solver uses the same distributed CRS matrix

```
void SolveScheme::
NormalLinearProblem(Solve *solvePtr)
{
        RoutineInitialize               ( solvePtr );
        RoutineHeader                   ( solvePtr );
   SolveParameters                      ( solvePtr );
        VariableDefinitions             ( solvePtr );
   SolveInitializer                     ( solvePtr );
   SolveDegreeOfFreedom                 ( solvePtr );
   SolveBoundaryDataPrepare             ( solvePtr );
   SolveMatrixAllocate                  ( solvePtr );
   SolveCallAssembleRoutine             ( solvePtr );
   SolveNeumanConditions                ( solvePtr );
   SolveDirichletConditions             ( solvePtr );
   SolveCallSolverRoutine               ( solvePtr );
   SolvePostProcess                     ( solvePtr );
   SolveTerminateSequence               ( solvePtr );
        RoutineTerminate                ( solvePtr );
   return ;
}
```

FIG. 5.2. *An example of an implementation-oriented pseudo-code from actual feelfem code*

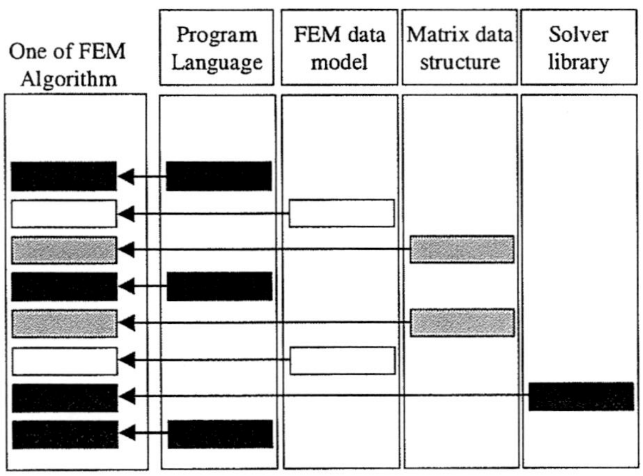

FIG. 5.3. *Layered implementation-oriented pseudo-code*

data structure, all we need to do is add a branch class to the Fortran90 - feelfem90DRAMA - Distributed CRS class inheritance tree, thanks to the layer structure of the code generator function classes. Currently, several parallel solvers including, PILUTS[8], parallel AMG[9], and MUMPS[10] are supported.

6.2. Examples. Let us consider actual examples of the feelfem system's advantages. From the system's input file shown in Fig.2.2 (127 lines), feelfem generates Fortran 90 with MPI program with 12990 lines for using the MUMPS solver. When using a simple skyline solver for one processor is specified, the generated Fortran 90 program has 12574 lines. If the linear tetrahedral elements are used, merely by changing "`fem u[T2],v[T2],w[T2];`" to "`fem u[T1],v[T1],w[T1];`", the generated code using the linear element for the MUMPS

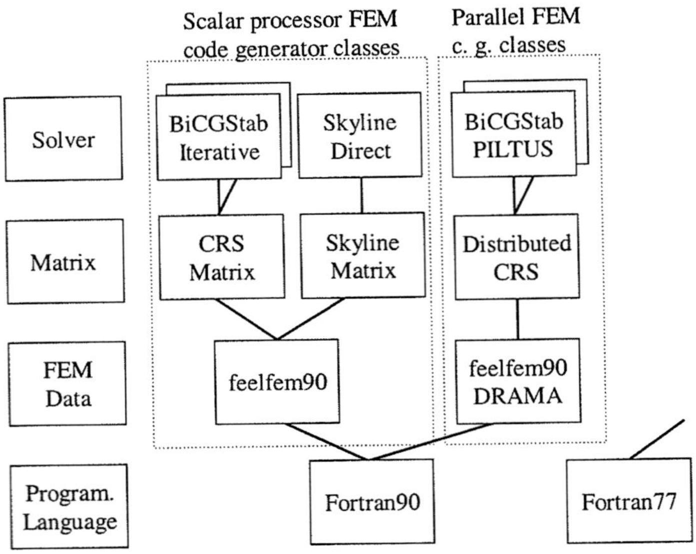

FIG. 6.1. *Inheritance tree of code generator function classes*

solver has 9731 lines and for the simple skyline solver has 9315 lines. Since the difference in both cases is 416 lines, it means the difference comes from only from mathematical program components.

The main part of the code generator for the MUMPS solver has 11272 lines in C++ program, while that for the skyline solver has 11082 lines. Since both code generators comprise quite a large number of lines but have many almost identical portions, we can make a code generator that needs MPI handling for MUMPS in just a few days, merely by copying the code generator for scalar processing with small modifications. The code generator functions are implemented in different classes, so there is no mutual interaction. That enables the code generator to be expanded without interfering with the existing code generator functions. This makes maintenance of the code generator very easy.

7. GiD Interface. GiD is a pre/post- processor developed at CIMNE in Barcelona, Spain. Since GiD is designed for easy use in various outer solvers, users only have to prepare several problem interface files to achieve strong interaction between their analysis programs and GiD. (Fig.7.1)

In feelfem, the interface files .prb, .mat, .cnd and .bas are automatically generated when users specify GiD as a pre/post processor in the feelfem script. In the feelfem environment, the .prb file is used to specify the initial values, and the .mat file is used to specify the material regions. Both specifications use the GiD GUI. The .cnd file is used to specify the boundary conditions, and users can also specify the boundary surfaces (3D case) or edges (2D case) by using the GiD GUI for boundary conditions. (Fig.3.1)

The codes generated by the feelfem system make output files for GiD for post processing. Other interface utilities, such as domain partition pictures, are also available. (Fig.7.2)

8. Conclusion. The feelfem system's use of object-oriented technology and its pseudo-code scheme representation mechanism give it great flexibility, enabling it to store newly developed numerical software easily. It is especially suitable for generating complicated parallel software that, once stored, can be easily reused. With its capability of handling

```
void SolveScheme::
NormalNonlinearProblem(Solve* solvePtr)
{
        RoutineInitialize          (solvePtr);
        RoutineHeader              (solvePtr);
    SolveParameters                (solvePtr);
        VariableDefinitions        (solvePtr);
    SolveInitializer               (solvePtr);
    SolveDegreeOfFreedom           (solvePtr);
    SolveBoundaryDataPrepare       (solvePtr);
    SolveMatrixAllocate            (solvePtr);
    SolveNonlinearInitialize       (solvePtr);
    SolveDirichletConditions       (solvePtr);
    SolveCallAssembleRoutine       (solvePtr);
    SolveNeumannConditions         (solvePtr);
    SolveDirichletConditions       (solvePtr);
    SolveCallSolverRoutine         (solvePtr);
    SolveNonlinearPostProcess      (solvePtr);
    SolveTerminateSequence         (solvePtr);
        RoutineTerminate           (solvePtr);
    return ;
}
```

FIG. 6.2. *Modification of a code generator from linear to nonlinear*

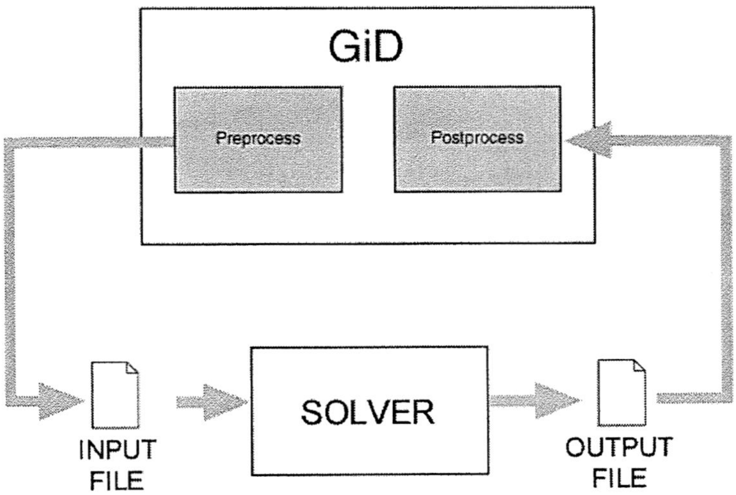

FIG. 7.1. *GiD interface model with an outer solver*

various FEM objects (e.g., quadratures, variational formulations, and numerical schemes), feelfem is well equipped to handle 'new' problems. In the feelfem system, mathematical algorithms expressed in feelfem script language, its parallel programming paradigms, and any combination of the two can be generated. With its stored knowledge database, the feelfem system has the potential to serve as a good prototyping tool for large scale scientific computing.

Currently, feelfem has strong interaction with the personal pre/post processor GiD, and thus provides users with an integrated environment for prototyping FEM analysis. The

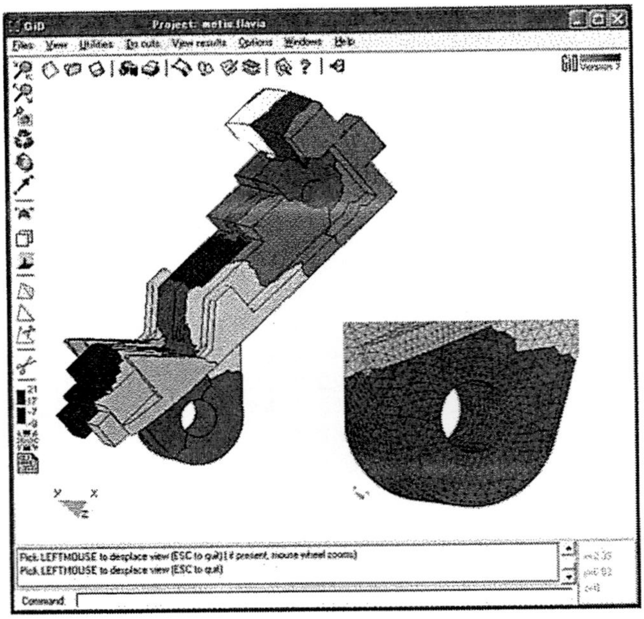

FIG. 7.2. *GiD is used to show domain partitioning*

feelfem system will be one of the GiD+ modules; readers are invited to use feelfem freely (to some extent) via http://gid.cimne.com.

REFERENCES

[1] "Solving Elliptic Problems Using ELLPACK", John R. Rice and Ronald F. Boisvert, Springer Verlag, 1984.

[2] "FEEL - A Tool for Finite Element Nalysis", H. Fujio and K. Hayami, Proc. Numer. Anal. Symp. Structural Anal.,17.pp.489-497,1993 (in Japanese)

[3] Diffpack http://www.nobjects.com/prodserv/diffpack/

[4] Deal II http://gaia.iwr.uni-heidelberg.de/ deal/

[5] GiD The personal pre/post processor http://gid.cimne.com

[6] GiNaC http://www.ginac.de

[7] "The Finite Element Method Using MATLAB", Second Edition, Young W. Kwon, Hyochoong Bang,2000

[8] Achim Basermann ,'Parallel Block ILUT Preconditioning for Sparse Eigenproblems and Sparse Linear Systems', Numerical Linear Algebra with Applications, 7:635-648, 2000

[9] AMG solver http://www.gmd.de/SCAI/Welcome.html

[10] MUMPS http://www.enseeiht.fr/lima/apo/MUMPS/

In: Applied Parallel and Distributed Computing ISBN 1-59454-174-4
Editors: Yi Pan and Laurence T. Yang , pp. 143-157

NUMERICAL CALCULATIONS OF ELECTROMAGNETIC PROBLEMS ON INFINIBAND–CLUSTERS

CARSTEN TRINITIS* AND ANDREAS BLASZCZYK†

Abstract. Accurate electromagnetic field simulation is a crucial step in the design and development in modern high–voltage systems. It enables the study of various design parameters without expensive experiments and allows the optimization of these systems in terms of space, cost, and energy efficiency. Such simulations, however, have high computational demands requiring efficient parallelization in order to become feasible in the standard design process.

Traditionally, massively parallel systems have been used for this kind of application, which are generally very expensive. During the last few years, clusters built from commodity PCs have emerged as an alternative, especially when coupled with high performance interconnection fabrics. Infiniband, a relatively new and promising technology is an ideal candidate for such an interconnection fabric.

This work presents first experiences with electromagnetic field simulations on a cluster with Infiniband interconnect. A real world example from the area of power transformer design, which has served as benchmark problem in previous publications, has been simulated on the Infiniband cluster. First measurements that have been carried out on our prototype Infiniband cluster are presented.

The research has been carried out in close cooperation between the Technische Universität München, which contributed the clustering technology, and ABB Corporate Research Switzerland, which contributed a state-of-the-art simulation code called POLOPT, which has been ported to the Infiniband cluster installed at TU Munich.

Key words. Electric field simulation, Cluster computing, Infiniband, Parallel computing, Interconnect technologies

1. Motivation. One of the most important stages in the development process of high voltage apparatus is the simulation of the electrostatic field distribution in order to detect critical areas that might have to be changed. When dealing with the design of electrical transformers, the precise, fast, and efficient calculation of eddy-current problems caused by electromagnetic effects is of essential importance in order to determine possible losses. An appropriate method for simulating both electrostatic and electromagnetic problems is the Boundary-Element method (BEM) [2]. Eddy currents are often generated in transformers and lead to power losses. For both electrostatic and electromagnetic problems, dedicated equation system solvers have been integrated into the framework of the boundary element field simulation code POLOPT [1]. POLOPT, which was originally developed at the University of Sarajevo and has been under further development at ABB corporate research centers Heidelberg/Germany and Baden/Switzerland [1] since the early 1990s, runs on a workstation and/or PC cluster architecture. For the electrostatic solver, reasonable results can be achieved with a Master-Slave approach using Fast Ethernet [3], [26], [4], [8], [27]. Due to the fact that the algorithm for solving electromagnetic problems is rather communication intensive, it is important to deploy a network with both high bandwidth and low latency. A networking technology that suits these requirements very well is Infiniband [13]. The performance of the Infiniband network is being compared to that of Ethernet, which is still being used as the standard interconnection technology for clusters. In future work, it is also intended to do such comparisons with other high-speed interconnects such as Gigabit Ethernet [11], SCI [15], or Myrinet [5]. However, with the current cluster installed at Technische Universität München, it is already possible to perform realistic eddy current calculations in a shorter amount of time. It has to be emphasized, however, that this paper is only intended to give first results obtained on the prototype Infiniband cluster installed at TU Munich

* Lehrstuhl für Rechnertechnik und Rechnerorganisation, LRR–TUM, Institut für Informatik, Technische Universität München, {trinitic}@cs.tum.edu

† ABB Corporate Research Center, Baden, Switzerland, Andreas.Blaszczyk@ch.abb.com

[1] http://www.abb.com/

[14]. Further research, together with an extension of our cluster, will give more detailed results in the near future.

The remainder of this paper is organized as follows. Section 2 provides some background about electromagnetic and electrostatic field problems, followed by a description of the corresponding simulation processes in Section 3. The parallelization of the codes are then discussed in Section 4. Section 5 introduces the compute platform used for this paper (i.e. PC clusters with Infiniband interconnect), and describes how it is used. The setup for the experiments is described in Section 6 followed by an outline of the work environment in Section 7. This setup is then used for first experiments testing the approach; these are presented in Section 8. The paper is then rounded up by a brief outlook and some concluding remarks in Section 9.

2. Background. The numerical analysis of three dimensional electrostatic and electromagnetic field problems has become an essential important phase of the design process of high voltage apparatus. One numerical method that is very often used for such problems is the Boundary Element Method [2] which is a very efficient method that allows solving complex three dimensional models with satisfactory accuracy. In contrast to two dimensional analysis the calculation of realistic three dimensional models is very CPU intensive.

2.1. Electrostatic problems. From a mathematical point of view, a field calculation problem can be stated as follows: The goal is to calculate the values of the potential

$$\Phi(x, y, z)$$

and the electric field strength

$$\vec{E}(x, y, z) = -\nabla\Phi \tag{2.1}$$

In order to achieve this one has to solve Laplace's differential equation

$$\Delta\Phi = 0 \tag{2.2}$$

For electrostatic fields this differential equation can be solved by

$$\Phi(\vec{r}_p) = \frac{1}{4\pi\epsilon}\int\int\int \frac{\rho(\vec{r}_q)}{|\vec{r}_p - \vec{r}_q|} dV \tag{2.3}$$

with $\vec{r}_p$ being the radius vector in the point of interest and $\vec{r}_q$ being the radius vector in the integration point. In reality electric fields are caused by applying voltage to electrode systems. The charge that causes the electric field is distributed over the electrode surfaces as an area charge with density ρ_A. For practical field problems the integration in (2.3) cannot be done analytically. The basic principle of all charge simulation methods is to approximate this real charge density distribution by simulation charges with charge densities that can easily be formulated. This approach makes it possible to calculate the simulation charges' potential functions analytically or numerically. Admissible simulation charges are point-, line-, area- or space charges. The potential that is generated by such a system of simulation charges can be calculated from the sum of each charge type's contribution:

$$\begin{aligned} \Phi(\vec{r}_p) &= \frac{1}{4\pi\epsilon}\Big[\sum_{i=1}^{n_p} \frac{Q_i}{|\vec{r}_p - \vec{r}_q|} + \sum_{i=1}^{n_l} \int \frac{\rho_{L_i}(\vec{r}_q)}{|\vec{r}_p - \vec{r}_q|} dL \\ &+ \sum_{i=1}^{n_a} \int\int \frac{\rho_{A_i}(\vec{r}_q)}{|\vec{r}_p - \vec{r}_q|} dA + \sum_{i=1}^{n_v} \int\int\int \frac{\rho_{V_i}(\vec{r}_q)}{|\vec{r}_p - \vec{r}_q|} dV \Big] \end{aligned} \tag{2.4}$$

with n_p being the number of point charges, n_l being the number of line charges, n_a being the number of area charges and n_v being the number of space charges, respectively. Each simulation source is defined by its geometry and charge density which makes it possible to calculate the integrals in (2.4). For a total of n_g simulation charges we get

$$\Phi(\vec{r}_p) = \sum_{i=1}^{n_g} p_i \cdot \rho_i \tag{2.5}$$

with p_i being the potential coefficients (which are independent on the geometry) and ρ_i being the charge density coefficients. Provided that the charge density coefficients/charge values are known we can calculate the potential in arbitrary points. If we want to calculate the charge values in the contour points with known boundary conditions (potential) we have to set up an equation of the form (2.5) for each contour point. Thus we obtain a linear equation system of the form

$$\mathbf{P} \cdot \mathbf{q} = \mathbf{\Phi_{KP}} \tag{2.6}$$

with $\mathbf{P}$ being the potential coefficient matrix, $\mathbf{q}$ being the vector of unknown charges and $\mathbf{\Phi}$ being the vector of potentials in the contour points. When solving the equation system (2.6) for the unknown vector $\mathbf{q}$ one can easily obtain the potential in arbitrary points using (2.5) and the electric field strength by differentiation of (2.5).

In summary, that the process of numerical field calculation is composed of three stages:

- Step 1: calculation of the coefficient matrix $\mathbf{P}$
- Step 2: solution of the linear equation system (2.6)
- Step 3: calculation of field and potential at points of interest

Such formulations of Laplace's equation are well suited for parallel computations [9]. Due to two important features a simple but efficient parallelization strategy can be applied:

1. All elements of the coefficient matrix $\mathbf{P}$ as well as the field values in arbitrary points can be calculated independently from each other
2. The solution of the linear equation system (2.6) can be found by means of iterative methods like the Generalized Minimal Residuals Method [22].

2.2. Electromagnetic problems. Eddy currents are often generated in transformers and cause power losses and heat problems. Faraday's Law implies that a changing flux produces an induced electric field even in empty space. If a metal plate is inserted into this empty space the induced electric field produces electric currents in the metal. These induced currents are called eddy currents (see figure 2.1). If the induced currents are created by a changing magnetic field then the Eddy currents will be perpendicular to the magnetic field. These induced electric fields are very different from electrostatic electric fields of point charges. First, they do not begin and end on charges but circle around themselves in loops. Secondly, the induced electric field is non-conservative, i.e. the work done by generated electric field can not be recovered except as heat. By constructing the transformer core of alternating layers of conducting and nonconducting materials, the size of the induced loops is reduced which in turn reduces the energy loss (see figures 2.2 and 2.3). The buzz that can often be heard near a transformer substation is due to alternating layers vibrating against each other.

From a mathematical point of view, an eddy current problem can be described as follows:

The conventional approach to the calculation of eddy currents is based on the formulation of the boundary value problem with respect to a vector magnetic potential. This is justified for two-dimensional problems when the vector magnetic potential has only one component. In three dimensions, however, the potential is a three dimensional vector like the field itself. Therefore one should use Maxwell's equations directly, with respect to field

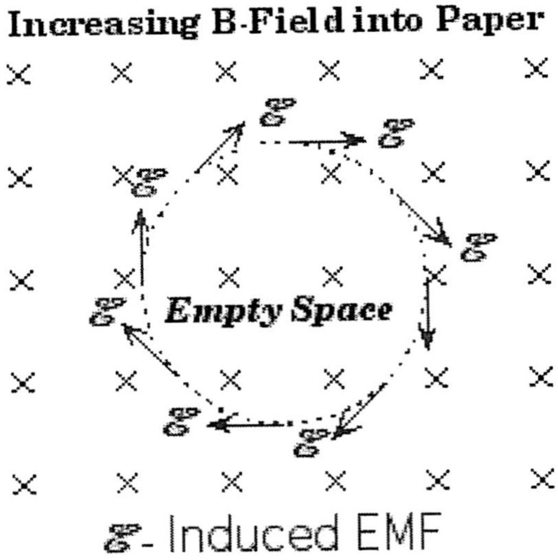

FIG. 2.1. *Eddy Current*

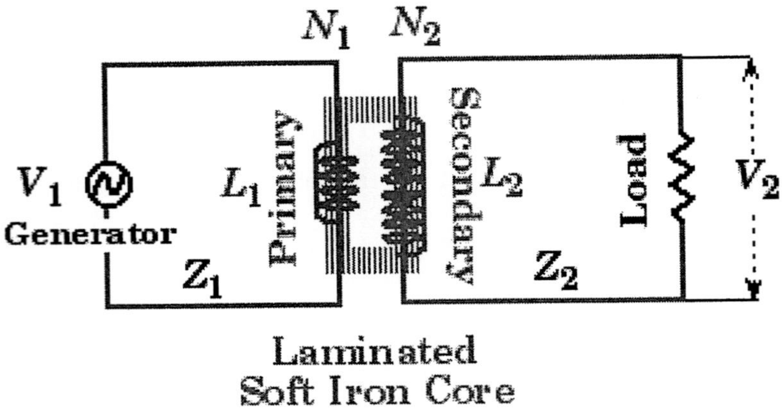

FIG. 2.2. *Transformer*

vectors. As can be seen in [10], this eventually yields a system of second kind boundary integral equations on a conductor surface by using the so called $\vec{H} - \phi$ formulation [17]. When applying the Boundary Element Method (BEM) for these equations, a linear equation system of the form

$$\left[\begin{array}{cc} A_1 & B_1 \\ \frac{\mu}{\mu_0} B_2 & A_2 \end{array} \right] \left(\begin{array}{c} j \\ \sigma \end{array} \right) = \left(\begin{array}{c} b_1 \\ b_2 \end{array} \right) \tag{2.7}$$

is obtained [10]. However, this equation system is still ill-conditioned for large $\frac{\mu}{\mu_0}$ so that it can not be solved with the General Minimal Residual Method (GMRES) [22], which is the solver being used in POLOPT. Therefore, a preconditioner is applied in [10] so that after preconditioning the equation system can be solved with GMRES. In order to reduce computation times, it is necessary to parallelize the solver. First, a coefficient matrix is generated by POLOPT which can be done in parallel since the generation of a matrix line

FIG. 2.3. *Transformer Core*

is independent from any other line. Then the parallel preconditioner and solver described in [10] are applied.

Typical sizes for the equation systems are in the range of 3-4-5 orders of magnitude with densely populated coefficient matrices.

2.3. A short note on GMRES. Many engineers are familiar with the Conjugate Gradient Method [12], which has been used successfully for many years to solve the large, sparse, positive definate (SPD) systems that result from certain finite element formulations. However, there are similar iterative techniques to solve the full, asymmetric, indefinate matrix equations one obtains from boundary integral formulations [16].

GMRES is designed for exactly such a purpose. Indeed, it is related to conjugate gradients insofar as both methods try to construct an orthogonal basis from a Krylov space consisting of the vectors $\{\mathbf{r}_0, \mathbf{A}\mathbf{r}_0, \mathbf{A}^2\mathbf{r}_0, ..., \mathbf{A}^{N-1}\mathbf{r}_0\}$ [28] where $\mathbf{A}$ is the N by N coefficient matrix in:

$$Ax = b \tag{2.8}$$

This set of vectors is typically orthonormalized into a basis $\mathbf{V}_k = span\{\mathbf{v}_0, \mathbf{v}_1, ..., \mathbf{v}_{k-1}\}$ by a Gramm-Schmidt process [24], where the vector $\mathbf{p}_k = \mathbf{v}_k \cdot |\mathbf{p}_k|$ is produced from

$$\mathbf{p}_k = \mathbf{A}\mathbf{v}_{k-1} - \sum_{j=0}^{k-1}(\mathbf{A}\mathbf{v}_i \cdot \mathbf{v}_j)\mathbf{v}_j \tag{2.9}$$

If $\mathbf{A}$ is (SPD), then the conjugate gradient method can be implemented as a three point recurrence: back orthogonalization to the entire space is limited to a few preceeding vectors. This is not the case for boundary element matrices, and we are obliged to orthogonalize new members of the subspace to all preceeding entries. Towards this end it is sometimes convenient to store the scalars indicated by $(\mathbf{A}\mathbf{v}_i \cdot \mathbf{v}_j)$ in $\mathbf{H}$, which can be straightforwardly shown to be an upper Hessenberg matrix. One better appreciates the advantage of this notation by writing the original system as

$$\mathbf{A}\mathbf{z} - \mathbf{r}_0 = 0 \tag{2.10}$$

with $\mathbf{z} = \mathbf{x}_g - \mathbf{x}_0$, $\mathbf{r}_0 = \mathbf{b} - \mathbf{A}\mathbf{x}_0$, where $\mathbf{x}_g$ is the current guess and $\mathbf{x}_0$ is the first one. Arnoldi's [6] original idea was to build successively better approximations by insisting that $(\mathbf{A}\mathbf{z}-\mathbf{r}_0)$ be orthogonal to $\mathbf{V}_k$ with k presumably much smaller than N. Vector $\mathbf{z}$ is assumed to be a member of the finite dimensional subspace spanned by $\mathbf{V}_k$, that is $\mathbf{z} = \sum_{i=0}^{k-1} \mathbf{v}_i y_i$. Consequently:

$$\begin{aligned} 0 &= (\mathbf{A}\mathbf{z} - \mathbf{r}_0)^T \mathbf{V} \\ &= (\mathbf{A}\mathbf{V}\mathbf{y})^T \mathbf{V} - \mathbf{r}_0{}^T \mathbf{V} \\ &= (\mathbf{V}^T \mathbf{A}\mathbf{V})\mathbf{y} - \mathbf{V}^T \mathbf{r}_0 \end{aligned}$$

The problem is now reduced to finding vector $\mathbf{y}$. Notice that $\mathbf{V}^T\mathbf{A}\mathbf{V}$ is the Hessenberg matrix we obtain from the Gramm-Schmidt process. The terms of the subdiagonal of $\mathbf{H}$ are $|\mathbf{p}|$'s.

The innovation of Saad and Schultz [22] was to augment $\mathbf{H}$ by $|\mathbf{p}_{\mathbf{k+1}}|$, the orthogonal vector formed in the (k^{th}) iteration. Then they solve the overspecified system by QR decomposition, which is effectively accomplished by a series of Given's rotations. This is GMRES. The algorithm is efficient because the residual can be measured *in situo* without actually finding $\mathbf{z}$ $\mathbf{x_g}$ at each step; moreover, it is more stable than the Arnoldi algorithm [25].

2.4. A few words about the boundary element method. In the Boundary Element Method integral equations are reduced to a system of algebraic equations by discretizing the model's surfaces with well selected, small curvilinear patches (boundary elements) on the interfaces between media with different material characteristics. The characteristics of the media are taken as constants for each relevant region in a model. Over a boundary element, the field is expressed as an analytical interpolation function between the field values at the nodes (element vertices).

The basis for establishing a system of integral equations is the introduction of equivalent electric surface charge densities, which are distributed:

- over boundary surfaces between dielectrics, taking into account the bound surface charge.
- over conductor-dielectric boundary surfaces, where the conducting body is at a known potential.
- over conductor-dielectric boundary surfaces, where the total quantity of electric charge on the conductor is known and may be zero.

The distribution of these equivalent surface charges over the model's boundary surfaces is fixed by the following conditions:

- boundary conditions on the electric field $\mathbf{E}$ and the electric displacement $\mathbf{D}$ between two dielectrics.

- prescribed values for the potential function on the conducting surfaces at fixed potentials.
- prescribed values for the net surface charges on the conductors at unknown potentials ("floating potential").

A proper numerical solution of these problems calls for an adequate approximation os both the geometry and the charge distribution. For the geometry approximation **POLOPT** uses triangular and quadrilateral curvilinear boundary elements, allowing suitable discretization of curved boundaries with a relatively small number of elements. The surface charges are approximated by a piece-wise linear function. The electric field in the region of interest can be considered as the result of the presence of the equivalent surface charges. These charges are the "sources" of the electric field (see chap. 3) [1].

3. Simulation Process. Traditionally, the development of high-voltage apparatus has been carried out by the electrical engineer who relied on his or her experience in designing the various components. Possible problems caused by too high electric field strengths leading to flashovers or eddy currents leading to power losses had to be detected in costly practical experiments. With the development of three dimensional electrostatic and electromagnetic field simulation software, it is possible to detect possible design flaws before actually building a prototype of the high-voltage apparatus.

3.1. Simulation stages. As a first stage, the mechanical design is specified using a commercial CAD-software like e.g. Pro/Engineer [21], SDRC I-DEAS [23] or CADfix [7] (see figure 3.1). This can also be carried out by staff other than those responsible for the actual

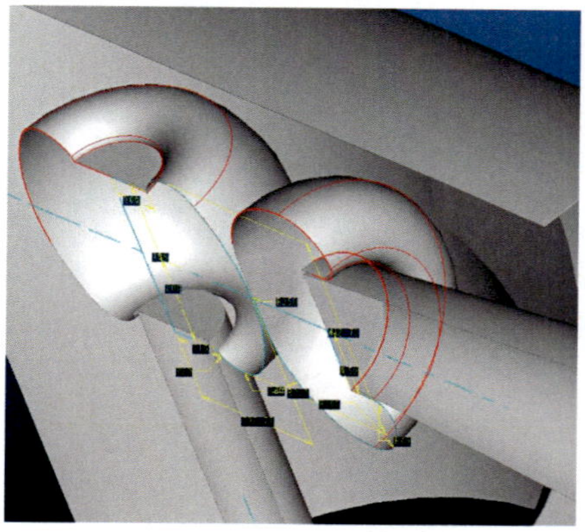

FIG. 3.1. *CAD Model as obtained from the Construction Department*

field simulation. In the second stage, the loads (i.e. potentials) and material properties are applied to the model, which is then being discretized (meshed) for numerical calculation (see figure 3.2). The discretized model with all loads and material properties is converted into a format suitable for the field calculation software, which, after running the numerical simulation, generates a result file that is converted into a format suitable for visualization in the CAD program (see figure 3.3). From these visualized results, the engineer can detect and eliminate possible design flaws in the components.

With respect to the practical elecrtical engineering problems that need to be solved at ABB, POLOPT with its electrostatic and electromagnetic solvers based on the Boundary Element Method (BEM) [2] has turned out to be much more effective than commercially available packages.

POLOPT's key advantage over the simulation packages mentioned above is its ability to run in parallel. Since both solvers are now parallelized based on the de facto Standard

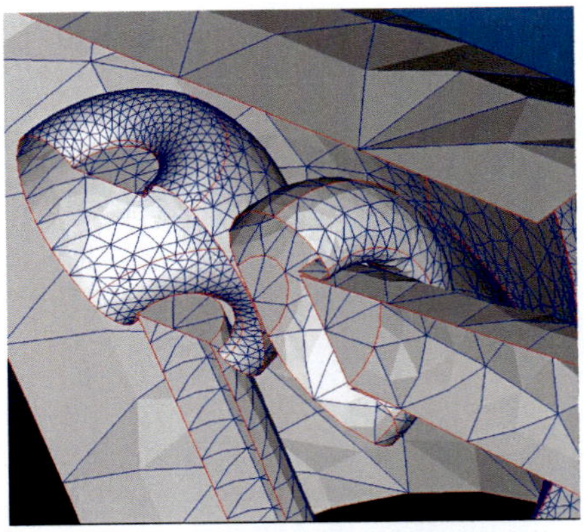

FIG. 3.2. *CAD Model meshed and ready for Numerical Simulation*

FIG. 3.3. *Visualization of Simulation Results*

MPI [18], the parallel version runs on virtually any parallel architecture, no matter if this is a cluster of PCs or a high performance mainframe computer.

4. Parallel Implementation of Polopt. For practical electrostatic and electromagnetic field problems as they are typically calculated at ABB Corporate Research, the size of the equation system that needs to be solved can be up to several thousand unknowns (orders of magnitude of $10^3 - 10^4$). Since this is very computation intensive, especially for electromagnetic problems, parallel solvers for both electrostatic and electromagnetic problems have been developed.

The parallel GMRES solver for electrostatic problems is described in detail in [3] and [4]. As described in section 3, the field calculation process consists of the following stages:

1. Initialization,
2. generation of the coefficient matrix,
3. solution of the linear equation system obtained form the previous step, and
4. potential and field calculation in points of interest.

By applying an iterative GMRES solver [22], steps 2-4 can be carried oput in parallel by using parallel matrix-vector multiplication routines from netlib [19].

5. InfiniBand Network Architecture. The description above has shown that both applications require significant computational power and main memory. In addition, especially the code of the electromagnetic solver also relies on a high–performance interconnection fabric in order to achieve reasonable performance. These requirements were tradi-

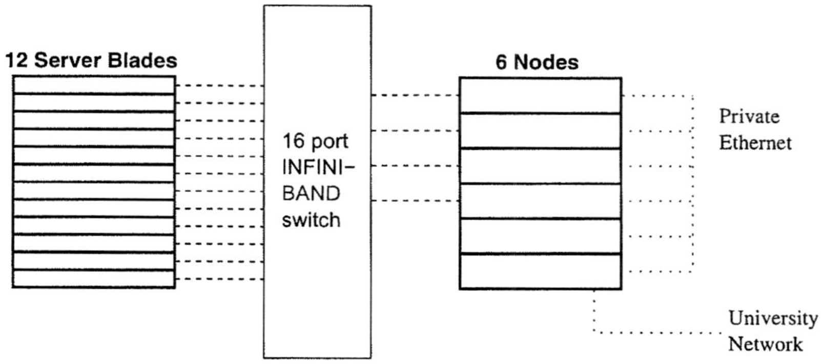

FIG. 6.1. *The InfiniBand cluster setup at LLR–TUM in a lab environment.*

	Server Blades	Nodes
Number of nodes	12	6
Processor	Intel Xeon DP 2.2 GHz	Intel Xeon DP 2.4 GHz
Number of Processors per node	1	2
L1 data cache size (line size)	8 Kbyte (32 bytes)	8 Kbyte (32 bytes)
L2 data cache size (line size)	512 Kbyte (32 bytes)	512 Kbyte (32 bytes)
Processor system bus	64 bit, 400 MHz data rate	64 bit, 400 MHz data rate
Main memory	2048 Mbyte	4096 Mbyte
Memory bus	128 bit, 200 MHz data rate	128 bit, 200 MHz data rate
Chipset	Serverworks Grand Champion LE	Intel E7500
Disk subsystem	diskless (booting from) Compact Flash card	IDE
Network	4X INFINIBAND	4X INFINIBAND & Fast Ethernet
Operating system	Linux Redhat 7.3	Linux Redhat 7.3
MPI software	MPICH	MPICH

TABLE 6.1
Configuration data of both types of nodes

tionally fulfilled only by classical massively parallel systems, like e.g. the Cray T3D/E or the SGI Origin 2000/3000. During recent years, however, a new class of architectures has emerged, breaking into this domain: clusters of inexpensive computers built with commodity off the shelf components connected via high–speed interconnects. These clusters combine both high performance, given by current state-of-the-art microprocessors and appropriate System Area Networks (SAN), with low cost, due to the commodity nature and thereby form a very attractive platform for the class of applications discussed here.

In the year 2000, an association of large and small IT companies has completed the first specification of the InfiniBand architecture. This architecture defines a System Area Network (SAN) that connects processing nodes and I/O nodes. Processing nodes use Host Channel Adapters (HCA) to attach to the network. Target Channel Adapters (TCA) connect I/O nodes to the fabric. Channel adapters are either connected directly or through switches. The basic InfiniBand connections are serial at data rates of 2.5 Gbps with low latency. Four or twelve of these serial point to point connections can be bundled, creating 4X connections at 10 Gbps or 12X connections at 30 Gbps respectivly. With its high bandwidth and low latency the InfiniBand architecture is an outstanding interconnect for high performance clusters.

6. Reference Clusters. For the evaluation of the work described above, LRR–TUM's InfiniBand research cluster has been used (see Figure 6.1). The configuration data of its key components are listed in Table 6.1.

The 12 *Server Blades* of the cluster are used exclusively for computation. The Server Blades are Nitro II InfiniBand Server Blades from Mellanox Technologies (www.mellanox.com). Each of the Server Blades has one Intel Xeon DP processor at 2.2 GHz, 2 GBytes of main memory, and uses a Serverworks Grand Champion LE chipset. In order to keep the design simple and avoid additional points of failure, the blades have no hard disk and no Ethernet connection. Instead, they boot from a Compact Flash card on each blade and then access remote file systems over the InfiniBand network. The Server Blades plug into the passive backplane of a 19 inch rackmount chassis, which provides power and their only network connection.

In addition to the 12 Server Blades, the cluster has 6 *Nodes* which are used mostly for interactive tasks, but can also be used for computation. Each of the Nodes has two Intel Xeon DP processors at 2.4 GHz and 4 GBytes of main memory. The main board of the Nodes is a Super P4DPi–G2 from SuperMicro Computer Co. with an Intel E7500 chipset and two Gigabit Ethernet ports. Each Node has a local IDE disk for booting and local files. In addition, file systems of some Nodes are mounted on all other Nodes and Server Blades in order to provide a common home directory and other common files. A MTPB23108 Host Channel Adapter (HCA) card from Mellanox Technologies is plugged into the 133 MHz PCI-X slot of the main board and provides two 4X InfiniBand ports.

A Nitrex II 16 port InfiniBand Switch Blade from Mellanox Technologies is the core of the InfiniBand fabric. The Switch Blade plugs into the passive backplane of the 19 inch rackmount chassis and connects the 12 Server Blades through the passive backplane. The remaining four ports of the Switch Blade are connected with cables to four of the Nodes. All InfiniBand connections are 4X with a theoretical peak bandwidth of 10 Gbps. In addition, the 6 Nodes are connected through a private Ethernet, and one of the Nodes serves as a gateway to the Ethernet of the University.

The operating system on all Nodes and Server Blades is Red Hat Linux release 7.3. The MPI implementation is MVAPICH (MPI for InfiniBand on VAPI Layer) from Ohio State University, which is a patch for MVICH (MPI for Virtual Interface Architecture) from National Energy Research Supercomputer Center (NERSC), that is based on MPICH 1.2.2 from Argonne National Laboratory. The compilers available are gcc version 2.96, PGI Fortran release 4.0-3, and Intel C++ and Fortran 7.0.

7. Production Environment. The ABB Corporate Research Center, which is located in Baden, Switzerland, focuses on the simulation of real world high voltage apparatus like transformers, insulators, switchgear etc.. The design engineer for such devices usually creates a CAD model using CAD packages described in section 3.

7.1. CAD frontend modelling systems. POLOPT provides interfaces for three different CAD systems which are being used at ABB: Pro/Engineer [21], SDRC-IDEAS [23] and CADFix [7]. All three systems provide modules for applying a boundary mesh (which is necessary for simulation), as well as for specifying boundary conditions and material-specific constants and interfaces for visualizing the results obtained by the POLOPT calculation. The most widely used CAD package is Pro/Engineer, since it allows for parametric modelling which makes it easy for the designer to change model dimensions in order to optinize the geometry of the design. The CAD frontend modelling system usually runs on a desktop PC, where the model is being created and then transferred to the POLOPT server which runs the actual simulation.

7.2. Data conversion. The discretized model with the boundary conditions and material constants is stored at the designer's desktop PC in a file format which is specific to the frontend modelling system. POLOPT then runs a data conversion module which converts the CAD-tool specific file into an input file format hat can be read by POLOPT.

After the calculation, the results file produced by POLOPT is converted into a file format that can be read and visualized by the CAD tool. This results file is then transferred back form the POLOPT server to the designer's desktop running one of the three CAD tools mentioned above.

7.3. Visualization and evaluation. All three CAD tools supported by POLOPT allow for efficient visualization and evaluation of the results obtained from the simulation. The field distributions as well as field lines can be visualized by spectral distributions corresponding to field strengths or potential values. Furthermore, plot graphs along areas of interest can be generated in order to determine potential hot spots in the high voltage design.

8. Application Examples and Results. For the simulations with our Infiniband-cluster, a transformer model, as it is also being used as a POLOPT benchmark at ABB corporate research, has been simulated using different configurations.

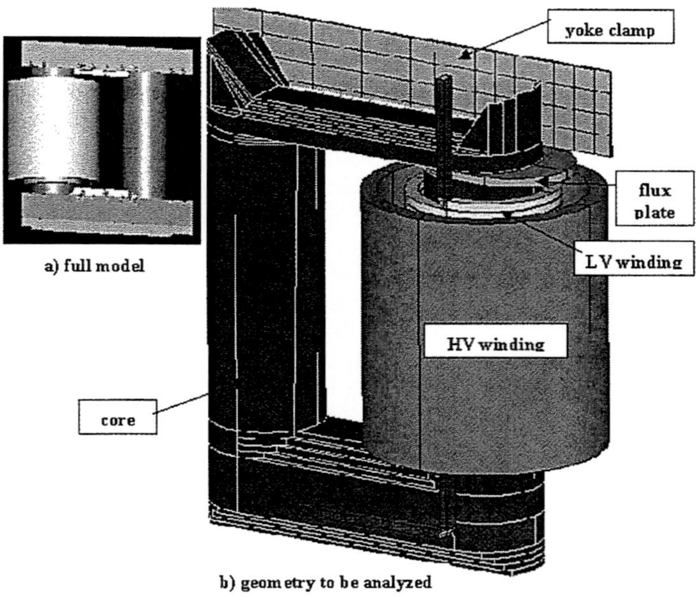

FIG. 8.1. *Transformer Model*

The transformer that has served as a benchmarking example is depicted in Figure 8. The task is to calculate the distribution of power losses caused by eddy currents in the yoke clamping plates in order to detect possible temperature hot spots. To guide the magnetic flux and to manipulate the loss distribution, the yoke is extended by a so called flux plate. The yoke clamps are modeled as solid parts. The full model consisting of the magnetic core, the yoke clamps, the flux plate and the HV windings has been analyzed with all materials assumed as linear. The obtained peak values were 10.071 kA for the Low Voltage winding (30 turns) and 482.175kA for the High Voltage winding (1 turn), respectively. From these values, the eddy currents in two different parts of the yoke clamp have been calculated. The required number of unknowns and the resulting working set sizes can be seen in Table 1.

The equation system size was 11547 unknowns, double precision complex (16 bytes) coefficients and a fully populated matrix.

The calculations have been performed on LRR-TUM's Infiniband cluster. Due to the high permeability values of the materials, it is necessary to actually solve the equation

Stage	4 Blades real/CPU	6 Blades real/CPU	8 Blades real/CPU	10 Blades real/CPU	12 Blades real/CPU
Init	9s/8s	8s/8s	9s/9s	9s/9s	9s/9s
Generate	296s/296s	196s/196s	148s/148s	118s/118s	99s/99s
Solve 1	**398s/398s**	**255s/255s**	**176s/175s**	**137s/136s**	**109s/109s**
Regenerate	22s/22s	14s/14s	10s/10s	8s/8s	7s/7s
Solve2	**486s/486s**	**308s/308s**	**218s/218s**	**164s/164s**	**130s/130s**
Field Calculation	264s/264s	177s/177s	138s/138s	111s/111s	89s/89s

TABLE 8.1

Computation times on server blades for transformer example

system twice [10]. This yields a 6 stage simulation process for the electromagnetic field calculations:

1. Initialization
2. Generation of the coefficient matrix
3. 1st Solution of the equation system
4. Regeneration of the coefficient matrix
5. 2nd solution of the equation system
6. Potential and field calculation in points of interest

As far as the interconnect is concerned, the interesting stages are stage 3 (Solution of the equation system) and stage 5 (2nd solution of the equation system) since the GMRES solver is very communication intensive at these stages. The model has been calculated on both parts of the Infiniband cluster described in section 5.

8.1. Server blades. With the server blades described in section 5, the model has been simulated on 4, 6, 8, 10, and 12 blades, respectively. Due to memory requirements (the coefficient matrix must fit into main memory), at least 4 server blades must be used for this benchmark problem. Since the server blades are only connected via Infiniband, Ethernet could not be used for these nodes. However, the configuration is a good environment to determine the parallel efficiency for POLOPT simulations on an Infiniband cluster. The simulations were run using 4-12 server blades connected via Infiniband in order to determine the parallel efficiency of the blade system. A minimum of 4 blades had to be used as the coefficient matrix being generated by POLOPT must fit into the compute nodes' main memory in order to prevent swapping.

The computation times obtained on the server blades are shown in table 2.

8.2. PC nodes. On the PC node part of the Infiniband cluster, the same problem was run using 2, 3 and 4 nodes with and without SMP support, respectively. Since the PC nodes are also equipped with Ethernet interfaces (the server blades are only connected via Infiniband), the Infiniband network techology's efficiency could be directly compared to that of Ethernet. For the Ethernet simulations, MPICH version 1.2.2.2 was used, whereas for Infiniband calculations, Ohio State University's MPVAPICH [20] based on the same version of MPICH served as the parallel library. The results are shown in table 3.

8.3. Observations. Two key facts can be seen from tables 2 and 3:

1. The blade system scales very well between 4 and 12 nodes,
2. There even is a superlinear speedup when taking 4 nodes as the base, and
3. The communication overhead (i.e. the time used for communication which is additional to the CPU time for the calculation) that is obtained in the two solution stages when using Fast Ethernet is almost zero for Infiniband.

Starting with the base calculation times for 4 blades, figures 8.2 and 8.3 show the parallel efficiency on the server blade system for solution phase 1 and solution phase 2, respectively.

Stage	2 Nodes Infiniband real/CPU	2 Nodes Ethernet real/CPU	4 Nodes Infiniband real/CPU	4 Nodes Ethernet real/CPU
Init	7s/7s	7s/7s	8s/8s	8s/8s
Generate	521s/519s	520s/518s	273s/273s	264s/256s
Solve 1	**704s/704s**	**760s/704s**	**297s/297s**	**419s/300s**
Regenerate	42s/42s	42s/42s	19s/19s	21s/21s
Solve2	**841s/840s**	**902s/840s**	**354s/354s**	**577s/409s**
Field Calculation	466s/466s	466s/465s	241s/241s	240s/239s

TABLE 8.2
Computation times on PC nodes for transformer example

An interesting effect that can be seen from the plots is that Infiniband shows a better parallel efficiency with a growing number of compute nodes. However, due to the fact that only 12 server blades were available, it was not possible to check this phenomenon for numbers of nodes greater than 12. Since the superlinear speedup that can be observed is probably due to cache sizes, it is currently analyzed with appropriate cache monitoring tools.

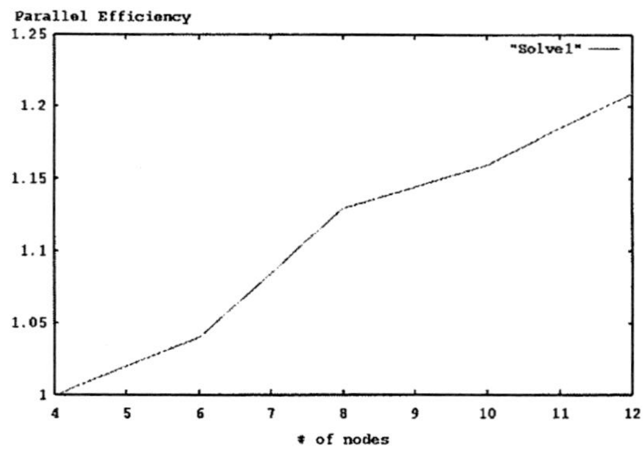

FIG. 8.2. *Parallel efficiency phase 1 (4-12 blades)*

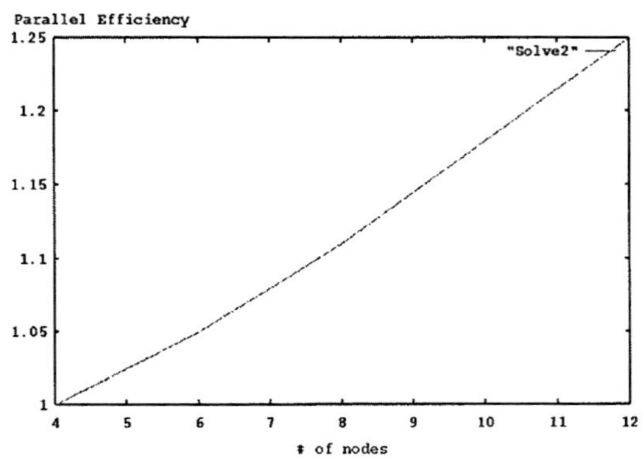

FIG. 8.3. *Parallel efficiency phase 2 (4-12 blades)*

When comparing the wallclock time and the CPU time in the solution phases on the PC nodes, it can be seen that for a growing number of nodes, the communication overhead is also growing when using Fast Ethernet. However, this overhead is almost zero for Infiniband interconnect, since both times are more or less equal, as can be seen in table 3.

9. Outlook and Conclusions. In this paper, first experiences with runnning an electric field simulation on an Infiniband cluster have been presented. The results obtained so far show that the Infiniband interconnect scales well with parallel efficencies greater that one for certain numbers of nodes. However, this effect, which is probably to to caching effects, is still to be investigated in further detail. Compared to Fast Ethernet, it could be shown that the communication overhead is almost zero for Infiniband interconnect.

However, in order to get up to date results, other interconnect technologies like Gigabit Ethernet [11], SCI [15] or Myrinet [5] also need to be investigated.

So far, Infiniband seems to be an appropriate interconnect technology for simulations as described in this paper. However, the results presented in this paper are only intended to present some preliminary results from the work in progress regarding field simulations on Infiniband.

At LRR-TUM, the Infiniband cluster [14] will be extended in the near future allowing for further investigations with a greater number of nodes as well as other inteconnect technologies. Furthermore, as technology evolves, we also expect better computation times when using new firmware versions for the Infiniband hardware.

REFERENCES

[1] Z. Andjelic. *POLOPT 4.5 User's Guide.* ABB Corporate Research Center Heidelberg, 1996.
[2] R. Bausinger and G. Kuhn. *Die Boundary-Element Methode (in German).* Expert Verlag, Ehingen, 1987.
[3] A. Blaszczyk, Z. Andjelic, P. Levin, and A. Ustundag. Parallel Computation of Electric Field in a Heterogeneous Workstation Cluster. In *Lecture Notes in Computer Science 919, HPCN Europe,* volume 919, pages 606–611. Springer Verlag, 1995.
[4] A. Blaszczyk and C. Trinitis. Experience with pvm in an industrial environment. In *Lecture notes in Computer Science 1156, EuroPVM'96,*, volume 1156, pages 174–179. Springer Verlag, 1996.
[5] N. Boden, D. Cohen, R. Felderman, J. S. A. Kulawik, C. Seitz, and W.-K. Su. Myrinet: A Gigabit–per–Second Local Area Network. *IEEE Micro,* 15(1):29–36, Feb. 1995.
[6] P. N. Brown. A theoretical comparison of the Arnoldi and GMRES algorithms. *SIAM J. Sci. Stat. Comput.*, 12(1):58–78, January 1991.
[7] Web page, FEGS Ltd. [Homepage], 2001, http://www.fegs.co.uk.
[8] M. Eberl, W. Karl, C. Trinitis, and A. Blaszczyk. Parallel computing on pc clusters - an alternative to supercomputers for industrial applications. In *Lecture Notes in Computer Science 1697, EuroPVM/MPI'99,* volume 1697, pages 493–498. Springer Verlag, 1999.
[9] A. B. et al. Parallel computation of electric field in a heterogeneous workstation cluster. In *Lecture Notes in Computer Science 919, HPCN Europe,* pages 606–611. Springer Verlag, 1995.
[10] G. Schmidlin, Ch. Schwab et al. Preconditioning second kind boundary integral equations for 3-d eddy current problems (unpublished). Technical report, ETH Zurich, Zurich, Switzerland, 2000.
[11] Web page, Gigabit Ethernet [Homepage], 2003, http://www.gigabit-ethernet.org.
[12] G. Golub and C. F. V. Loan. *Matrix Computions.* The Johns Hopkins University Press, Baltimore, second edition, 1989.
[13] Web page, Infiniband Trade Association [Homepage], 2003, http://www.infinibandta.org/.
[14] Web page, Infiniband Cluster at TUM [Homepage], 2003, http://infiniband.cs.tum.edu/.
[15] IEEE Computer Society. IEEE Standard for the Scalable Coherent Interface (SCI). IEEE Std 1596-1992, 1993. IEEE 345 East 47th Street, New York, NY 10017-2394, USA.
[16] J. H. Kane, D. E. Keyes, and K. G. Prasad. Iterative solution techniques in boundary element analysis. *International Journal for Numerical Methods in Engineering,* 31:1511–1536, 1991.
[17] I. Mayergoyz. Eddy current problems and the boundary integral equation method. *Computational Electromagnetics,* pages 163–171, 1996.
[18] Message Passing Interface Forum (MPIF). MPI: A Message-Passing Interface Standard. Technical Report, University of Tennessee, Knoxville, June 1995. http://www.mpi-forum.org.
[19] Web page, The Netlib Repository [Homepage], 2000, http://www.netlib.org.
[20] Web page, Ohio State University [Homepage], 2003, http://nowlab.cis.ohio-state.edu/projects/mpi-iba/.
[21] Web page, Parametric Technology Corporation [Homepage], 2000, http://www.ptc.com.
[22] Y. Saad and M. Schultz. GMRES: A generalized minimal residual algorithm for solving nonsymmetric linear systems. In *SIAM J.Sci. Stat. Comput.*, pages 856–869. 1989.
[23] Web page: SDRC [Homepage], 2001, http://www.sdrc.com.

[24] G. Strang. *Linear Algebra and Its Applications*. Harcourt, Brace, Jovanovich, Publishers, San Diego, 3rd edition edition, 1988.

[25] C. Trinitis. Comparison of several minimization algorithms for electric field optimization. In *10th International Symposium on High Voltage Engineering (ISH'97)*, volume 3, pages 49–52, 1997.

[26] C. Trinitis. *Feldoptimierung von dreidimensionalen Isoliersystemen in der Hochspannungstechnik*. PhD thesis, Technische Universität München, Germany, 1998.

[27] C. Trinitis. Field optimization of three dimensional high voltage equipment. In *11th International Symposium on High Voltage Engineering (ISH'99)*, volume 2, pages 2.75–2.78, 1999.

[28] R. Weiss. *Convergence Behavior of Generalized Conjugate Gradient Methods*. PhD thesis, Technische Universität Karlsruhe, December 1990.

In: Applied Parallel and Distributed Computing
Editors: Yi Pan and Laurence T. Yang , pp. 159-168
ISBN 1-59454-174-4

THE PARALLEL WAVEFORM ICGS METHOD FOR TRANSIENT SIMULATION OF SEMICONDUCTOR DEVICES ON DISTRIBUTED MEMORY ARCHITECTURES

LAURENCE TIANRUO YANG*

Abstract. In this paper, the parallelization aspects of the accelerated waveform relaxation algorithms for the transient simulation of semiconductor devices on parallel distributed memory computers are mainly studied. These methods are competitive with standard pointwise methods on serial architectures, but are significantly faster on parallel computers. Here we are making use of an improved parallel version of the Conjugate Gradient Squared method (ICGS) combining elements of numerical stability and parallel algorithm design, for solving the resulting sequence of time-varying sparse linear differential-algebraic initial-value problems (IVP) arising at each linearization step with waveform Newton. We reorganize the algorithm such that all inner products, matrix-vector multiplications and vector updates of a single iteration step are independent and communication time required for inner product can be overlapped efficiently with computation time of vector updates. Therefore, the bottleneck of the performance, namely the cost of global communication on parallel distributed memory computers can be significantly reduced. The resulting ICGS algorithm maintains the favorable properties of the original algorithm while not increasing computational costs. Compared with other accelerated approaches such as convolution SOR and waveform GMRES techniques on waveform relaxation algorithm and pointwise methods, some very preliminary experimental results carried out on a massively parallel systems have demonstrated the advantages of the proposed approach.

Key words. Transient simulation of semiconductor devices, Accelerated waveform relaxation algorithms, Improved Conjugate Gradient Squared method, Linear systems, Inner products, Global communications

1. Introduction. Due to the increasing availability of parallel computers and the computational expense and growing importance of performing semiconductor device transient simulation, it has been suggested that efficient parallel algorithms should be developed and used for these simulation problems. Although several approaches have been shown that SIMD type machines are effective for device transient simulation [6, 21], it is more important to spend our efforts on the increasingly more popular and cost-effective MIMD type architectures such as distributed memory computers.

The pointwise Newton-GMRES algorithm has been considered as the most efficient serial algorithm for device transient simulation. The block-Jacobi preconditioned GMRES [17] is used to solve the linear systems arisings at each Newton iteration of each timestep of an implicit integration formula applied to (2.1) in the algorithm. The inner products are needed heavily in the pointwise Newton-GMRES method for each GMRES iteration. On parallel distributed memory computers, the matrices and vectors are distributed over the processors, so that even when the matrix operations can be implemented efficiently by parallel operations, we still can not avoid the global communication required for inner product communications. Many works have demonstrated that the parallel performance on this kind of architecture is always limited because of the global communication required for the inner products while the matrix-vector multiplication only requires local communication, i.e. communication with only a few processors. In a word, these global communication costs become relatively more and more important when the number of the parallel processors is increased and thus they have the potential to affect the scalability of the algorithm in a negative way [4, 5]. Although many approaches have been proposed in which communication operations can be overlapped with local computation [1, 5, 23, 24], the communication latency is still so large that it can not be hidden by the relatively small amount of computation done at a single timestep. In order to achieve high scalable performance on this type of architecture, a numerical algorithm should try to avoid frequent global communications between processors

*Department of Computer Science, St. Francis Xavier University, P.O. Box 5000, Antigonish, B2G 2W5, NS, Canada, Email: lyang@stfx.ca

due to inner products on distributed memory computers. The waveform relaxation (WR) approach to solve time-dependent problems is such a method, because in parallel waveform relaxation, iterates are communicated between processors only after having been computed over a time interval [7, 13, 22].

Similar with other iterative methods, rapid convergence determines the numerical efficiency of the waveform relaxation. In the literature, there are several approaches to accelerated waveform relaxations, such as multigrid [8], Krylov-subspace [9, 10], and convolution SOR techniques [14, 15]. In [16], the authors mainly focus on one method, namely waveform GMRES (WGMRES), an extension of the generalized minimum residual algorithm (GMRES) [17], of the Krylov-subspace methods to accelerate the convergence of waveform relaxation algorithms. The GMRES method yields an optimal reduction of the residual norm for a given number of iterations. The method requires the computation of an orthogonal basis of the Krylov subspace. For this, a number of inner products, increasing with the iteration count, needs to be computed. Additional time-consuming computational kernels are vector updates and matrix-vector products. In many situations, especially when matrix operations are well-structured, these two operations are suitable for implementation on vector and share memory parallel computers. But for parallel distributed memory machines, although these two operations can be avoided by using waveform relaxation method accelerated by waveform GMRES technique instead of pointwise Newton-GMRES, the global communication required by inner products during waveform GMRES technique still dominates parallel performance and makes the performance on this kind of architecture very limited accordingly.

In this paper, we will look at another type of method for acceleration from Krylov subspace family which requires less inner product operations, namely the conjugate gradient squared algorithm [20], for the resulting large and sparse linear systems with unsymmetric coefficient matrices arising at each linearization step with waveform Newton. Recently, Maheswaran et al. [11] propose a new modified parallel version, we refer to the Modified Conjugate Gradient Squared (MCGS) method, where the synchronization overhead is effectively reduced by a factor of two. This is achieved by changing the computation sequence in the CGS method. Based on their similar ideas, we propose a new Improved Conjugate Gradient Squared (ICGS) method which is reorganized without changing the numerical stability so that all the computational kernels, namely inner products, matrix-vector multiplications and vector updates of a single iteration step are independent, and subsequently communication time required for inner product can be overlapped efficiently with computation time of vector updates. Therefore, the cost of global communication on parallel distributed memory computers can be significantly reduced. The resulting CGS algorithm maintains the favorable properties of the CGS algorithm while not increasing computational costs.

The remaining part of the paper is organized as follows. Some background about device transient simulation will be described shortly in section 2. Then the accelerated waveform relaxation method with several acceleration techniques such as convolution SOR and waveform GMRES methods will also be presented briefly in section 3. In section 4, we will describe the corresponding proposed efficient parallel waveform ICGS method. In section 5, the parallel implementation details including data distribution and communication scheme will be addressed briefly. Finally, the very preliminary experimental comparison of parallel performance of proposed method with other accelerated approaches such as convolution SOR and waveform GMRES techniques on waveform relaxation algorithm and pointwise methods will be demonstrated as well.

2. Device Transient Simulation. Based on the background described in [10, 16], charge transport within a semiconductor device is assumed to be governed by the possion equation, and the electron and hole continuity equations [2, 19]. Given a two-dimensional rectangular discretization mesh, the device equation system is typically discretized with finite-difference formula applied to the Possion equation, and an exponentially fit finite-difference formula applied to the continuity equations (the Scharfetter-Gummel method [19]). On an N-node mesh, this spatial discretization yields a sparse differential-algebraic initial-value problem (IVP) consisting of 3N equations in 3N unknowns, denoted by [10, 16]:

$$\begin{aligned} F_1(u(t), n(t), p(t)) &= 0, \\ \frac{d}{dt}n(t) + F_2(u(t), n(t), p(t)) &= 0, \\ \frac{d}{dt}p(t) + F_3(u(t), n(t), p(t)) &= 0, \end{aligned} \tag{2.1}$$

where

$$F_i(u(0), n(0), p(0)) = 0, \quad i = 1, 2, 3$$

and $t \in [0, T]$, and $u(t), n(t), p(t)$ are vectors of normalized potential, electron concentration, and hole concentration, respectively. Here F_1, F_2 and F_3 are specified component-wise as [10, 16]:

$$\begin{aligned} F_{1_i}(u_i, n_i, p_i, u_j) &= \frac{kT}{q}\sum_j \frac{d_{ij}\epsilon_{ij}}{L_{ij}}(u_i - u_j) - qA_i(p_i - n_i + N_{D_i} - N_{A_i}), \\ F_{2_i}(u_i, n_i, u_j, n_j) &= \frac{kT}{qA_i}\sum_j \frac{d_{ij}\mu_{n_{ij}}}{L_{ij}}[n_i B(u_i - u_j) - n_j B(u_j - u_i)] + R_i, \\ F_{3_i}(u_i, p_i, u_j, p_j) &= \frac{kT}{qA_i}\sum_j \frac{d_{ij}\mu_{n_{ij}}}{L_{ij}}[p_i B(u_j - u_i) - p_j B(u_i - u_j)] + R_i, \end{aligned}$$

The sums above are taken over the silicon nodes j adjacent to node i. For each node j adjacent to node i, L_{ij} is the distance from node i to node j, d_{ij} is the length of the side of the Voronoi box that encloses node i and bisects the edge between node i and j, and ϵ_{ij}, $\mu_{n_{ij}}$ and $\mu_{p_{ij}}$ are the dielectric permittivity, electron and hole mobility, respectively, on the edge between nodes i and j. The Bernoulli function, $B(x) = x/(e^x - 1)$, is used to exponentially fit potential variation to electron and hole concentration variations, and efficiently upwinds the current equations.

3. Accelerated Waveform Methods. Usually the differential-algebraic equation (DAE) system (2.1) is solved by discretizing the system in time with a low-order implicit integration method. The standard approach used to solve the resulting sequence of non-linear algebraic systems is to use some variants of Newton's method and/or relaxation [2, 12]. As we mentioned above, this approach is very limited on parallel distributed memory computers with a high communication costs.

A more effective approach to solve (2.1) on parallel distributed memory computers is to use waveform relaxation (WR) to decompose the DAE system into subsystems before time discretization [7]. The WR algorithm has several computational advantages such as avoiding factoring large and sparse matrices, exploiting multi-rate behavior, using different timesetps to resolve different solution components, and finally well suitable for parallel implementations because of a low global communication/computation ratio. However we apply to solve the device equation system (2.1), the WR algorithm converge slowly unless acceleration techniques, such as convolution SOR, or waveform GMRES, are used [10, 16].

Convolution SOR (CSOR) is a generalized waveform extension of the well-known successive overrelaxation (SOR) method to accelerate the convergence of relaxation methods for solving linear system of equations. The CSOR method can be described shortly as follows based on the materials from [10, 16]. We mainly consider the problem of numerically solving the linear initial-value problem:

$$\frac{d}{dt}x(t) + Ax(t) = b(t), \quad x(0) = x_0, \tag{3.1}$$

where $A \in \Re^{n\times n}$, $b(t) \in \Re^n$ is given for all $t \in [0, T]$, and $x(t) \in \Re^n$ is to be computed. Detailed descriptions about CSOR are presented in [16]. In generally, in iteration $k+1$, each waveform $\hat{x}_i^{k+1}$ is computed as in ordinary Gauss-Seidel WR, and then is moved slightly in iteration direction by convolution with CSOR parameter, namely function $\omega(t)$. The convolution allows the CSOR method to correctly account for the frequency-dependence of the spectrum of the Gauss-Jacobi WR operator by, in effect, using a different SOR parameter for each frequency.

Here we would like to pay more attention to another efficient acceleration technique, namely waveform CGS (conjugate gradient squared) for solving (3.1). With the splitting like $A = M - N$, the basic iteration can be expressed as follows [10, 16] :

$$\frac{d}{dt}x^{k+1}(t) + Mx^{k+1}(t) = Nx^k(t) + b(t).$$

The solution x to (3.1) is thus a fixed point of the WR algorithm [10, 14], satisfying the integral operator equation

$$(I - K)x = \psi. \tag{3.2}$$

Here we follow the notations described in [16] where K is defined by

$$(Kx)(t) = \int_0^t e^{(s-t)M} Nx(s)ds,$$

and

$$\psi(t) = e^{-tM}x(0) + \int_0^t e^{(s-t)M} b(s)ds.$$

Krylov subspace methods can be used to accelerate the convergence of WR, but as K is not self-adjoint, a variant suitable for non-self-adjoint operators must be used [10, 16]. In [16], Reichelt et al. [16] have used waveform GMRES (WGRMES), an extension of the generalized minimum residual algorithm to successfully accelerate the convergence on MIMD parallel computers such as Intel iPSC/860. However, on distributed memory computers, the performance of their approach on this kind of architecture is still very limited because they still can not avoid the large global communication required for inner product during waveform GMRES accelerated technique. In next subsections, we will shortly introduce the parallel ICGS method which requires less inner products and its mathematical background. Here we use A to express the coefficient matrix instead of $I - K$ throughout the left of paper.

4. The CGS and ICGS Methods. The Conjugate Gradient Squared (CGS) algorithm [20] for the solution of the linear equations

$$Ax = b, \quad \text{where} \quad A \in \Re^{n\times n} \quad x, b \in \Re^n. \tag{4.1}$$

is described in the Algorithm 1. Here x_0 is any initial guess for the solution and $r_0 = b - Ax_0$ is the initial residual. An arbitrarily chosen vectors $\tilde{r}_0$ such that $\tilde{r}_0^T r_0 \neq 0$ are input to the algorithm, in addition to vector b and the sparse matrix A.

Algorithm 1 The Classical CGS Method

$r_0 = b - Ax_0; q_0 = p_{-1} = 0;$
$\rho_{-1} = 1; \rho_0 = \tilde{r}_0^T r_0;$
for n = 1, 2, 3, ... **do**
  $\beta = \frac{\rho_n}{\rho_{n-1}};$
  $u_n = r_n + \beta q_n;$
  $p_n = u_n + \beta(q_n + \beta p_{n-1});$
  $v_n = Ap_n;$
  $\sigma = \tilde{r}_0^T v_n;$
  $\alpha = \frac{\rho_n}{\sigma};$
  $q_{n+1} = u_n - \alpha v_n;$
  $f_{n+1} = u_n + q_{n+1};$
  $r_{n+1} = r_n - \alpha A f_{n+1};$
  $x_{n+1} = x_n + \alpha f_{n+1};$
  $\rho_{n+1} = \tilde{r}_0^T r_{n+1};$
  $e_{n+1} = r_{n+1}^T r_{n+1};$
  if $(|e_{n+1}| < tol)$ **then**
    STOP
  end if
end for

Recently, Maheswaran et al. [11] propose a new modified parallel version of the Conjugate Gradient Squared method. We refer it as the MCGS method where the synchronization overhead is effectively reduced by a factor of two. This is achieved by changing the computation sequence in the CGS method. Based on their similar ideas, we propose a new Improved Conjugate Gradient Squared (ICGS) method. The basic idea in reformulating the ICGS algorithm is to merge the main computational kernels such as vector updates, matrix-vector multiplications and inner products so that they can be executed in parallel per iteration of the algorithm. If we reorganize the vectors w_{n+1}, x_{n+1} and r_{n+1} of the MCGS algorithm [11], we can get the following for the vector w_{n+1}:

$$w_{n+1} = Aq_{n+1} = A(u_n - \alpha y_n). \tag{4.2}$$

If we define $s_n = Ar_n$ and $t_n = Ay_n$, we can get from (4.2):

$$w_{n+1} = s_n + \beta w_n - \alpha t_n. \tag{4.3}$$

Similarly for the vector x_{n+1}, if we insert $q_{n+1} = u_n - \alpha y_n$ into the expression, we will have

$$x_{n+1} = x_n + \alpha(u_n + q_{n+1}) = x_n + \alpha(2u_n - \alpha y_n), \tag{4.4}$$

and for the vector r_{n+1}, if we combine w_{n+1} in equation (4.3), we have

$$\begin{aligned} r_{n+1} &= r_n - \alpha(s_n + \beta w_n + w_{n+1}) \\ &= r_n - \alpha(2s_n + 2\beta w_n - \alpha t_n). \end{aligned} \tag{4.5}$$

Based on the equations (4.3), (4.4), (4.5) and complicated mathematical derivations, the ICGS algorithm can be depicted as follows:

Under the assumptions, the Improved Conjugate Gradient Squared (ICGS) method can be efficiently parallelized as follows:

- The inner products of a single iteration step (16), (17), (18), (19) and (20) are independent(parallel).

Algorithm 2 The Improved CGS Method

1: $\gamma_{-1} = 1; p_0 = 0; q_0 = 0; w_0 = 0;$
2: $w_{-1} = 0; y_{-1} = 0; r_0 = b - Ax_0; s_0 = Ar_0;$
3: $\gamma_0 = \tilde{r}_0^T r_0; \eta_0 = \tilde{r}_0^T s_0;$
4: $\mu_0 = \tilde{r}_0^T w_0; \lambda = \tilde{r}_0^T y_{-1}; \rho_{-1} = 1;$
5: **for** n = 1, 2, 3, ... **do**
6: $\quad \beta_n = \frac{\gamma_n}{\gamma_{n-1}};$
7: $\quad \sigma_n = \eta_n + \beta_n(2\mu_n + \lambda_n \beta_n);$
8: $\quad u_n = r_n + \beta_n q_n;$
9: $\quad y_n = s_n + 2\beta_n w_n + \beta_n^2 y_{n-1};$
10: $\quad s_n = Ar_n;$
11: $\quad t_n = Ay_n;$
12: $\quad w_n = Aq_n;$
13: $\quad w_{n+1} = s_n + \beta_n w_n - \alpha_n t_n;$
14: $\quad r_{n+1} = r_n - \alpha_n(2s_n + 2\beta_n w_n - \alpha_n t_n);$
15: $\quad x_{n+1} = x_n + \alpha_n(2u_n - \alpha_n y_n);$
16: $\quad \rho_{n+1} = \tilde{r}_0^T r_{n+1};$
17: $\quad \eta_{n+1} = \tilde{r}_0^T s_{n+1};$
18: $\quad \mu_{n+1} = \tilde{r}_0^T w_{n+1};$
19: $\quad \lambda_{n+1} = \tilde{r}_0^T y_n;$
20: $\quad e_{n+1} = r_{n+1}^T r_{n+1};$
21: $\quad$ **if** $(|e_{n+1}| < tol)$ **then**
22: $\quad\quad$ STOP
23: $\quad$ **end if**
24: **end for**

- The matrix-vector multiplications of a single iteration step (10), (11) and (12) are independent(parallel).
- The vector updates (13), (14) and (15) are independent, (8) and (9) are independent(parallel).
- The communications required for the inner products (16), (17), (18), (19) and (20) can be overlapped with the update for x_{n+1} in (15).

Therefore, the cost of communication time on parallel distributed memory computers can be significantly reduced.

5. Parallel Implementation.

5.1. Data distribution. To cope with large and sparse matrices arising from the simulation, if we are working on different computer system architectures or dealing with different algorithms or data, the appropriate storage schemes should be considered differently. In this paper, we use one of the most common format called CRS format (compressed row storage). The main reason is that this type of storage scheme is very suitable for both regularly and irregularly structured large and sparse matrices. The detailed description can be found in the literature. Briefly, the non-zeros of a large and sparse matrix are stored in row-wise in three one-dimensional arrays. The values of the non-zeros are contained in array *value*. The corresponding column indices are contained in array *col_ind*. The elements of *row_ptr* point to the position of the beginning of each row in *value* and *col_ind*.

In order to efficiently parallelize the ICGS algorithm on a parallel architecture, we first need to decide the data distribution of matrix and vector arrays, hopefully optimally, to each processor and then determine an efficient communication scheme by taking into account different sparsity patterns, not only for matrix-vector multiplication but also for inner products, to minimize the overall execution time. In this paper, we will mainly follow the approach has been used in [3] for data distribution and communication scheme which do not require any knowledge of the matrix sparsity pattern. The communication scheme are automatically determined by the analysis of the indices of the non-zero matrix elements.

In the following part, we will use the same notations introduced in [3] for short illustrations. Let n_k and e_k denote the number of rows and no-zeros of processor k, where $k = 0, \ldots, p-1$, respectively. e and n are the total number of corresponding numbers. g_k is the index of the first row of processor k, and z_i is the number of non-zeros of row i. We can get the following relations: $n = \sum_{k=0}^{p-1} n_k, e = \sum_{k=0}^{p-1} e_k, g_k = 1 + \sum_{i=0}^{k-1} n_i, e_k(g_k, n_k) = \sum_{i=gk}^{gk+nk-1} z_i$ Based on the analysis, the total costs of each iteration can be described as $c_1\ s\ e + c_2\ n + c_3$ where the first term corresponds to the number of operations for s matrix-vector multiplications, the second term corresponds to the number of vector updates. Since we are mainly dealing with large and sparse matrices, the constants can be neglected. Now we can estimate the contribution of the operations executed on processor k to the total number of operations by

$$\zeta \approx \frac{c_1\ s\ e_k + c_2\ n_k}{c_1\ s\ e + c_2\ n} = \frac{s\ e_k + \xi\ n_k}{s\ e + \xi n},$$

where $\xi = c_2/c_1$ depends on both the iterative methods and also the processor architecture. Ideally, the computational load balance should be distributed in such a way that each processor only gets p-th fraction for the total number of operations. Based on this, we can use the following strategy to distribute the rows of the matrix and the vector components [3]:

$$n_k = \begin{cases} \min\limits_{1 \le t \le n - g_k + 1} \{t | \frac{s\ e_k(t) + \xi\ t}{s\ e + \xi\ n} \ge \frac{1}{p}\} & k = 0, 1, \ldots, q \\ n - \sum_{i=0}^{q} n_i & k = q+1 \\ 0 & k = q+2, \ldots, p-1 \end{cases}$$

Since our main target is large and sparse matrices and we assume $p \ll n$, the relation $q = p-1$ or $q+1 = p-1$ always hold. It can be shown that for $\xi = c_2/c_1 \to 0$, each processor will get nearly the same number of non-zeros which means that the execution time of the vector updates in negligible compared to the execution of matrix-vector multiplications. It also can be shown that for $\xi = c_2/c_1 \to \infty$ each processor will get nearly the same number of rows which means that the execution time of the matrix-vector multiplications only contribute to a very small part of the total execution time.

5.2. Communication schemes. After the discussion of data distribution, we also need to investigate a suitable communication scheme by preprocessing the distributed column index arrays for efficient matrix-vector multiplications since on a distributed memory systems, its computation requires communication due to the partial vector on each processor. We will use an approach similar to that proposed in [3] for our communication schemes.

If we decide to implement the matrix vector multiplication row-wisely, components of the vector x of $y = Ax$ are communicated. We firstly analyze the arrays *col_ind* on each processor to determine which elements result in access to non-local data. Then, the processors exchange information to decide which local data must be sent to which processors. Based on the above analysis, we will reorder these two arrays *col_ind* and *value* in such a way that the data that results in access to processor l is collected in block l, called *local block*. The motivation behind this reordering is to perform computation and communication overlapped. The elements of block l succeed one another row-wise with increasing column index per row. The detailed description can be found in [3].

For the parallel implementation of this operation, each processor executes asynchronous receive-routines to receive necessary non-local data. Then all components of the vector x that are needed on other processors are sent asynchronously. After the required data are

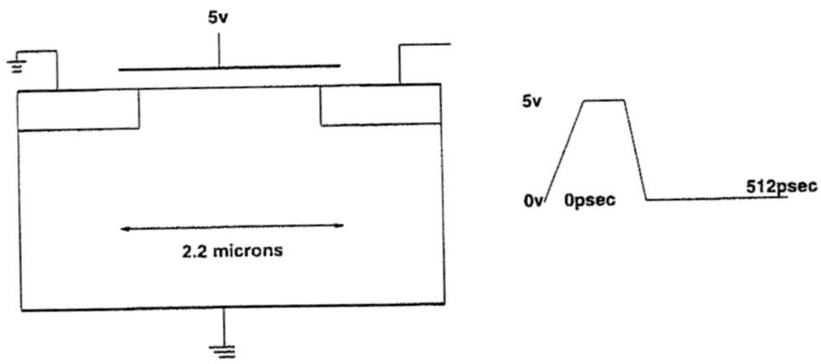

FIG. 6.1. *Illustration of the drain-driven karD*

TABLE 6.1
Description of three different devices

Device	Description	Mesh	Unknowns
ldd	lightly-doped drain	15×20	656
soi	silicon-on-insulator	18×24	856
kar	abrupt junction	19×31	1379

available, each processor will perform operations with it local block. After that, as soon as non-local data arrive, processor continue the matrix vector operation by accessing the elements of the corresponding blocks. It will be repeated until the whole operation is completed. According to the communication scheme described, the communication and computation are performed overlapped so that waiting time can be reduced.

6. Experimental Results. The three different MOS devices *ldd*, *soi* and *kar* described in Table 6.1 are used to construct six simulation examples suggested in [16], each device being subjected to either a drain voltage pulse with the gate held high (the *D* examples), or a gate voltage pulse with the drain held high (the *G* examples). The (*karG64* and *soiG64*) examples are constructed by refining the meshes of *karG* and *soiG* to contain 64 vertical lines. Zero-volt Dirichlet boundary conditions are imposed by ohmic contacts at the source and along the bottom of the substrate and Neumann reflecting boundary conditions are imposed along the left and right sides. The description of device and illustration of the drain-driven *karD* example are described in Figure 6.1 and Table 6.1 which are taken from [16].

We have compared our approach with parallelized pointwise Newton/GMRES, WRN [18], WN/WGMRES, and WRN with CSOR acceleration by some preliminary results. The backward Euler method with 256 fixed timesteps is used for all experiments, on a simulation interval of 51.2 or 512 picoseconds. Although the use of global uniform timesteps precludes multirate integration, it also simplifies the problem of load-balancing. The convergence criterion for all experiments is that the maximum relative error of any terminal current over the simulation interval be less than 10^{-4}. The initial guess for WRN and for the accelerated waveform methods is produced by performing 16 or 32 WR iterations beginning with flat waveform extended from the initial conditions.

Compared with the published results on the execution times in wall clocks seconds required to complete a transient simulation of the *karD*, *soiG*, *lddD* and *karG64* examples using WRN, WRN with CSOR acceleration, pointwise Newton/GMRES, WN/WGMRES respectively in [16, 18], based on the preliminary experimental results we conducted, we can see that pointwise-GMRES does exhibit some speedup when parallelized, but the speedup flattens out after four processors. Compared with that of original WRN method, the execution time of WRN with acceleration technique CSOR is obviously shorter. WN/WGMRES approach proposed in [16] is better than WRN with CSOR acceleration technique. Our approach need shortest execution times to complete a transient simulation which is consistent with our expectations where the inner products, even matrix-vector multiplications are totally independent and therefore can be executed simultaneously. Further extensive results are needed to be done to make complete comparison with those previously mentioned methods.

REFERENCES

[1] Z. Bai, D. Hu, and L. Reichel. A newton basis GMRES implementation. Technical Report 91-03, University of Kentucky, 1991.

[2] R. E. Bank, W. C. Coughran, W. Fichtner, E. Grosse, D. Rose, and R. Smith. Transient simulation of silicon devices and circuits. *IEEE Transactions on Computer-Aided Design of Integrated Circuits and Systems*, 4:436–451, October 1985.

[3] A. Basermann, B. Reichel, and C. Schelthoff. Preconditioned CG methods for sparse matrices on massively parallel machines. *Parallel Computing*, 23(3):381–398, 1997.

[4] L. G. C. Crone and H. A. van der Vorst. Communication aspects of the conjugate gradient method on distributed memory machines. *Supercomputer*, X(6):4–9, 1993.

[5] E. de Sturler. A parallel variant of the GMRES(m). In *Proceedings of the 13th IMACS World Congress on Computational and Applied Mathematics*. IMACS, Criterion Press, 1991.

[6] C. L. Gardner, P. J. Lanzkron, and D. J. Rose. A parallel block iterative method for the hydrodynamic device model. *IEEE Transactions on Computer-Aided Design of Integrated Circuits and Systems*, 10:1187–1192, September 1991.

[7] E. Lelarasmee, A. E. Ruehli, and A. L. Sangiovanni-Vincentelli. The waveform relaxation method for time domain analysis of large scale integrated circuits. *IEEE Transactions on Computer-Aided Design of Integrated Circuits and Systems*, 1:131–145, July 1982.

[8] C. Lubich and A. Osterman. Multi-grid dynamic iteration for parabolic equations. *BIT*, 27:216–234, 1987.

[9] A. Lumsdaine. *Theoretical and practical aspects of parallel numerical algorithms for initial value problems*. PhD thesis, Massachusetts Institute of Technology, Cambridge, MA 1992.

[10] A. Lumsdaine, M. Reichelt, and J. White. Conjugate direction waveform methods for transient two-dimensional simulation of MOS devices. In *Proceedings of International Conference on Computer-Aided Design*, pages 116–119, Santa Clara, California, November 1991.

[11] M. Maheswaran, K. J. Webb, and H. J. Siegel. MCGS: a modified conjugate gradient squared algorithm for nonsymmetric linear systems. *International Journal of Supercomputing*, 2000.

[12] K. Mayaram and D. Pederson. CODECS: A mixed-level device and circuit simulator. In *Proceedings of International Conference on Computer-Aided Design*, pages 112–115, Santa Clara, California, November 1988.

[13] U. Miekkala and O. Nevanlinna. Convergence of dynamic iteration methods for initial value problems. *SIAM Journal on Scientific Computing*, 8:459–482, July 1987.

[14] M. Reichelt. *Accelerated waveform relaxation techniques for the parallel transient simulation of semiconductor devices*. PhD thesis, Massachusetts Institute of Technology, 1993.

[15] M. Reichelt, J. White, and J. Allen. Waveform frequency-dependent overrelaxation for transient two-dimensional simulation of MOS devices. In *Proceedings of Workshop on Numerical Modeling of Process and Devices for Integrated Circuits*, pages 161–166, May 1992.

[16] M. W. Reichelt, A. Lumsdaine, and J. K. White. Accelerated waveform methods for parallel transient simulation of semiconductor devices. In *Proceedings of the International Conference on Computer-Aided Design*, pages 270–274, 1993.

[17] Y. Saad and M. Schultz. GMRES: a generalized minimal residual algorithm for solving nonsymmetric linear systems. *SIAM Journal on Scientific and Statistical Computing*, 7:856–869, 1986.

[18] R. Saleh and J. White. Accelerating relaxation algorithms for circuit simulation using waveform-newton and step size refinement. *IEEE Transactions on Computer-Aided Design of Integrated Circuits and Systems*, 9:951–958, September 1990.

[19] S. Selberherr. *Analysis and Simulation of Semiconductor Devices*. Springer-Verlag, New York, 1984.

[20] P. Sonneveld. CGS: a fast Lanczos-type solver for nonsymmetric linear systems. *SIAM Journal on Scientific and Statistical Computing*, 10:36–52, 1989.

[21] D. Webber, E. Tomacruz, R. Guerrieri, T. Toyabe, and A. Sangiovanni-Vincentelli. A massively parallel algorithm for three-dimensional device simulation. *IEEE Transactions on Computer-Aided Design of Integrated Circuits and Systems*, 10:1201–1209, September 1991.

[22] J. K. White and A. Sangiovanni-Vincentelli. *Relaxation Techniques for the Simulation of VLSI Circuits*. Kluwer Academic Publishers, 1987.

[23] T. Yang. Solving sparse least squares problems on massively parallel distributed memory computers. In *Proceedings of International Conference on Advances in Parallel and Distributed Computing*

(APDC-97), pages 170–177, March 19-21, 1997. Shanghai, P.R.China.

[24] T. Yang and H. X. Lin. The improved quasi-minimal residual method on massively distributed memory computers. In *Proceedings of the International Conference on High Performance Computing and Networking (HPCN-97)*, pages 389–399, April 28-30, Vienna, Austria 1997.

In: Applied Parallel and Distributed Computing
Editors: Yi Pan and Laurence T. Yang , pp. 169-183
ISBN 1-59454-174-4

DISTRIBUTED PARALLEL SOLVER FOR MULTIPHASE FLOW IN POROUS MEDIA

ZHANGXIN CHEN*, WENJUN LI†, AND GUANREN HUAN‡

Abstract. In this paper we develop a distributed parallel solver for multiphase flow in porous media. In this solver we parallelize an iterative flexible GMRES (FGMRES) and use a block ILU as its parallel preconditioner. We present numerical results for realistic simulation models on linux parallel PC clusters.

Key words. Distributed parallel solver, Oil reservoir simulator, GMRES, Multiphase flow

1. Introduction. With the development of new oil reservoir simulators, new requirements from reservoir engineering, such as extremely large regions of oil reservoir fields to simulate and very fine grids to use, have lead to tremendously large sizes of simulation models that involve as many as millions of unknowns and to very complex models, such as those with unstructured grids and poorly conditioned partial differential equations. On the other hand, shortening of simulation time and history match requires reliable, fast, and accurate algorithms for solving large-scale systems arising from numerical reservoir simulations.

Scalar computers have been greatly utilized in numerical reservoir simulations. However, parallel PC clusters offer a great potential for the solution of large-scale systems. When the scale of an oil reservoir simulation becomes tremendously large, to increase capability and speed of a simulator, the choice of a parallel computing frame for the simulator is very important.

In general, parallelization of an oil reservoir simulator is divided into two steps. The first step involves parallelization of a linear solver. A good parallel solver can apply to different simulation models. The second step involves parallelization of the rest of a code. This step depends on the underlying simulation model.

The systems of algebraic equations arising from the numerical discretization of the governing equations for multiphase flow have peculiar properties. The coefficient (stiffness) matrices of these systems are sparse but nonsymmetric and indefinite, for example. While sparse, their band structure is usually spoiled by wells that perforate into many gridblocks and/or by irregular gridblock structure. What is more, for reservoir simulation problems with a number of gridblocks of order $100,000$, about $80\% - 90\%$ of the total simulation time is spent on the solution of linear systems. Hence the choice of a linear solver and its parallelization are very important to the numerical simulation of multiphase flow. In this paper we concentrate on the development of a distributed parallel solver for a multiphase flow model used in numerical reservoir simulations. The development is based on our recent research work for an oil reservoir simulator [3]. In particular, we parallelize an iterative FGMRES (flexible generalized minimum residual) algorithm and use a block ILU as its parallel preconditioner. Numerical results are presented for a realistic simulation model on linux parallel PC clusters.

The rest of the paper is organized as follows. In the next section we introduce a distributed parallel linear solver. Then, in the third section we present a simulation model and numerical results. Finally, we make concluding remarks and mention future research in the last section.

*Department of Mathematics, Box 750156, Southern Methodist University, Dallas, TX 75275-0156, USA. (zchen@mail.smu.edu).
†Department of Mathematics, Box 750156, Southern Methodist University, Dallas, TX 75275-0156, USA. (wli@mail.smu.edu).
‡Department of Mathematics, Box 750156, Southern Methodist University, Dallas, TX 75275-0156, USA. (ghuan@mail.smu.edu).

2. Distributed Parallel Linear Solver. In an oil reservoir simulator, distributed parallelization of a linear solver includes three major parts (see Fig. 2.1, where np is the number of processors). The first part is to transfer a set of sequential data to a set of distributed data, such as a coefficient matrix (A), a right-hand side vector (b), and a solution vector (x). The second part involves parallel computation for solving a linear system. The third part is to merge the data of the solution vector. The first part is only necessary for the first step of parallelization mentioned in the previous section, but not necessary for the second step of parallelization because all data are in distributed data storage in each processor after the second step. At each time step for a time-dependent problem, the third part is not necessary for a parallel simulator if the solution vector does not need to output. Thus these two parts can be removed when the entire parallelization has been done for an oil reservoir simulator. Below our discussion falls into three parts: distributed parallel data storage, parallelization of FGMRES, and parallelization of preconditioners.

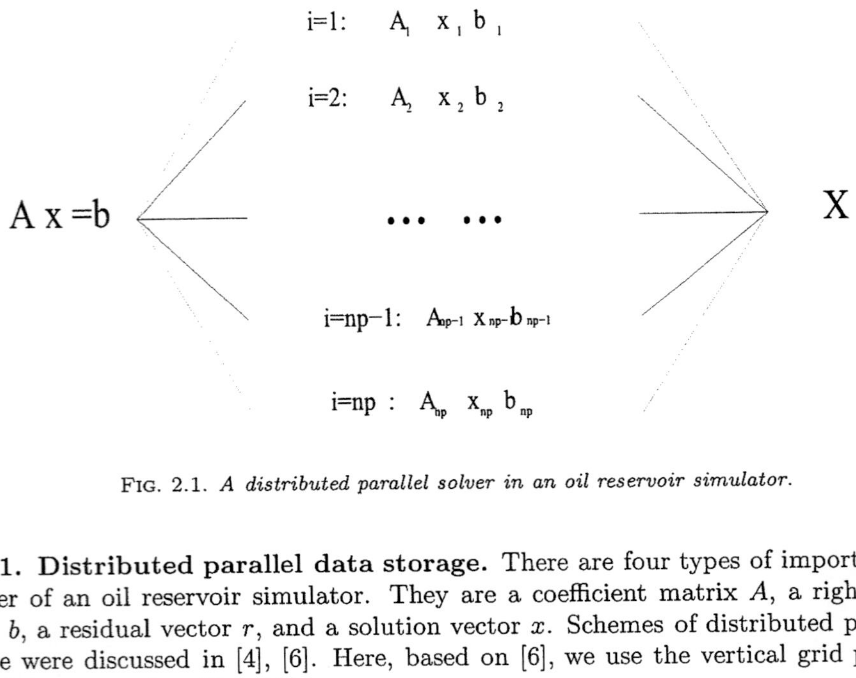

FIG. 2.1. *A distributed parallel solver in an oil reservoir simulator.*

2.1. Distributed parallel data storage. There are four types of important data in a solver of an oil reservoir simulator. They are a coefficient matrix A, a right-hand side vector b, a residual vector r, and a solution vector x. Schemes of distributed parallel data storage were discussed in [4], [6]. Here, based on [6], we use the vertical grid partitioning for each processor (see Fig. 2.2).

In each processor i, $i = 1, \ldots, np$, matrix A_i and vectors r_i, b_i, x_i are stored separately. We define the index of rows of matrix A_i as ind_{A_i} and the index of vectors r_i, b_i, and x_i as ind_{r_i}, ind_{b_i}, and ind_{x_i}, respectively. Define ind_{ij} as the index set of the boundary grids between subdomains i and j. For $i \neq j$, their indices satisfy the following relations:

$$ind_{A_i} \cap ind_{A_j} = \emptyset, \tag{2. 1}$$
$$ind_{b_i} \cap ind_{b_j} = \emptyset, \tag{2. 2}$$
$$ind_{r_i} \cap ind_{r_j} = \emptyset, \tag{2. 3}$$
$$ind_{x_i} \cap ind_{x_j} = ind_{ij}. \tag{2. 4}$$

As an example, we consider a region with a 10×10 grid for a two-dimensional problem (in the yz-plane); Figs. 2.3–2.5 show the partitions for a different number of processors.

Vector x_i does not only include the components whose indices belong to processor i, it also include the components whose indices belong to the boundary grids of its neighboring

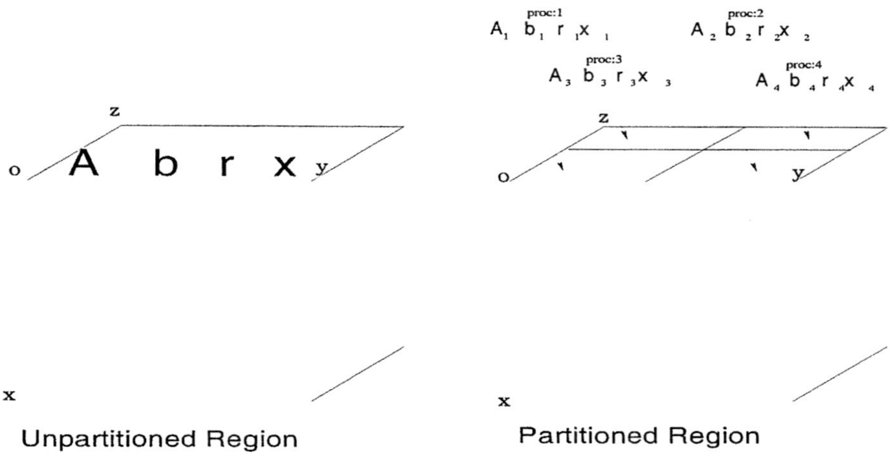

FIG. 2.2. *A partitioned region for distributed parallel computing in an oil reservoir simulator.*

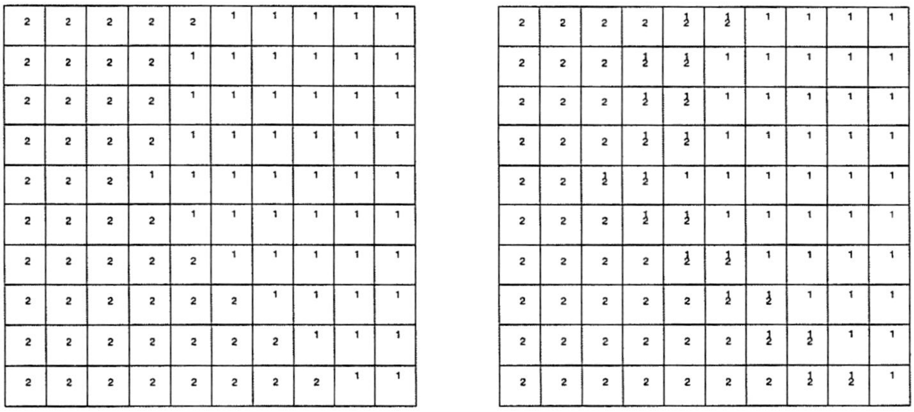

FIG. 2.3. *Partition for 2 processors, left: index sets for A_i,b_i,r_i; right: index sets for x_i.*

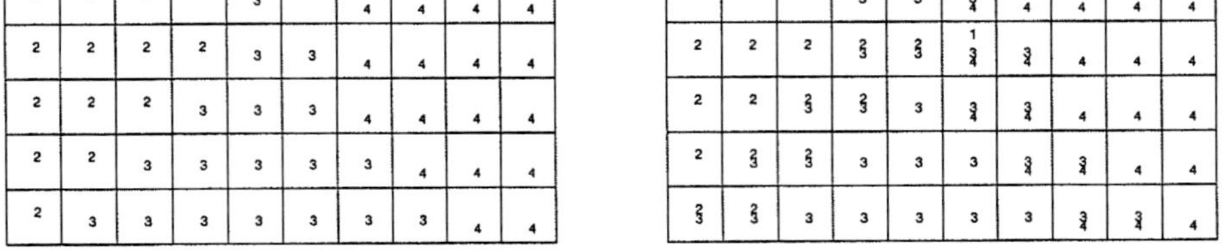

FIG. 2.4. *Partition for 4 processors, left: index sets for A_i,b_i,r_i; right: index sets for x_i.*

processors. Thus, at each iterative step, updating vector x_i needs communication from its neighboring processors. We show this communication in Figs. 2.6 and 2.7.

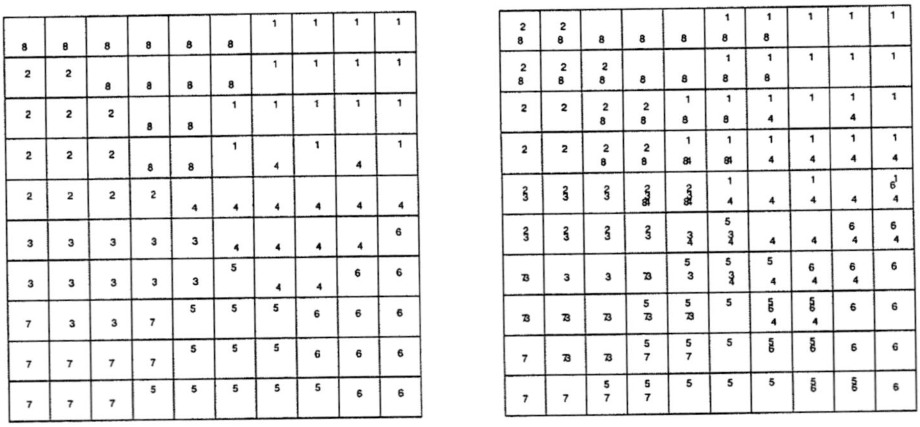

FIG. 2.5. *Partition for 8 processors, left: index sets for A_i,b_i,r_i; right: index sets for x_i.*

FIG. 2.6. *Partition of a region and its corresponding vector x_i.*

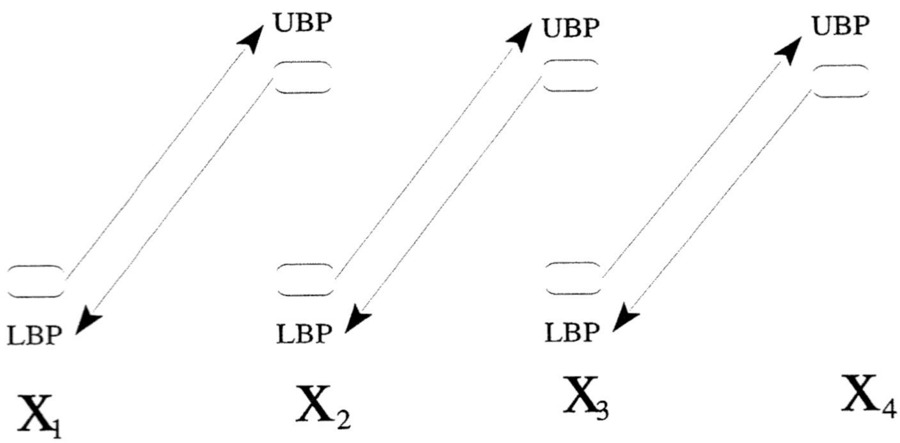

FIG. 2.7. *Communication among processors.*

Algorithm 1: Right-preconditioned FGMRES(m)

1. **Start:** Choose an initial guess x_0 and the dimension of the Krylov subspace m.
   Set up a $(m+1) \times m$ matrix $\hat{H}_m$ with zero entries.
2. **Arnoldi process:**
   (a) Compute $r_0 = b - Ax_0$, $\beta = \|r_0\|_2$, and $v_1 = r_0/\beta$
   (b) For $j = 1, \ldots, m$, do
   - Computer $z_j = M_j^{-1} v_j$
   - Computer $w_j = Az_j$
   - For $i = 1, \ldots, j$, $\begin{cases} h_{ij} := (w_j, v_i) \\ w_j := w_j - h_{ij} v_i \end{cases}$
   - Computer $h_{j+1,j} = \|w_j\|_2$ and $v_{j+1} := w_j / \|w_j\|_2$

   (c) Define $Z_m = [z_1, \ldots, z_m]$.
3. **Update:** $x_m = x_0 + Z_m y_m$, where
   $$y_m = \text{argmin} \|\beta e_1 - \hat{H}_m y\|_2$$
4. **Restart:** If convergent, stop; else, $x_0 = x_m$ and go to 2.

2.2. Parallelization of the FGMRES. The ORTHOMIN (orthogonal minimum residual) [10] has been applied to petroleum reservoir simulations and is still widely used in this area due to its ability to solve efficiently sparse, nonsymmetric systems of algebraic equations. However, it is well known that the GMRES [9] is more efficient and robust, particularly for the solution of large systems. We have recently applied this algorithm and its variation FGMRES to realistic petroleum reservoir simulations [3], [5].

Algorithm 2: Distributed parallel right-preconditioned FGMRES(m)

- For processor k, $k = 1, \ldots, np$, do
  1. **Start:** Choose an initial guess $x_0^{\{k\}}$ and the dimension of the Krylov subspace m.
     Set up a $(m+1) \times m$ matrix $\hat{H}_m$ with zero entries.
  2. **Arnoldi process:**
     (a) Compute $r_0^{\{k\}} = b^{\{k\}} - A^{\{k\}} x_0^{\{k\}}$

     (b) Compute $\|r_0^{\{k\}}\|_2^2$, compute the sum of $\|r_0\|_2^2 = \sum_{k=1}^{np} \|r_0^{\{k\}}\|_2^2$ in processor 1, and broadcast $\|r_0\|_2$ to every processor .

     (c) Compute $v_1^{\{k\}} = r_0^{\{k\}} / \|r_0\|_2$, $\beta = \|r_0\|_2$

     (d) For $j = 1, \ldots, m$, do
     - Compute $z_j^{\{k\}} = M_j^{\{k\}^{-1}} v_j^{\{k\}}$
     - Update $z_j^{\{k\}}$ and compute $w_j^{\{k\}} = A^{\{k\}} z_j^{\{k\}}$
     - For $i = 1, \ldots, j$,
       Compute $(w_j^{\{k\}}, v_i^{\{k\}})$, compute the sum

       $$h_{ij} = \sum_{k=1}^{np} (w_j^{\{k\}}, v_i^{\{k\}})$$

       in processor 1, and broadcast h_{ij} to every processor.
     - For $i = 1, \ldots, j$, compute $w_j^{\{k\}} = w_j^{\{k\}} - h_{ij} v_i^{\{k\}}$
     - Compute $\|w_j^{\{k\}}\|_2^2$, compute the sum of

       $$\|w_j\|_2^2 = \sum_{k=1}^{np} \|w_j^{\{k\}}\|_2^2$$

       in processor 1, and broadcast $h_{j+1,j} = \|w_j\|_2$ to every processor .
     - Compute $v_{j+1}^{\{k\}} = w_j^{\{k\}} / \|w_j\|_2$

     (e) Define $Z_m^{\{k\}} = [z_1^{\{k\}}, \ldots, z_m^{\{k\}}]$
  3. **Update:** $x_m^{\{k\}} = x_0^{\{k\}} + Z_m^{\{k\}} y_m$, where $y_m = \text{argmin}\|\beta e_1 - \hat{H}_m y\|_2$
  4. **Restart:** If convergent, stop; else, $x_0^{\{k\}} = x_m^{\{k\}}$ and go to 2.

The right-preconditioned FGMRES solves a modified linear system:

$$AM^{-1}(Mx) = b. \tag{2. 5}$$

Its algorithm is classically described as in Algorithm 1, where $\hat{H}_m$ is upper Hessenberg from the Gram-Schmidt process. The Arnoldi process simply constructs an orthogonal basis for the preconditioned Krylov subspace

$$\kappa_m = \text{span}\left\{ r_0, AM_1^{-1} r_0, \ldots, (AM_1^{-1}) \cdots (AM_{m-1}^{-1}) r_0 \right\}.$$

The difference between the GMRES and FGMRES is that for the GMRES, all the $M_i = M$ are the same, and $z_i = M^{-1}v_i$ need not be stored during computations. The FGMRES is more flexible and suitable than the GMRES in the solution of difficult problems with complex preconditioners.

The main operations in Algorithm 1 are: (1) vector updates, (2) dot products, (3) matrix-vector products, and (4) preconditioning operations. Therefore, the FGMRES needs to be parallelized in the following four operations:

- Vector updates: Vectors in each processor are assumed to be in the same fashion. Each vector except those that multiply a matrix can be updated by an iterative step in its processor. The vector that multiplies a matrix, such as z, must be updated by two steps: one is the iterative update and the other is the global update by communication with the neighboring subdomains.
- Dot products: A global dot product is obtained from subvectors' dot-product in each processor.
- Matrix-vector products: They can be done in each processor without communication with neighboring processors after the vector has been updated.
- Preconditioning operations: The details are in the next subsection.

We assume that $A^{\{k\}}$ and $r^{\{k\}}$ are the submatrix of A and subvector of r in processor k. The parallelized right-preconditioned FGMRES(m) is described in Algorithm 2.

2.3. Parallelization of preconditioners. In our oil reservoir simulator [3], there are two types of preconditioners, ILUT [7] and ILUK [8]. Based on them, block Jacobi preconditioners are constructed as our distributed parallel preconditioners.

In processor k, submatrix $A^{\{k\}}$ of A is stored. We define the column index set of $A^{\{k\}}$ as $indC_{A_k}$. It can be divided into two sets ind_{localA_k} and $ind_{neighborA_k}$ such that

$$ind_{localA_k} \cup ind_{neighborA_k} = indC_{A_k}, \tag{2. 6}$$

$$ind_{localA_k} \cap ind_{neighborA_k} = \emptyset, \tag{2. 7}$$

$$ind_{A_k} \cap ind_{localA_k} = ind_{localA_k}, \tag{2. 8}$$

$$ind_{A_k} \cap ind_{neighborA_k} = \emptyset. \tag{2. 9}$$

Thus we see that $ind_{neighborA_k}$ is the index set of the neighboring subdomain boundary grids. It is associated with the off-diagonal block submatrices $A^{\{k\}}_{kl}$, $k \neq l$. ind_{localA_k} is associated with the diagonal block submatrix $A^{\{k\}}_{kk}$. Generally, submatrices $A^{\{k\}}_{ij}$ are sparse, and some of off-diagonal submatrices are zero. An example for four processors is shown in Fig. 2.8. The parallel preconditioning operations are given in Algorithm 3, where the steps (a)–(c) are the same as in Algorithm 2.

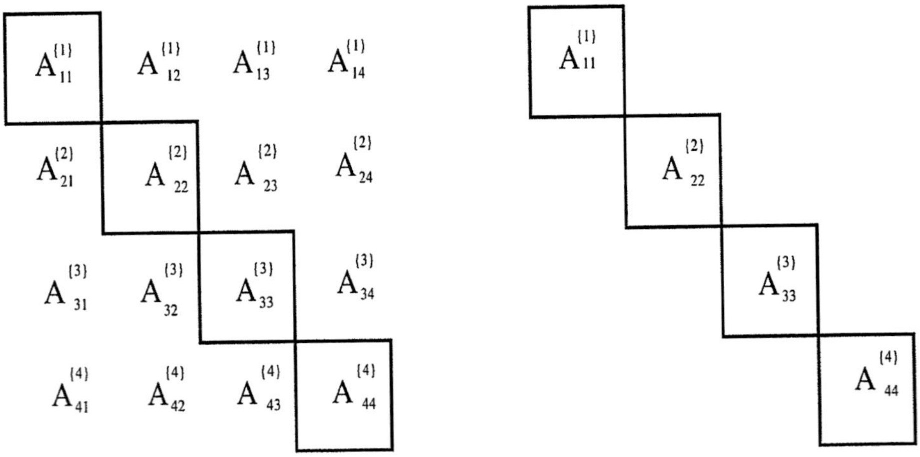

FIG. 2.8. *For 4 processors, left: block coefficient matrix; right: block Jacobi preconditioner.*

Algorithm 3: Parallel Jacobi preconditioning operations

1. For processor k, $k = 1, \ldots, np$, do
   - **Before the Arnoldi process:**
     Compute the preconditioner M_k as an ILU factorization $L^{\{k\}}U^{\{k\}}$ of $A_{kk}^{\{k\}}$ using the ILUT or ILUK method.
   - **During the Arnoldi process:**
     (a) ......
     (b) ......
     (c) ......
     (d) For $j = 1, \ldots, m$, do
       – Compute the vector $v_j^{\{k\}}$
       – Solve y from $L^{\{k\}}y = v_j^{\{k\}}$
       – Solve $z_j^{\{k\}}$ from $U^{\{k\}}z_j^{\{k\}} = y$
       – Update $z_j^{\{k\}}$ using communication with neighboring subdomains.
       – Computer $w_j^{\{k\}} = A^{\{k\}}z_j^{\{k\}}$

3. Numerical Experiments. In this section we report numerical results obtained for solving two-phase flow in porous media. The space discretization of the governing equations for this flow is based on a block-centered finite difference method with harmonically averaged coefficients (equivalently, a mixed finite element method). The solution scheme is based on an iterative IMPES (implicit in pressure and explicit in saturation) solution method [2]. The linear solver is based on the distributed parallel solver developed in the previous section. The numerical experiments are carried out on a linux parallel PC cluster: ROCKETCALC with 8 nodes; each node has Intel Pentium, 2GHz, 2G RAM, and integrated Intel 100Mbps ethernet.

3.1. Differential model. The flow of two-phase immiscible fluids in a porous medium $\Omega \subset \Re^d$ $(d \leq 3)$ is given by the mass balance equation for each of the fluid phases

$$\phi \frac{\partial(\rho_\alpha s_\alpha)}{\partial t} + \nabla \cdot (\rho_\alpha \mathbf{u}_\alpha) = \rho_\alpha q_\alpha, \quad \alpha = w, o, \tag{3.1}$$

where $\alpha = w$ denotes the wetting phase (e.g., water), $\alpha = o$ indicates the nonwetting phase (e.g., oil), ϕ is the porosity of the medium, and ρ_α, s_α, $\mathbf{u}_\alpha$, and q_α are, respectively, the density, saturation, volumetric velocity, and external volumetric flow rate of the α-phase. The volumetric velocity $\mathbf{u}_\alpha$ is given by the Darcy law

$$\mathbf{u}_\alpha = -\frac{K_{r\alpha}}{\mu_\alpha} \mathbf{K} \nabla (p_\alpha - \rho_\alpha g Z), \quad \alpha = w, o, \tag{3.2}$$

where $\mathbf{K}$ is the absolute permeability of the porous medium, p_α, μ_α, and $K_{r\alpha}$ are the pressure, viscosity, and relative permeability of the α-phase, respectively, g denotes the gravitational constant, Z is the depth, and the z-coordinate is in the vertical downward direction. In addition, the constraint for the saturations is

$$s_w + s_o = 1, \tag{3.3}$$

and the two pressures are related by the capillary pressure function

$$p_c(s_w) = p_o - p_w. \tag{3.4}$$

These equations can be written as a pressure equation for p_o and a saturation equation for s_w [1]. For this model, our experiments are done with the length of simulation time of $T = 3,050.00$ (days) and the time step of 50.0 (days). The flow under consideration is uniform in the z-direction, so the computation can reduce to a two-dimensional domain.

3.2. Numerical results. Numerical results are given in terms of four groups. The number of grids is from 100×100 to 300×300 for all four groups.

- The first group uses ILUK(2), and the results are given in Figs. 3.1–3.3.
- The second group uses ILUK(6), and the results are given in Figs. 3.5–3.7.
- The third group uses ILUT(3), and the results are given in Figs. 3.8–3.10.
- The fourth group uses ILUT(21), and the results are given in Figs. 3.11–3.13.

In these figures, we compute the speed-up factors as follows: $S_{np} = T_1/T_{np}$, where T_k is the time cost for the number k of processors and S_{np} is used for computing the total speed-up or the solver speed-up, and $M_{np} = N_1/N_{np}$, where N_k is the number of iterations for the number k of processors and M_{np} is used for computing the MatVect (matrix-vector multiplication) speed-up, $k = 1, \ldots, np$. The index for a preconditioner is given by the rule: $prec = 21, 25$ for ILUK(2) and ILUK(6), and $prec = 31, 36$ for ILUT(6) and ILUT(21), respectively. As an illustration, the daily oil production rate and oil recovery curves for the first group are presented in Figs. 3.4 for different numbers of processors.

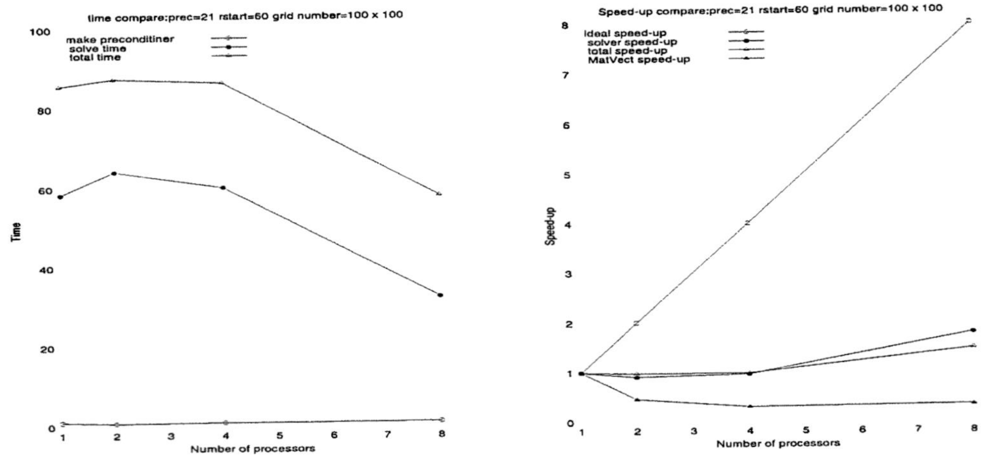

FIG. 3.1. *Number of grids:* 100 × 100, *Nrst=60, and Prec=21.*

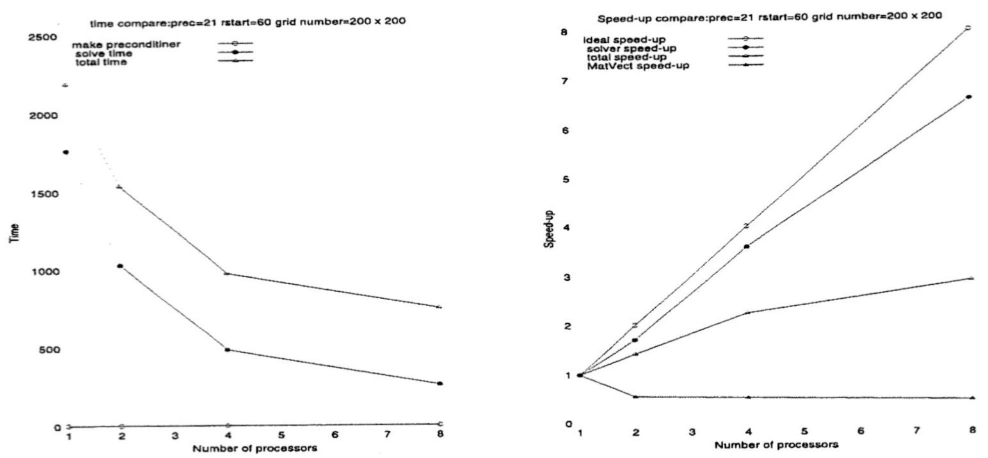

FIG. 3.2. *Number of grids:* 200 × 200, *Nrst=60, and Prec=21.*

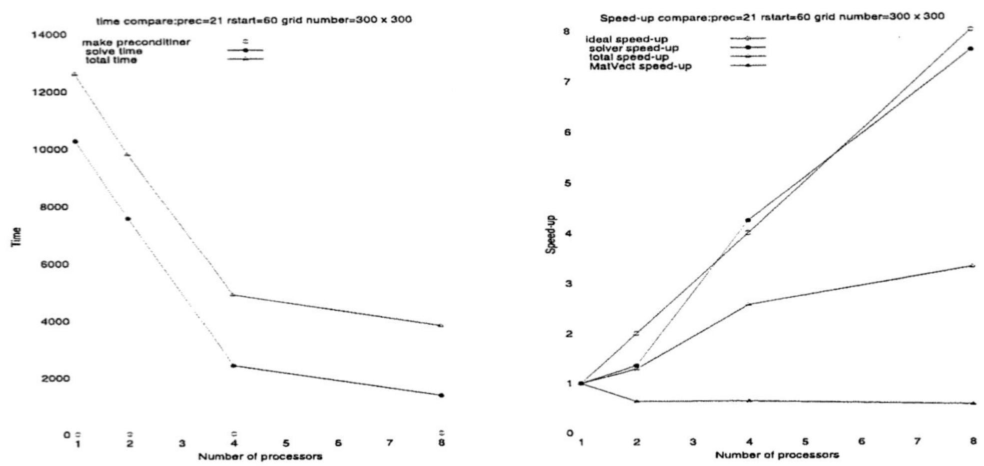

FIG. 3.3. *Number of grids:* 300 × 300, *Nrst=60, and Prec=21.*

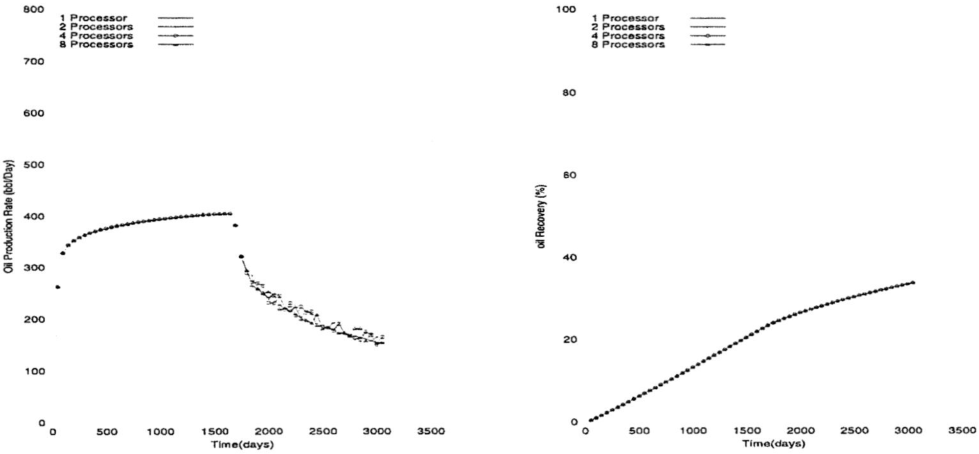

FIG. 3.4. *Number of grids:* 300 × 300, *Nrst=60, and Prec=21.*

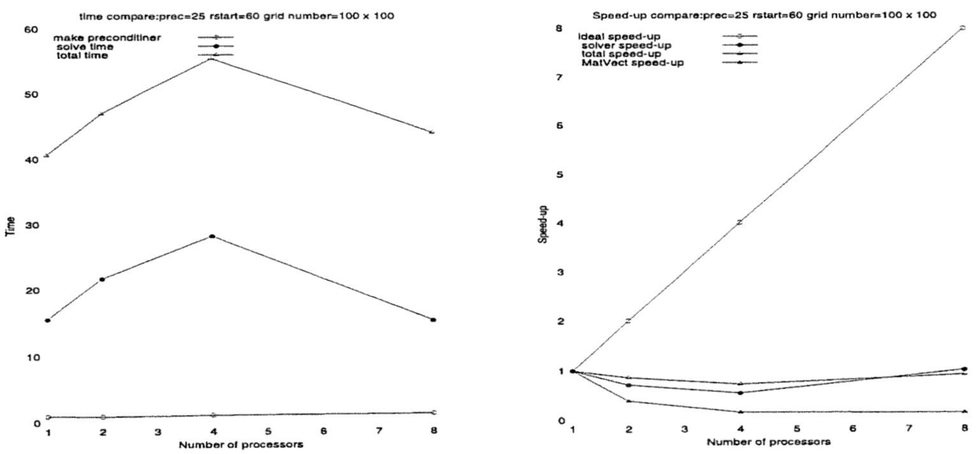

FIG. 3.5. *Number of grids:* 100 × 100, *Nrst=60, and Prec=25.*

3.3. Conclusions. From above numerical results, we can make the following remarks:

- In terms of the oil recovery and production rates, the results of our sequential and parallel FGMRES with different preconditioners match very well.
- The speed-up of the parallel solver is better than that of total simulator. This is because the time of spending on scattering and merging data at the start and end of our parallel solver increases with the increasing number of processors. This situation will be improved after we parallelize our entire simulator because these kinds of scattering and merging data will be removed in the parallel simulator.
- The block Jacobi preconditioners obtained from low order ILUK or ILUT, such as ILUK(2) and ILUT(3), have good speed-up with increasing the scale of test problems for the same model. This is due to the fact that the global property of the Jacobi preconditioners has not been destroyed much for the whole solver.
- The block Jacobi preconditioners obtained from higher order ILUK or ILUT, such as ILUK(6) and ILUT(21), do not have good speed-up. The reason is that the global property of the block Jacobi preconditioners has been destroyed dramatically with increasing the number of processors for the same model problem.

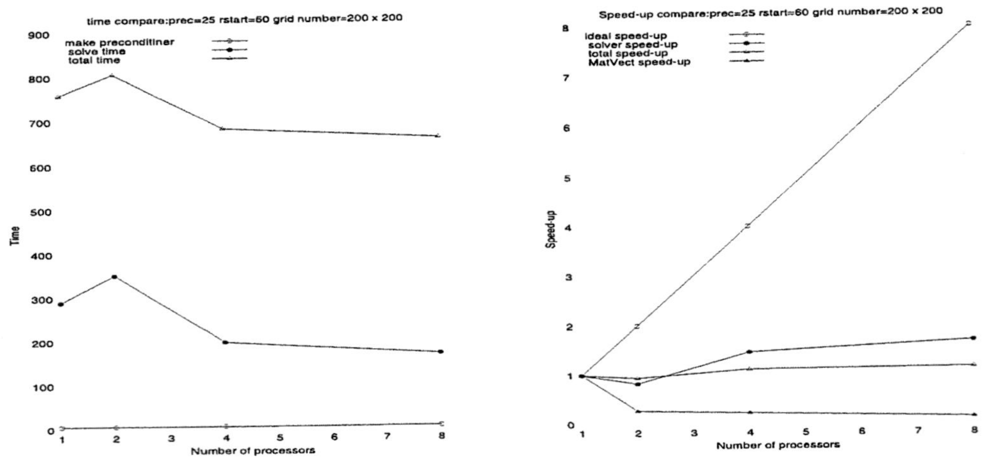

FIG. 3.6. *Number of grids:* 200 × 200, *Nrst=60, and Prec=25.*

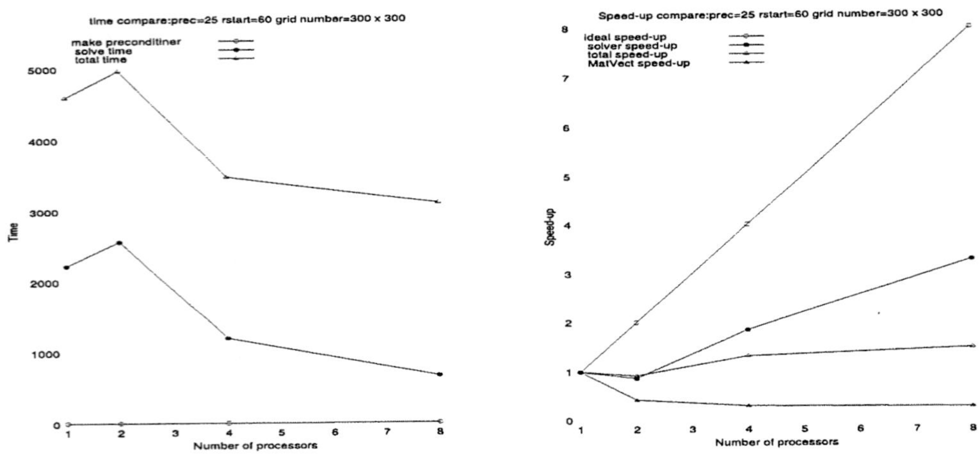

FIG. 3.7. *Number of grids:* 300 × 300, *Nrst=60, and Prec=25.*

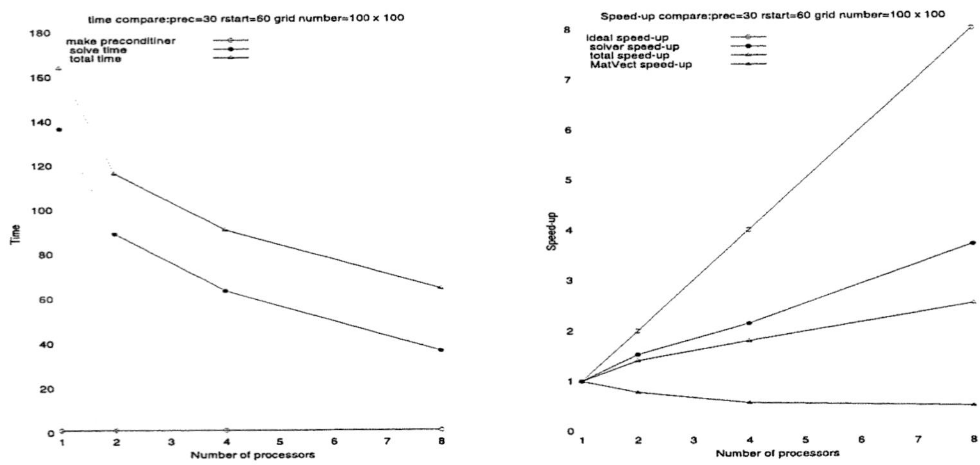

FIG. 3.8. *Number of grids:* 100 × 100, *Nrst=60, and Prec=30.*

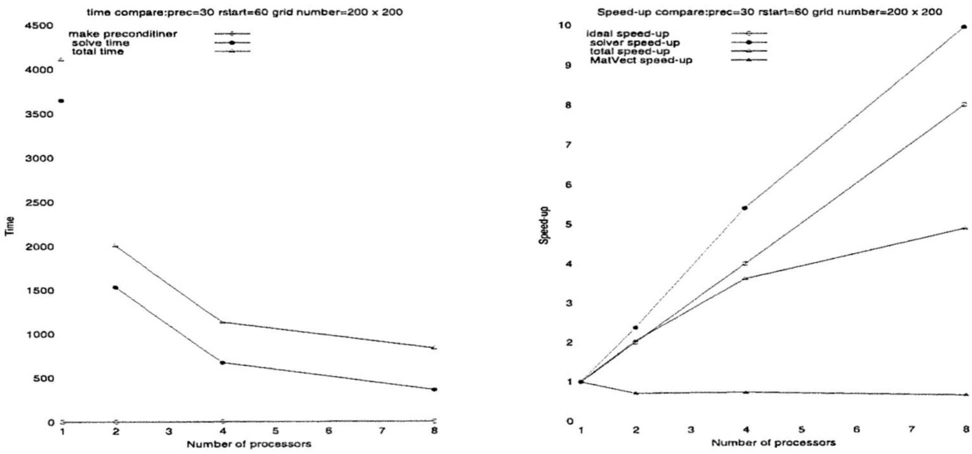

FIG. 3.9. *Number of grids:* 200 × 200, *Nrst=60, and Prec=30.*

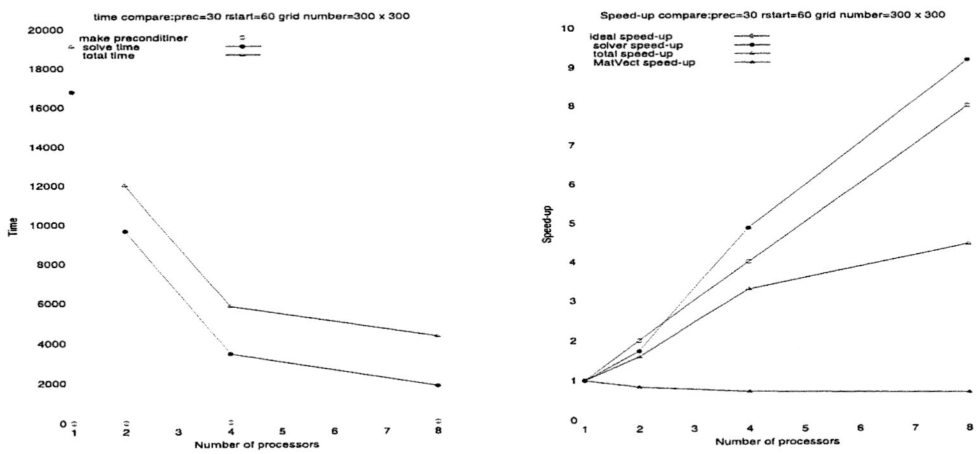

FIG. 3.10. *Number of grids:* 300 × 300, *Nrst=60, and Prec=30.*

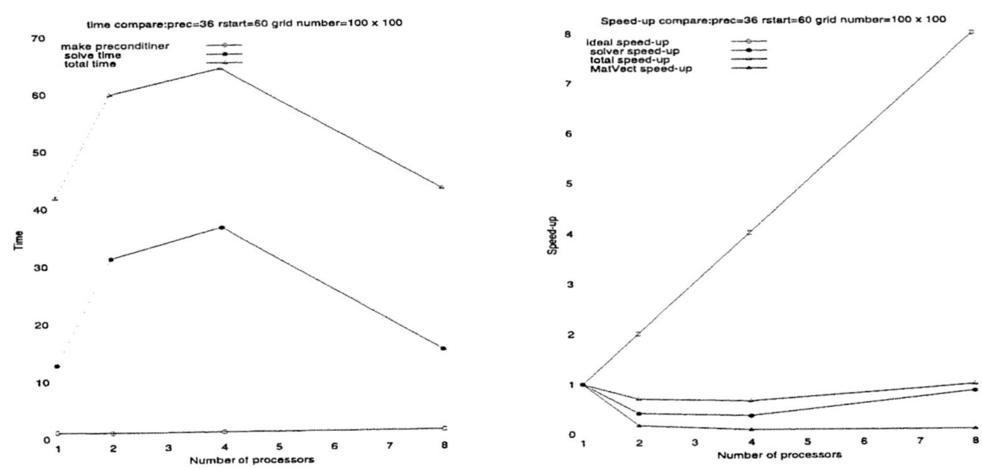

FIG. 3.11. *Number of grids:* 100 × 100, *Nrst=60, and Prec=36.*

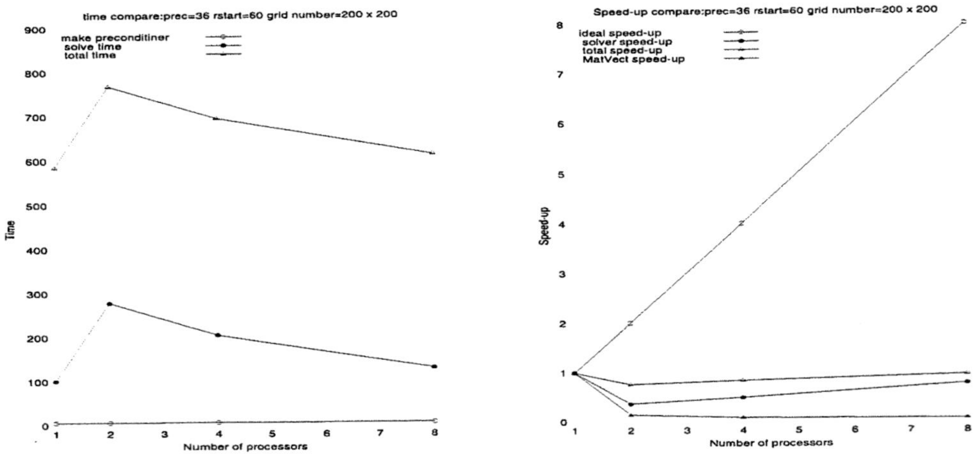

FIG. 3.12. *Number of grids:* 200 × 200, *Nrst=60, and Prec=36.*

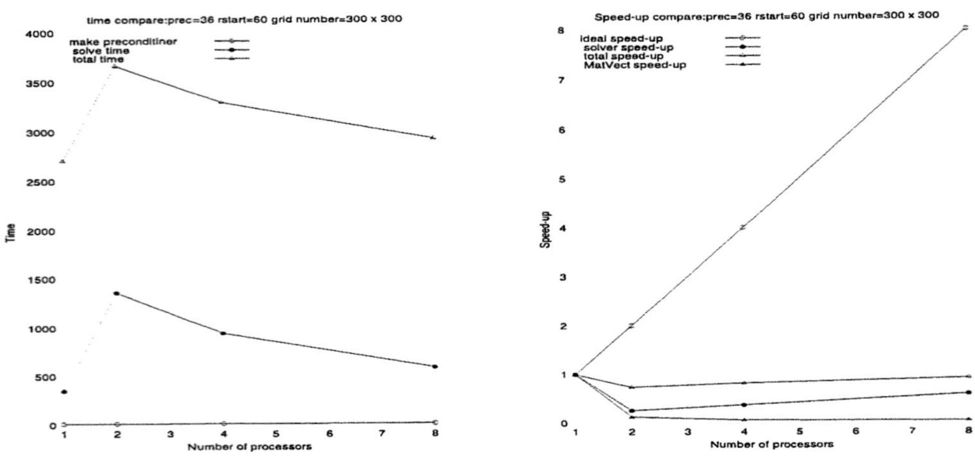

FIG. 3.13. *Number of grids:* 300 × 300, *Nrst=60, and Prec=36.*

- The parallelized FGMRES has a good parallel character. When a block Jacobi preconditioner is weak, the speed-up of the parallel solver is mainly picked up by the FGMRES.

4. Concluding Remarks. We have developed a distributed parallel solver for multiphase flow in porous media, and presented numerical experiments. The concluding remarks can be made as in Section 3.3. In this paper the experiments are carried out for two-phase flow. In the future we will investigate the application of this parallel solver to more advanced flow models such as the black oil and compositional models. Also, we will work on parallelization of the entire reservoir simulators. Finally, we have used the finite difference method for discretization of the governing equations of the two-phase flow model on structured grids. We are investigating the application of the control volume finite element method to this model on unstructured grids and the application of parallel solvers to the solution of the resulting systems on unstructured grids.

REFERENCES

[1] Z. CHEN, *Degenerate two-phase incompressible flow I: Existence, uniqueness and regularity of a weak solution*, J. Diff. Equations, 171 (2001), pp. 203–232.

[2] Z. CHEN, G. HUAN, AND B. LI, *An improved IMPES method for two-phase flow in porous media*, Transport in Porous Media 54 (2004), 361-376.

[3] Z. CHEN, G. HUAN, B. LI, W. LI, S. BUITRAGO, D. ESPIN, AND H. KLIE, *Comparison of practical approaches to reservoir simulation*, Proceedings of the 2nd Meeting on Reservoir Simulation, Universidad Argentina de la Empresa, Buenos Aires, Argentina, Nov. 5-6, 2002, CD-ROM.

[4] W. LI, *Parallel pre-symmetrized iterative algorithm on nonsymmetric linear systems* (in Chinese), The Sixth Chinese Parallel Computing Academy Annual Conference, pp. 67–72, September 2000, Changsha, China.

[5] W. LI, Z. CHEN, AND G. HUAN, *Comparison of the GMRES and ORTHOMIN for the black oil model in porous media*, to appear.

[6] W. LI AND L. T. YANG, *An improved parallel pre-symmetrized iterative algorithm on a kind of non-symmetric linear systems*, The 2002 International Conference on Parallel Processing (ICPP-02), pp. 240–245, August 2002, Vancouver B.C., Canada.

[7] Y. SAAD, *ILUT: A dual threshold incomplete ILU factorization*, Numer. Linear Algebra Appl., 1 (1994), pp. 387–402.

[8] Y. SAAD, *Iterative Methods for Sparse Linear Systems*, Boston, MA, PWS Pub. Co., 1996.

[9] Y. SAAD AND M. H. SCHULTZ, *GMRES: A generalized minimal residual algorithm for solving non-symmetric linear systems*, SIAM J. Sci. Statist. Comput., 7 (1986), pp. 856–869.

[10] P. K. W. VINSOME, *ORTHOMIN, an iterative method for solving sparse sets of simultaneous linear equations*, in Proc. Fourth Symposium on Reservoir simulations, Society of Petroleum Engineers of AIME, 1976, pp. 149–157.

INDEX

A

B

C

D

E

F

S

T

V

W

X